Cambridge IGCSE® and O Level

Economics

Revision Guide

Colin Bamford

Shaftesbury Road, Cambridge CB2 8EA, United Kingdom

One Liberty Plaza, 20th Floor, New York, NY 10006, USA

477 Williamstown Road, Port Melbourne, VIC 3207, Australia

314–321, 3rd Floor, Plot 3, Splendor Forum, Jasola District Centre, New Delhi – 110025, India

103 Penang Road, #05-06/07, Visioncrest Commercial, Singapore 238467

Cambridge University Press & Assessment is a department of the University of Cambridge.

We share the University's mission to contribute to society through the pursuit of education, learning and research at the highest international levels of excellence.

www.cambridge.org
Information on this title: www.cambridge.org/9781108440417

© Cambridge University Press & Assessment 2018

This publication is in copyright. Subject to statutory exception and to the provisions of relevant collective licensing agreements, no reproduction of any part may take place without the written permission of Cambridge University Press & Assessment.

First published 2018

20 19 18 17 16 15 14 13 12 11 10

Printed in Great Britain by Ashford Colour Press Ltd.

A catalogue record for this publication is available from the British Library

ISBN 978-1-108-44041-7 Paperback

Cambridge University Press & Assessment has no responsibility for the persistence or accuracy of URLs for external or third-party internet websites referred to in this publication, and does not guarantee that any content on such websites is, or will remain, accurate or appropriate. Information regarding prices, travel timetables, and other factual information given in this work is correct at the time of first printing but Cambridge University Press & Assessment does not guarantee the accuracy of such information thereafter.

IGCSE® is a registered trademark

All exam-style questions and sample answers in this title were written by the author. In examination, the way marks would be awarded to answers like these may be different.

....

NOTICE TO TEACHERS IN THE UK
It is illegal to reproduce any part of this work in material form (including photocopying and electronic storage) except under the following circumstances:

(i) where you are abiding by a licence granted to your school or institution by the Copyright Licensing Agency;
(ii) where no such licence exists, or where you wish to exceed the terms of a licence, and you have gained the written permission of Cambridge University Press;
(iii) where you are allowed to reproduce without permission under the provisions of Chapter 3 of the Copyright, Designs and Patents Act 1988, which covers, for example, the reproduction of short passages within certain types of educational anthology and reproduction for the purposes of setting examination questions.

Contents

Introduction		v
How to use this book		viii

Section 1: The basic economic problem — 1

Chapter 1	The nature of the economic problem	2
Chapter 2	Factors of production	6
Chapter 3	Opportunity cost	12
Chapter 4	Production possibility curves	15
Exam-style structured questions for Section 1		19

Section 2: The allocation of resources — 21

Chapter 5	Microeconomics and macroeconomics	22
Chapter 6	The role of markets in allocating resources	25
Chapter 7	Demand	29
Chapter 8	Supply	36
Chapter 9	Price determination	42
Chapter 10	Price changes	45
Chapter 11	Price elasticity of demand	48
Chapter 12	Price elasticity of supply	53
Chapter 13	Market economic system	57
Chapter 14	Market failure	60
Chapter 15	Mixed economic system	65
Exam-style structured questions for Section 2		69

Section 3: Microeconomic decision makers — 71

Chapter 16	Money and banking	72
Chapter 17	Households	75
Chapter 18	Workers	79
Chapter 19	Trade unions	85
Chapter 20	Firms	89
Chapter 21	Firms and production	95
Chapter 22	Firms' costs, revenue and objectives	99
Chapter 23	Market structure	103
Exam-style structured questions for Section 3		107

Section 4: Government and the macroeconomy — 109

Chapter 24	The role of government	110
Chapter 25	The macroeconomic aims of government	113
Chapter 26	Fiscal policy	119
Chapter 27	Monetary policy	126
Chapter 28	Supply-side policies	130

Chapter 29	Economic growth	133
Chapter 30	Employment and unemployment	139
Chapter 31	Inflation and deflation	144
Exam-style structured questions for Section 4		149

Section 5:	Economic development	151
Chapter 32	Living standards	152
Chapter 33	Poverty	155
Chapter 34	Population	159
Chapter 35	Differences in economic development between countries	164
Exam-style structured questions for Section 5		167

Section 6:	International trade and globalisation	171
Chapter 36	International specialisation	172
Chapter 37	Free trade and protection	175
Chapter 38	Foreign exchange rates	180
Chapter 39	Current account of balance of payments	186
Exam-style structured questions for Section 6		191

Suggested answers	193
Glossary	223
Index	231
Acknowledgements	235

Introduction

Revision is a continual process. Of course, it is something you do in order to prepare for examinations, but it is good practice to consistently look over your work and refresh your knowledge of economics. That is what this Revision Guide is for.

It is designed to help you revise all the topics in your IGCSE and O Level Economics course. The Revision Guide follows the structure of the course closely. It is divided into 39 chapters. Each of the chapters summarises a key economic topic and is based on a section of the syllabus. In addition, every chapter includes:

- a sample question accompanied by an exemplar answer and a skills focus that highlights aspects of the answer – to help you to develop your approach to answering a particular style of question
- tips to remind you of a key point, advise you of a common error or offer guidance on how to approach a question
- a progress check – questions to check your understanding
- a revision checklist – a short summary of what you should know
- structured skills practice – questions for you to answer with tips to guide you on how to approach a question
- exam-style multiple choice questions – to give you extra practice.

There are exam-style structured questions at the ends of Sections 1–6 to give you practice in answering a data response question and a four-part question.

At the end of the Revision Guide, suggested answers are provided for the structured skills practice questions, exam-style multiple choice questions and exam-style structured questions. Comments on the answers to the exam-style structured questions show how the answer could be improved.

How to revise in an effective way

Multiple choice questions

These are an excellent way of revising topics since they require you to check how much you know and understand about what you have studied during your Economics course. You will find examples of multiple choice questions at the end of each chapter, in the accompanying Workbook and the Coursebook.

Multiple choice questions consist of:

- a stem or introduction that states what is required
- four possible choices or responses – A, B, C, D.

You may find the following steps helpful to think about when answering multiple choice questions:

i   Carefully read the question and each of the four possible answers.
ii Look for any 'terms' that you recognise and think about what they mean.
iii Cross out any of the choices that strike you as being more obviously incorrect.
iv Choose the answer that makes most sense.

In your examination, you may have a relatively high number of multiple choice questions to respond to in the given time, so it might be best to make an educated guess if you are struggling to answer a particular question.

Some multiple choice questions test your knowledge and understanding. For example:

1 Why is the Human Development Index (HDI) a better indicator of comparative living standards than the gross domestic product (GDP) per head?
   A it includes international trade
   B it includes more measures of living standards
   C it is measured in money terms
   D it is more directly linked to economic growth.

> **TIP**
>
> If you go to Chapter 32.1 in the Coursebook, you will see a subsection that defines the HDI. The definition does not mention trade (A), money terms (C) or economic growth (D), so these three responses can all be eliminated. This leaves B as the correct answer.

Most multiple choice questions require knowledge and understanding combined with application to a particular topic. For example:

2 What is the **most** likely result of an increase in interest rates?
   A a fall in consumer spending
   B a fall in productivity
   C a rise in borrowing
   D a rise in investment.

> **TIP**
>
> You should be able to answer this question once you have completed Chapter 27 in the Coursebook. (Note how 'most' is highlighted in bold – this is to help you.) An increase in interest rates benefits people with savings but makes it less attractive to borrow money, so options C and D can be eliminated. There is no obvious link with productivity (B). This leaves A as the correct answer.

Structured questions

Paper 2 of IGCSE and O Level Economics consists of structured questions which take the form of a 'command word' and an instruction. Section A consists of a set of compulsory structured questions that are drawn from source material and take the form of text, usually with some accompanying data. Section B consists of structured questions which have four parts that require responses.

In answering structured questions, you need to demonstrate knowledge and understanding, analysis and evaluation as determined by the command word in the question.

Assessment objectives and command words

Command word	What it means
Analyse	Examine in detail to show meaning, and to identify elements and the relationships between them
Calculate	Work out from given facts, figures or information
Define	Give the precise meaning
Describe	State the points of a topic, giving the characteristics and main features
Discuss (whether or not)	Write about issues or topics in depth in a structured way
Explain	Set out purposes or reasons/make the relationships between things evident/state why and/or how and support with relevant evidence
Give	Produce an answer from a given source or recall/memory
Identify	Name/select/recognise
State	Express in clear terms

Source: Cambridge Assessment International Education

Some structured questions are drawn from source material. One or two questions may require a simple calculation or interpretation of the data. Remember to refer to this source material in your answers.

When answering four-part questions, it is important to read carefully any contextual information provided and think about what the command word in each question is asking of you.

Exam-style structured questions for you to practise can be found at the ends of Sections 1–6. Each mainly draws upon knowledge from the section. Additional skills practice focusing on answering structured questions can be found towards the end of each chapter.

A final thought

There is no substitute for practice. In any examination, correct timing is vital for success. Remember to look carefully at the total time you have been given to complete each paper and how many questions you are expected to answer in that time, as well as how many marks they are worth.

When revising, time yourself whenever possible so that you become familiar with how long you should write on particular types of question. In this way, there is less chance that you will run out of time and so jeopardise the mark you might have been awarded.

All exam-style questions and sample answers in this title were written by the author. In examinations, the way marks are awarded may be different.

How to use this book

Learning summary – Learning summaries are designed to remind you of key economic concepts that you should have learnt. If you cannot remember them, make sure you re-visit them during your revision.

Terms – Definitions of key terms throughout will remind you of important economic terms that you should know.

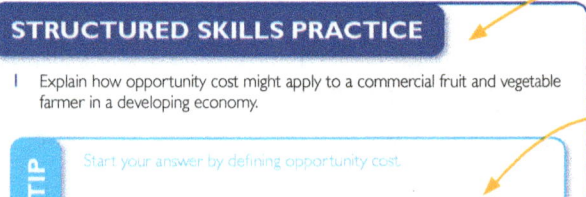

Structured skills practice – This feature serves as a reminder on how to interpret and answer structured question types.

Tip – Tip boxes remind you of a key point, advise you of a common error or offer guidance on how to approach a question.

Sample question and answer – Each chapter in the revision guide contains a sample question based on the information in that chapter, accompanied by an exemplary answer written by the authors.

Skills focus – Skills focus boxes contain helpful information about how to approach particular question types. Aspects of an answer may be highlighted to help make sure you understand exactly what a question is asking.

Sample question
Mauritius, an island in the Indian Ocean, has an economy which is heavily dependent on international tourism. Identify **two** examples for each of the four factors of production that are likely to have been responsible for the development of an international tourism business in Mauritius.

Sample answer:
Mauritius has sandy beaches and sunny weather (land) and an abundant supply of skilled and unskilled labour. Capital includes an international airport and hotels. In terms of enterprise, international companies are prepared to invest and take risks to develop the international tourism business, as well as local entrepreneurs who are increasing the scale of their businesses.

SKILLS FOCUS
There are other possibilities in each case. Note that land as a factor of production is best remembered as 'a natural resource'.

Progress check
Answer the following questions to check your understanding:
1 Define opportunity cost.
2 Suppose a small business has accumulated $10 000 to spend on its development. How can opportunity cost be applied to this situation?

Progress check – You will find short, straight-forward questions at regular intervals to help you check your understanding of the topics you should have learnt.

Exam-style multiple choice questions practice – Exam-style multiple choice questions appear at the end of each chapter where you can practice applying your knowledge and understanding of a particular topic.

Exam-style multiple choice questions
1 Why does the economic problem occur?
  A resources are limited; wants are limited
  B resources are limited; wants are unlimited
  C resources are unlimited; wants are limited
  D resources are unlimited; wants are unlimited

2 Which is **not** an economic good?
  A a free sample of a new type of soap
  B a local bus service
  C medical care provided free to young children
  D sunlight that helps crops to grow

Exam-style structured questions practice – Exam-style structured questions appear at the end of each section and are designed to help you practice applying your structured question skills as well as your economics knowledge.

Exam-style structured questions for Section 4
Data response question
Read the source material carefully before answering the question.

Source material: Economic growth in Pakistan since 2012
Pakistan's economic growth since 2012 has been very encouraging. It has increased from 3.8% in

Four-part question
This question is introduced by stimulus material. In your answer, you may refer to this material and/or to other examples that you have studied.

In 2017, the average rate of unemployment in Malaysia was 3.5%. It was reported that industrial output was increasing but there had been a drop in palm oil production and some service sector activities such as tourism. An even bigger concern was the rate of graduate unemployment, estimated to be as high as 18% among young graduates.

Revision checklist – Short, bullet-pointed summaries provide a useful overview of the key learning points you should know after studying a chapter.

Section 1:
THE BASIC ECONOMIC PROBLEM

Chapter 1

The nature of the economic problem

Learning summary

By the end of this chapter, you should understand:

- what is meant by wants and how these differ from needs
- why resources are scarce and why this can explain the so-called 'economic problem'
- the difference between economic goods and free goods.

1.1 Needs and wants

There is a fundamental difference between needs and wants. A need is something we must have in order to survive, for example food, clothing and somewhere to live. A **want** is something we would like to have in order to make our lives more enjoyable.

> **TERM**
>
> Wants: desires for goods and services.

1.2 The economic problem

Each of us faces the so-called '**economic problem**' – see Figure 1.1. This is because we do not have the income to satisfy all of our wants. It leads to a situation of **scarcity**. The economic problem affects individuals, businesses and government, none of which has the **resources** to meet all of their needs.

> **TERMS**
>
> Economic problem: unlimited wants exceeding finite resources.
>
> Scarcity: a situation where there is not enough to satisfy everyone's wants.
>
> Resources: factors used to produce goods and services.

> **TIP**
>
> Make sure you know the difference between something that is a need and something that is a want.

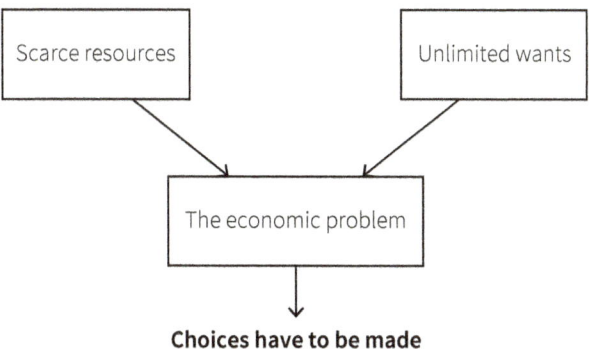

Figure 1.1 The economic problem

Sample question

Refer to Figure 1.1. Describe how the economic problem affects each of the following in a country that you have studied:

i   a typical family
ii the owner of a takeaway food stall
iii the government.

Sample answer:

i   A family's needs have to be satisfied from the income of family members – this can include benefits that are provided in kind or in monetary terms by the government. Wants are likely to be greater – a person might like a more up-to-date mobile phone, a new bicycle or to be able to watch a top football game. The economic problem is that a family may not have sufficient income to be able to do all of these.

ii The food stall owner might like to have some new cooking equipment or use some savings to purchase a second food stall. If unlimited resources were available it would be fine, but as this is unlikely the owner has to choose which of the options to pursue.

iii A government's income mainly comes from taxation which is then used to fund services such as hospitals and schools, to construct new roads or upgrade railway lines. Government revenue is limited – not all wants can be satisfied so, inevitably, choices have to be made.

SKILLS FOCUS

In each case, wants are unlimited, yet resources are limited whether family income, savings or a government's income from taxation. The point about unlimited wants and limited resources is fundamental when answering the sample question.

1.3 Economic goods and free goods

Almost everything that is provided is an **economic good**. This is because resources are required to produce such goods – these resources include raw materials, labour and business know-how. **Free goods** are different – no resources are required to produce such goods.

> ### TERMS
>
> **Economic good:** a product which requires resources to produce it and therefore has an opportunity cost.
>
> **Free good:** a product which does not require any resources to make it and so does not have an opportunity cost.

Progress check

Answer the following questions to check your understanding:

1. What is the difference between a need and a want?
2. What is the economic problem?
3. Give an example of a free good and an economic good.

Sample question

Describe whether each of these is an economic good or a free good:

i. a mobile phone
ii. rain water used to irrigate food crops
iii. free medicines for the elderly.

Sample answer:

i. A mobile phone is an economic good. This is because all sorts of resources, human and physical, are required in its production and sale to customers.

ii. Rain water could be either a free good or an economic good. The rain water itself is a free good when it falls directly onto crops. If a man-made irrigation system is required to make use of the rain water, then it becomes an economic good.

iii. Although elderly people are not charged for medicines, they are an economic good. This is because many resources and scientific expertise are required to manufacture the medicines before they are distributed to the elderly.

SKILLS FOCUS

The key point in each case is that an economic good requires resources to produce it.

Revision checklist

You should know:

- [ ] The fact that needs are essential while wants are not, means that we cannot always have everything we would like.
- [ ] This underpins the economic problem of unlimited wants in relation to scarce resources.
- [ ] Resources are required to produce economic goods, even though a charge may not be made for them.

STRUCTURED SKILLS PRACTICE

1. Explain how the economic problem might apply to a small clothing manufacturer in Bangladesh.
2. The Indian government provides 2.5 million farmers with free power to irrigation pumps. Explain why free power is an economic good.

TIP: This question could mislead. Think about whether any resources are being used.

Exam-style multiple choice questions

1. Why does the economic problem occur?
   - A resources are limited; wants are limited
   - B resources are limited; wants are unlimited
   - C resources are unlimited; wants are limited
   - D resources are unlimited; wants are unlimited

2. Which is **not** an economic good?
   - A a free sample of a new type of soap
   - B a local bus service
   - C medical care provided free to young children
   - D sunlight that helps crops to grow

Chapter 2: Factors of production

Learning summary

By the end of this chapter, you should understand:

- what is meant by factors of production
- the nature of land, labour, capital and enterprise, and be able to give examples of each
- what influences the mobility of factors of production
- the causes of changes in the quantity and quality of factors of production.

2.1 Factors of production

The term **factors of production** is used in economics to describe the resources that are needed to produce the many goods and services that are made in all types of economy. They are limited in supply.

Most economists identify four main factors of production, as shown in Figure 2.1.

> **TERM**
>
> Factors of production: the economic resources of land, labour, capital and enterprise.

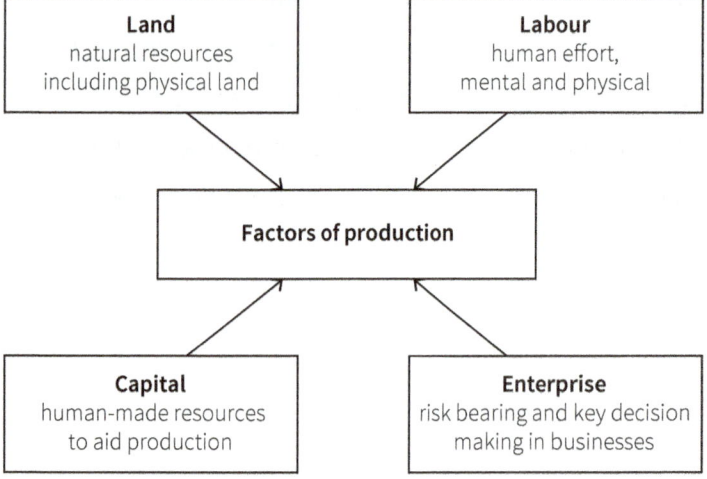

Figure 2.1 The four factors of production

Land covers any natural resource which is used in production. So besides the land itself, it also includes what is beneath the land (e.g. coal), what occurs naturally on the land (e.g. rainforests) and the seas, oceans and rivers, and what is found in them (e.g. fish).

Labour covers all human effort. This includes both the mental and the physical effort involved in producing goods and services.

Capital is any human-made (manufactured) good used to produce other goods and services. It includes, for example, offices, factories, machinery, railways and tools.

Enterprise is the willingness and ability to bear uncertain risks and to make decisions in a business. **Entrepreneurs** are the people who organise the other factors of production and who crucially bear the risk of losing their money if their business fails. Entrepreneurs decide what to produce by taking into account consumer demand and how to produce it.

> **TERM**
>
> Entrepreneur: a person who bears the risks and makes the key decisions in a business.

> **TIP**
>
> Remember:
> - Land is more than just a physical resource.
> - Labour is more than simply the number of workers.
> - Capital should not be confused with money used in the production process.
> - Enterprise involves risk and uncertainty.

Sample question

Mauritius, an island in the Indian Ocean, has an economy which is heavily dependent on international tourism. Identify **two** examples for each of the four factors of production that are likely to have been responsible for the development of an international tourism business in Mauritius.

Sample answer:

Mauritius has sandy beaches and sunny weather (land) and an abundant supply of skilled and unskilled labour. Capital includes an international airport and hotels. In terms of enterprise, international companies are prepared to invest and take risks to develop the international tourism business, as well as local entrepreneurs who are increasing the scale of their businesses.

> **SKILLS FOCUS**
>
> There are other possibilities in each case. Note that land as a factor of production is best remembered as 'a natural resource'.

2.2 Mobility of the factors of production

Mobility refers to the extent to which it is possible to change how or where a factor of production can be used. The extent of mobility varies for each factor of production.

TERMS

Occupationally mobile: capable of changing use.

Geographically immobile: incapable of moving from one location to another location.

Figure 2.2 compares the extent of **occupational and geographical mobility** of the factors of production.

IMMOBILE → MOBILE	
Mobility of land	• Geographically immobile, although a piece of land can be used to support various activities such as a factory or an office block
Mobility of labour	• Some geographical and occupational mobility is possible, e.g. migration of workers to countries such as the UK, Singapore and Dubai • May also be immobile for occupational reasons (e.g. a dentist could become a labourer on a construction site, but you would not want an unqualified labourer to be your dentist) and for personal or family reasons
Mobility of capital	• Can be very mobile, e.g. the globalisation of manufacturing and service sector activity • Mobility depends on the type of capital, because some capital resources cannot be moved
Mobility of enterprise	• Very geographically and occupationally mobile because entrepreneurs have the skills to organise different types of business in almost any location anywhere in the world

Figure 2.2 Mobility of factors of production

2.3 Quantity and quality of the factors of production

The quantity and quality of an economy's factors of production are important enablers in allowing it to grow and develop. For many less developed economies, the lack of adequate factors of production can be a reason why development is restricted.

- 'Quantity' refers to the *volume of resources* available through an economy's factors of production.
- 'Quality' means *how useful or productive* its factors of production are. This is particularly relevant in the case of an economy's **labour force** and capital.

> **TIP**
>
> Be careful not to confuse **productivity** with production, which is defined as the output arising from the use of factors of production.

> **TERMS**
>
> Labour force: people in work and those actively seeking work.
>
> Productivity: the output per factor of production in an hour.

Table 2.1 summarises how quantity and quality can apply to the factors of production.

Table 2.1 How quantity and quality apply to the factors of production

Factor of production	Quantity	Quality
Land	Fixed in general terms – subject to depletion through over-use	Has modest scope for improvement
Labour	Dependent on the size of population and other determinants of the labour force	Dependent on the education, training, experience and health of the labour force
Capital	Influenced by investment	Affected by technological advances which produce higher-quality output
Enterprise	Influenced by favourable economic conditions which develop entrepreneurs	Dependent on experience but also willingness to bear risks

> **Progress check**
>
> Answer the following questions to check your understanding:
>
> 1 Give an example of each factor of production for a food stall trader in a local market.
>
> 2 Why might an agricultural worker be occupationally and geographically immobile?
>
> 3 Give examples of how the quality of labour in an economy might be improved.

Sample question

As the size of the global population continues to grow, there is an ever-increasing need to increase food production. Explain how the quantity and quality of the factors of production can be used to expand production.

Sample answer:

The factors of production – land, labour, capital, enterprise – are the resources required to produce goods and services. There are many possibilities to improve their quantity and quality which will lead to an increase in food production.

Land can be reclaimed for agriculture. The fertility of land can be improved and land pollution can be reduced.

In the case of labour, more workers can be employed to increase food production and the skill level of the agricultural workforce can be improved by training.

Capital can be used to purchase more machinery in order to increase crop yields and older machinery can be replaced with modern, more efficient equipment.

Entrepreneurs (enterprise) can be encouraged to invest in agriculture and more can be done to enhance awareness of business opportunities.

SKILLS FOCUS

Note how an example of quantity and quality is given for each factor of production, as required by the question. This is good examination technique and shows that both aspects of the question have been considered.

Revision checklist

You should know:

- There are four factors of production – land, labour, capital and enterprise.
- These are the key resources that are required to produce goods and services in any type of economy.
- The factors of production vary in terms of their mobility.
- Changes in the quantity and quality of factors of production lead to changes in the ways in which goods and services are produced.

STRUCTURED SKILLS PRACTICE

1. Explain why Japanese car manufacturers have moved their production and assembly of vehicles to other Asian locations.

   Refer to the factors of production in your answer. A good starting point is to recognise that other Asian locations are likely to have lower labour costs and lower costs of setting up a production plant.

Exam-style multiple choice questions

1. Which factor of production is an airport?

   A capital

   B enterprise

   C labour

   D land

2. Which of these is **not** a likely cause of the geographical immobility of labour in a developing economy?

   A a lack of information about job opportunities

   B a reluctance to move away from family and friends

   C a worker has appropriate skills

   D the cost of moving from a rural area to a city.

3. Which is an important characteristic of an entrepreneur?

   A being happy just to make a decent living

   B being willing to take risks and bear the consequences

   C being willing to work only between 9 am and 5 pm

   D hating to invest in new ideas.

Chapter 3: Opportunity cost

Learning summary

By the end of this chapter, you should understand:

- what is meant by opportunity cost
- how opportunity cost applies in different contexts
- how opportunity cost influences the decision making of consumers, workers, producers and governments.

3.1 Opportunity cost

Opportunity cost is an important topic, particularly in microeconomics. It is also relevant in macroeconomics when considering the choices that governments face.

As shown in Chapter 1, economic resources are scarce and, because of this, choices inevitably have to be made. Opportunity cost is relevant when considering these choices in order to come up with the best alternative.

> **TERM**
>
> **Opportunity cost:** the best alternative forgone.

Look at these examples to see how opportunity cost affects decision making.

- *For yourself.* You have a big decision ahead of you! Once you have finished your IGCSEs or O Levels, if you choose to continue at college, the opportunity cost is the best alternative which is getting a job.
- *For a government.* Every year governments have to address how much tax revenue they should spend on the services they provide such as education, healthcare, infrastructure and so on. As finances are limited, choices have to be made. If there is a pressing need for more to be spent on healthcare, there will have to be less spending on education, assuming this is the best alternative forgone.

> **TIP**
>
> Opportunity cost is expressed in terms of the best alternative action. It is usually a physical alternative and not expressed in monetary terms.

Sample question

In the 2017/18 federal budget, Pakistan's finance minister announced the following:

- outlay of 4.75 trillion rupees (Rs) and tax revenue of Rs 4.33 trillion
- a 40% increase in development expenditure
- an increase in the minimum wage to Rs 15 000
- allocation of Rs 121 billion to an Income Support Programme for 5.5 million beneficiaries
- some income and purchase taxes to be increased to pay for additional government spending

Explain how opportunity cost can be applied to the many decisions that the finance minister has to make in preparing the federal budget.

Sample answer:

The finance minister is faced with having to make many choices, in terms of how to spend the outlay and how to raise the required tax revenue. For example, should more handouts be given to small farmers or should the minimum wage be increased? Should high income earners pay more tax or should the tax on petrol be increased? Such decisions need to be thought through carefully.

SKILLS FOCUS

This is a typical situation involving opportunity cost. The sample answer looks at its application to both sides of the budget. The finance minister can make changes to taxation or government spending or, what is most likely, a combination of both.

Progress check

Answer the following questions to check your understanding:

1. Define opportunity cost.
2. Suppose a small business has accumulated $10 000 to spend on its development. How can opportunity cost be applied to this situation?

Revision checklist

You should know:

- ☐ Opportunity cost involves sacrificing the best alternative in favour of a preferred action.
- ☐ Opportunity cost applies to the decisions made by consumers, producers and governments.

STRUCTURED SKILLS PRACTICE

1 Explain how opportunity cost might apply to a commercial fruit and vegetable farmer in a developing economy.

TIP Start your answer by defining opportunity cost.

Exam-style multiple choice questions

1 A student decides to go to college to study A Levels. The fees will be $1000 a year for two years. The student's alternative is to get a job that will pay $5000 a year. What is the opportunity cost of going to college?

A $8000
B $10 000
C $12 000
D $15 000

2 A construction worker has been offered three new jobs. The worker ranks the jobs in preferred order and decides to take a job as a lorry driver. What might be the opportunity cost?

A the difference in pay between a construction worker and a lorry driver
B the more regular work as a lorry driver
C the second ranked job as a security guide
D the wage as a construction worker

Production possibility curves

Learning summary

By the end of this chapter, you should understand:

- what is meant by a production possibility curve
- how to use, draw and interpret production possibility curves
- the causes and consequences of shifts in a production possibility curve.

4.1 Production possibility curves (PPC)

> **TERM**
>
> Production possibility curve (PPC): a curve that shows the maximum output of two types of product and the combination of those products that can be produced with existing resources and technology.

Figure 4.1 is a typical example of a PPC. It shows:

- how the country's resources can be used to produce either 300 million capital goods (such as machinery) or 200 million consumer goods (such as food or clothing)
- that any point on the PPC, for example A or B, represents a situation where all resources are being fully used
- that not all resources are being used at point C, which is inside the PPC
- that point D, outside the PPC, is not achievable given current resources and technology.

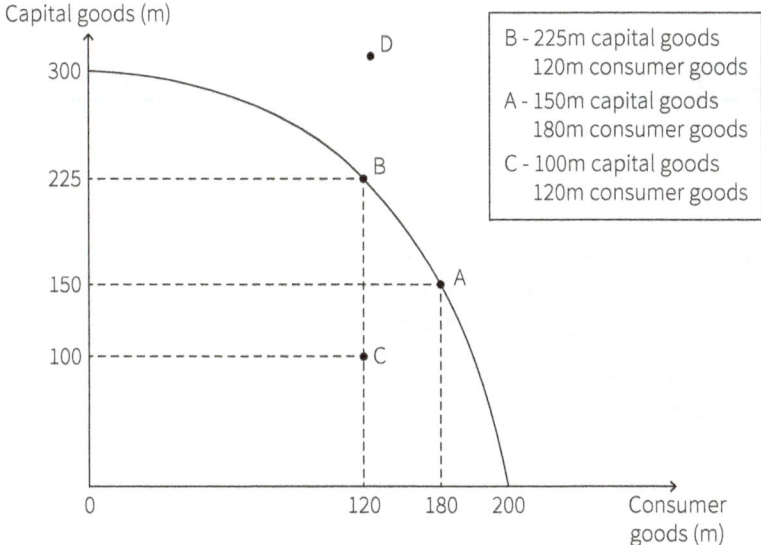

Figure 4.1 A production possibility curve – the figures in the box show the maximum output for capital and consumer goods at points A, B and C

> **TIP**
>
> Remember to label the x and y axes correctly on a production possibility curve, otherwise the diagram will make no sense. The axes must be labelled with two different goods. A common mistake is to label the axes price and quantity. Include '0' for the origin.

Sample question

The diagram shows a production possibility curve.

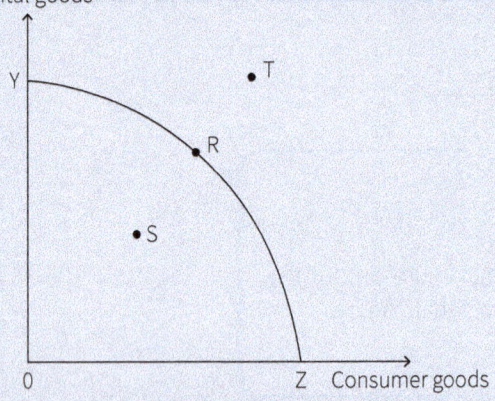

i What is the maximum amount of consumer goods that can be used?

ii What does this imply for the production of capital goods?

iii At which point on the diagram is production efficient?

iv At which point on the diagram could production be increased?

v At which point on the diagram is the level of production not possible?

Sample answer:

i Z

ii No capital goods can be produced as all available resources are being used to produce consumer goods.

iii R

iv S

v T

SKILLS FOCUS

The purpose of this sample question is to enable you to identify the characteristics of PPCs. These are the aspects that you will need to know.

4.2 Movements along a PPC

A movement along a PPC shows how resources can be reallocated. This is shown in Figure 4.1 where a movement along the PPC from A to B leads to more resources being allocated to capital goods with fewer resources being available for consumer goods.

Moving from A to B results in a loss of 60 million units of capital goods. This lost production is the opportunity cost of moving from A to B.

4.3 Shifts of a PPC

A shift of a PPC is different. It represents a situation where more resources (shift to right) or fewer resources (shift to left) become available. These shifts are shown in Figure 4.2.

(a) Shift to right – possible reasons include increase in labour force, improved technology and improved education

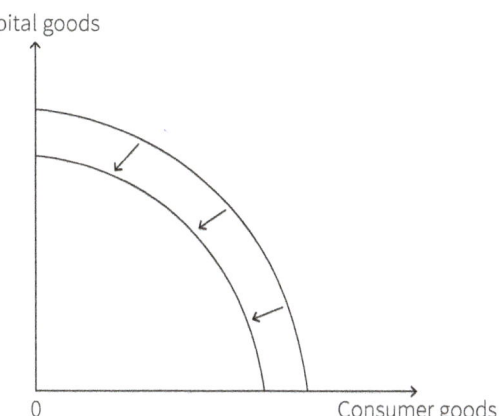

(b) Shift to left – possible reasons include net outward migration, capital stock not being replaced and natural disasters

Figure 4.2 Shifts in PPC

Progress check

Answer the following questions to check your understanding:

1. Draw a production possibility curve (PPC).
2. On this diagram, show a movement along the PPC and an outward shift of the PPC. Explain what each means.

Revision checklist

You should know:

- ☐ A production possibility curve can be used to show how resources in an economy can be allocated.
- ☐ There is a difference between a movement along a PPC and a shift of the PPC.
- ☐ Opportunity cost can be applied to the reallocation of resources.

STRUCTURED SKILLS PRACTICE

1 In 2016, the Nigerian economy experienced negative growth of 3% mainly due to falling oil prices. There was also a reallocation of productive resources from the oil sector to the non-oil sector. Analyse these two changes, using a production possibility curve (PPC) diagram.

TIP You should draw a PPC for each change.

Exam-style multiple choice questions

1 In 2016, the Philippines experienced a tsunami that had a devastating effect on its economy. How might this be shown on a production possibility curve (PPC)?

A as a movement of the point of production away from the PPC

B as a shift to the left of the PPC

C as a shift to the right of the PPC

D with no change in the position of the PPC

2 Using all available resources, an economy produces different combinations of capital goods and consumer goods as shown on its production possibility curve (PPC) diagram below.

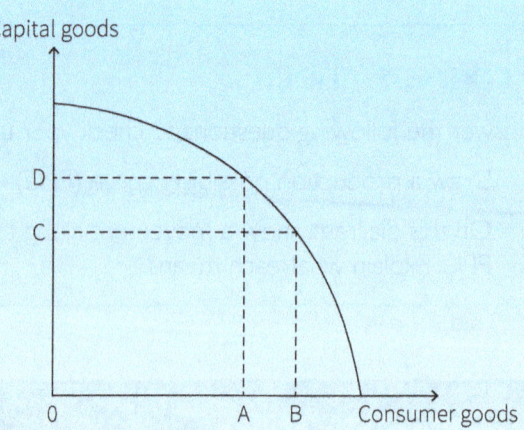

What is the opportunity cost of increasing the production of consumer goods from A to B?

A AB

B CD

C 0A

D 0C

Exam-style structured questions for Section 1

Data response question

Read the source material carefully before answering the question.

Source material: Zambia's health sector budget issues

Zambia is a lower middle income economy in Africa. Since 2012, its economy has faltered, resulting in a depreciation of its currency, the kwacha. Typically, families have experienced a fall in incomes, which in turn has put pressure on the government's budget.

Health is an important area of government spending (see Figure S1.1). The Zambian government is committed to providing universal free care irrespective of income or wealth, although a nominal charge is made for some services. The budget allocation of 8.3% of total spending in 2016 was well below the target of 15% recommended by the African Union countries' Abuja Declaration of 2001. Increasing this percentage will not be easy in the current economic climate.

About 60% of the health budget is spent on labour costs. Due to rising import prices for essential drugs, very little is left for new hospitals and up-to-date equipment. It is clear that if the government cannot pay, any new funding will have to come from out-of-pocket charges for patients. This would not be popular as citizens in Zambia already pay double that of those in neighbouring lower middle income countries for the same medical services.

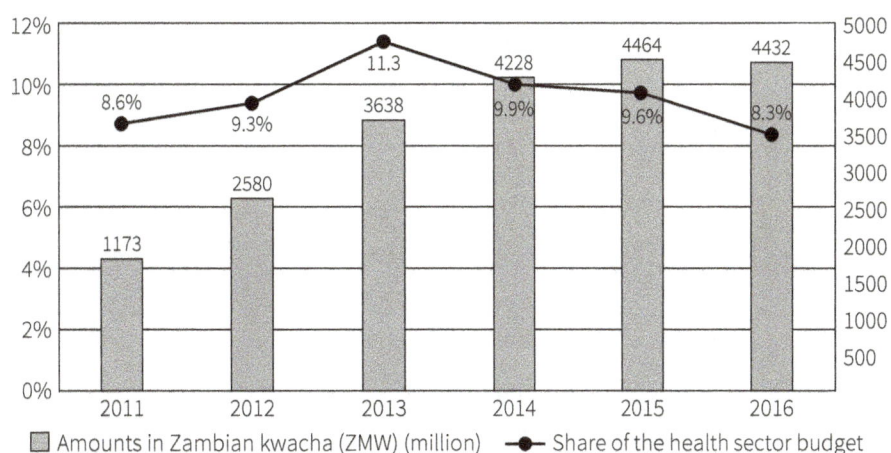

Figure S1.1 Zambia's health budget and its percentage share of the national budget

Source: Annual national budget speeches for Zambia from 2011 to 2016.

Answer all parts of the question. Refer to the source material in your answers.

a Calculate the approximate decrease in the share of the health sector budget from 2013 to 2016. [1]

b Describe the change in the amount of money allocated to the health sector from 2011 to 2016. [2]

c Explain what additional information you would need to be more certain about the change in spending on healthcare services. [2]

d Explain **two** factors of production that are necessary for the provision of healthcare services. [4]

e Explain whether free healthcare is a free good or an economic good. [4]

f Analyse how a fall in expenditure on healthcare might affect the production possibility curve in Zambia. [5]

g Discuss whether or not opportunity cost can be used by the Zambian government when faced with having to make difficult budgetary decisions. [6]

h Discuss whether or not the Zambian government should increase out-of-pocket charges for those using certain healthcare services. [6]

Four-part question

This question is introduced by stimulus material. In your answer, you may refer to this material and/or other examples that you have studied.

In 2017, migrant workers comprised about one-third of Singapore's three million labour force. Many migrant workers are from Bangladesh, India, Malaysia and the Philippines, and work in construction, shipbuilding and hotels. Strict laws govern their numbers and how long they are able to stay in Singapore.

a Define 'enterprise'. [2]

b Explain why some factors of production are more mobile than others. [4]

c Analyse why some workers may wish to migrate to countries such as Singapore. [6]

d Discuss whether or not a country such as Singapore should regulate the number of migrant workers. [8]

Section 2:
THE ALLOCATION OF RESOURCES

Chapter 5: Microeconomics and macroeconomics

Learning summary

By the end of this chapter, you should understand:

- ☐ what is meant by microeconomics and macroeconomics, and the difference between them
- ☐ who are the key decision makers in microeconomics and macroeconomics.

5.1 Microeconomics and macroeconomics

The difference between **microeconomics** and **macroeconomics** is in their names – 'micro' means small-scale, while 'macro' means large-scale.

TERMS

Microeconomics: the study of the behaviour and decisions of households and firms, and the performance of individual markets.

Macroeconomics: the study of the whole economy.

Market: an arrangement which brings buyers into contact with sellers.

TIP

You should now realise that not all economic problems and issues can be classified as simply microeconomics or macroeconomics.

Microeconomics – involves how individuals, households and firms behave in **markets**, for example:

- Why do individuals buy more of a particular product when its price falls?
- What happens to the demand for cars when household income increases?
- What happens to food prices when there is a drought?
- Why do star football players get paid huge wages?

Macroeconomics – involves a wide range of topics in all sorts of economies, for example:

- Why has India's economic growth increased above that of China in recent years?
- What are the main causes of inflation in Pakistan?
- How important is international tourism for the economy of Mauritius?
- What might be the effects if the EU imposes a tariff on UK vehicle exports when the UK leaves the EU?

> ## Sample question
> Explain how each of the following situations can involve microeconomic and macroeconomic concepts:
>
> i   a rise in the price of imported Chinese television sets in Malaysia
>
> ii a reduction in the rate of interest in Malaysia.
>
> **Sample answer:**
>
> i   A rise in the price of imported Chinese televisions will lead to a fall in the quantity demanded (micro). Consumers will be likely to switch to locally manufactured televisions as these will now be relatively cheaper (micro). This will likely increase employment in Malaysian manufacturers (macro) and increase the surplus in the balance of trade (macro).
>
> ii A reduction in the rate of interest in Malaysia will increase the funds available for lending to consumers (macro). Consumers will now purchase 'big ticket' items such as televisions and cars (micro). This will increase total demand (macro) and if these are produced in Malaysia, there will be an increase in employment in these industries (macro).
>
> ### SKILLS FOCUS
> Both examples show how, in seemingly simple situations, microeconomic and macroeconomic concepts are interwoven.

> ## Progress check
> Answer the following questions to check your understanding:
>
> 1 Give an example of a microeconomic issue and a macroeconomic issue that is currently affecting your household.
>
> 2 Give **four** examples of markets.

5.2 Decision makers in microeconomics and macroeconomics

Decision makers are often called **economic agents**. They include individuals, households, firms and governments.

> ### TERM
> Economic agents: those who undertake economic activities and make economic decisions.

Revision checklist

You should know:

- [ ] Microeconomics is the study of individual markets, while macroeconomics is the study of the whole economy.
- [ ] A decision maker is also called an economic agent.

STRUCTURED SKILLS PRACTICE

1. i Give two examples of macroeconomic decisions that have to be taken by a government.
   ii Explain whether the decision in each case involves an opportunity cost.

TIP Remember that opportunity cost is the best alternative that is forgone. Any government decision involving funding is likely to have an opportunity cost.

Exam-style multiple choice questions

1. The government of Qatar fixes the wages of migrant labour on government construction projects. Which branch of economics is this?

   A microeconomics only

   B macroeconomics only

   C microeconomics with some macroeconomics

   D macroeconomics with some microeconomics

2. Which economic agents influence food prices in Pakistan?

	Pakistan households	Pakistan farmers	Pakistan government
A	No	Yes	No
B	Yes	Yes	Yes
C	No	No	Yes
D	Yes	No	No

The role of markets in allocating resources

Learning summary

By the end of this chapter, you should understand:

- the key allocation decisions that have to be made in all economic systems
- the nature of the market mechanism
- how the price system provides answers to key allocation decisions.

6.1 The three fundamental economic questions

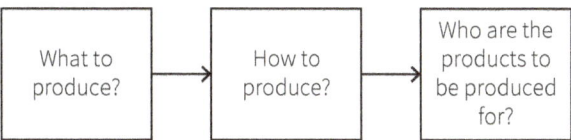

Figure 6.1 The three fundamental economic questions

The questions shown in Figure 6.1 arise because of the basic economic problem that was described in Chapter 1.

6.2 Economic systems

> **TERM**
>
> Economic system: the institutions, organisations and mechanisms that influence economic behaviour and determine how resources are allocated.

The answers to the three economic questions depend on the type of **economic system**.

There are three main types of economic system – see Figure 6.2. The difference between them depends on the respective roles and importance of government and the **price mechanism**.

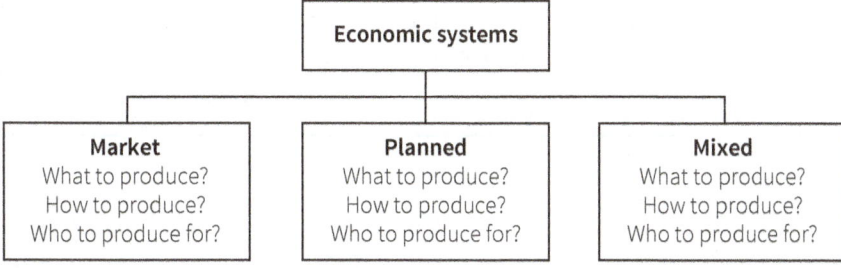

Figure 6.2 The three main types of economic system

TERM

Price mechanism: the system by which the market forces of demand and supply determine prices.

Sample question

Most countries have mixed economic systems. The size of the private sector varies. The diagram shows government spending as a percentage of total expenditure for selected countries in 2014.

i Identify the evidence to suggest that the governments of Kiribati, Cuba and France provide most goods and services.

ii State how most goods and services are allocated in Pakistan.

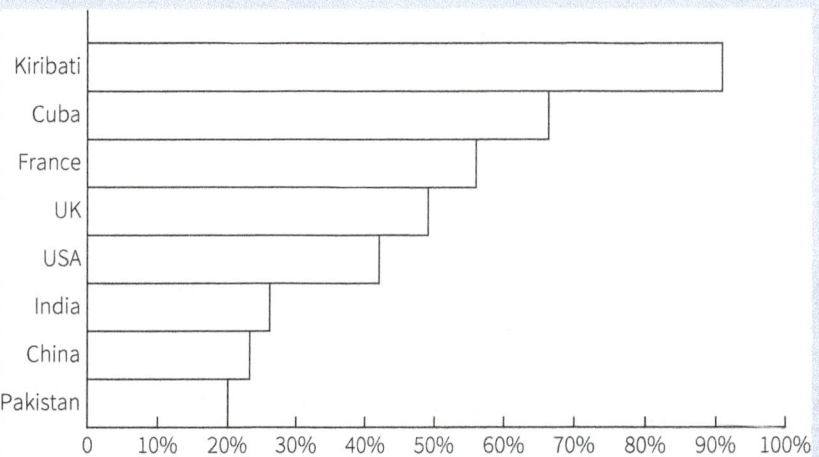

Government spending as a percentage of total expenditure, 2014

Sample answer:

i In each of the named countries, the percentage of government spending is above 50% of total expenditure.

ii Most goods and services in Pakistan are allocated through the market mechanism.

SKILLS FOCUS

The data may seem surprising, especially for China where only about a quarter of total spending comes from the government. This reflects the growing importance of the private sector and the market in what has been, and still is, a rapidly growing economy. Note that the data is in the form of percentages and therefore does not take into account the different sizes of these economies.

6.3 The price mechanism in a market economic system

In a market economic system, consumers and producers signal their preferences through the price mechanism. Government intervention is minimal. The price mechanism works automatically whereby prices are determined by the interaction of **demand** and **supply**.

> **TERMS**
>
> Demand: the willingness and ability to buy a product.
>
> Supply: the willingness and ability to sell a product.

Figure 6.3 shows two ways in which the price mechanism works when there is a shortage of supply and an oversupply of cooking oil in the market. In both cases, **market equilibrium** is restored after a time lag.

> **TERMS**
>
> Market equilibrium: a situation where demand and supply are equal at the current price.
>
> Market disequilibrium: a situation where demand and supply are not equal at the current price.

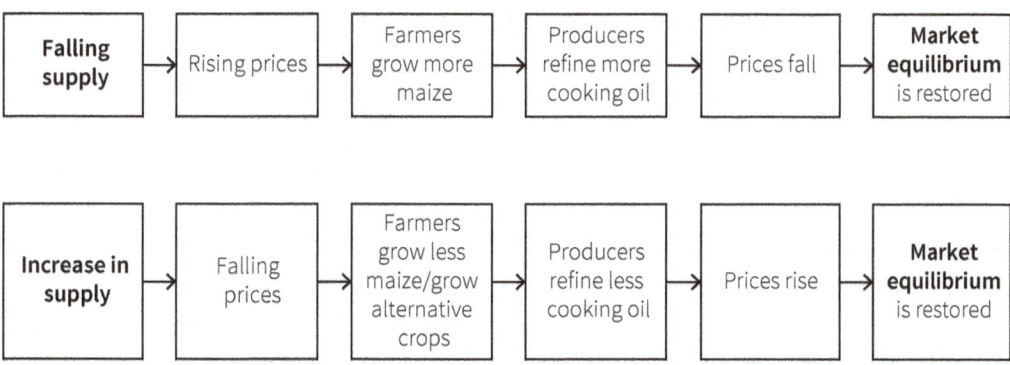

Figure 6.3 Price mechanism at work in a market economy

> **TIP**
>
> Remember that in a market economy it is always assumed that prices are determined by the twin forces of demand and supply.

Progress check

Answer the following questions to check your understanding:

1. What are the three fundamental economic questions?
2. What are the two main features of any economic system?
3. When is a market in equilibrium?
4. Refer to Figure 6.3. Draw similar diagrams to show how the price mechanism works when:
    i demand falls
    ii demand increases.

Revision checklist

You should know:

- [ ] Most countries have mixed economic systems. This is so in developed and developing economies.
- [ ] The price mechanism is central to the allocation of resources.
- [ ] Where there is no government intervention, prices are determined where demand and supply are equal.

STRUCTURED SKILLS PRACTICE

1. Pakistan is a typical example of an economy where the market has an increasing role in the allocation of resources. Explain in principle how this is likely to have come about.

    **TIP** The key phrase in this question is 'how this is likely to have come about'. Your answer should explain how the roles of government and the price mechanism have changed over time.

Exam-style multiple choice question

1. Recent clinical studies have shown that the excessive consumption of sugar is not good for health. Which is the **least** likely response from the market?

   A consumers increase their demand for low sugar drinks

   B sugar farmers in the Carribbean plant fewer sugar canes

   C sugar refiners reduce their production

   D the market price for sugar increases.

Demand

Chapter 7

Learning summary

By the end of this chapter, you should understand:

- what is meant by demand and how to draw a demand curve
- the link between individual and market demand in terms of aggregation
- how to distinguish between extensions and contractions in demand
- the causes of shifts in the demand curve.

7.1 Definition of demand

When economists refer to **demand**, they mean effective demand. It means that individuals must be able to afford a product and that a firm is prepared to sell this product to them.

> **TERM**
>
> Demand: the willingness and ability to buy a product.

7.2 Demand and price

Demand and price are inversely related. In other words, demand for a product will increase or rise as price falls and will decrease or fall as price rises. If a product has similar competing products, as its price rises, consumers may decide to switch to a competing product. If the price of the competing product rises, consumers are most likely to reduce their demand for it.

7.3 Individual and market demand

Individual demand is the amount of a product an individual would be willing and able to buy, at different prices. The **market demand** for a product is arrived at by the aggregation of the demand of all potential consumers or buyers. So if, say, 100 people are buyers of a given product, the sum of the demand from each makes up the market demand.

> **TERMS**
>
> Individual demand: a consumer's demand for a product.
>
> Market demand: total demand for a product.

A *demand schedule* is a table of data which shows how much of a product is demanded at different prices. Table 7.1 shows an example for the weekly demand for cinema tickets.

Table 7.1 A demand schedule showing weekly demand for cinema tickets

Price ($)	40	28	22	16	12	10
Quantity demanded in '000s	300	400	500	750	1000	1200

This data can be plotted on a simple graph and joined up to give a *demand curve*. This is shown in Figure 7.1.

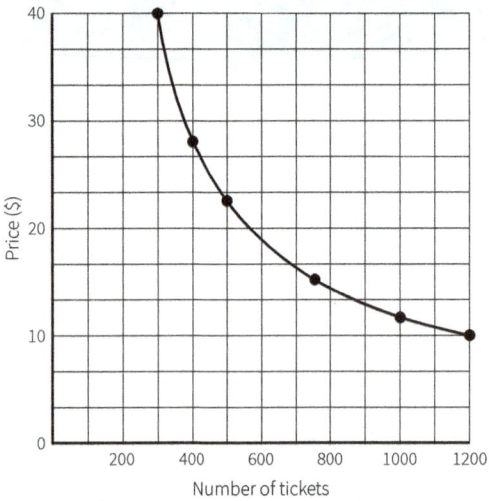

Figure 7.1 A demand curve showing weekly demand for cinema tickets

When drawing a demand curve, always make sure that price is on the vertical (y) axis and that quantity demanded is on the horizontal (x) axis. Check that you have labelled each correctly and remember to show the origin (0).

Figure 7.1 shows:

- how many cinema tickets are demanded at any price in the range $10 to $40
- that no tickets will be bought if the price exceeds $40.

It is often convenient to show a demand curve as a straight line (yet still refer to it as a demand 'curve').

The effect of change in price on demand

A demand curve diagram can be used to demonstrate how a change in the price of a product affects the quantity that is demanded. This is shown by a movement along the demand curve, up or down.

TERMS

Extension in demand: a rise in the quantity demanded caused by a fall in the price of the product itself.

Contraction in demand: a fall in the quantity demanded caused by a rise in the price of the product itself.

TIP

Both **extension in demand** and **contraction in demand** refer to 'quantity demanded'.

Sample question

Refer to the weekly demand for cinema tickets in Figure 7.1. Reproduce the demand curve and then identify:

i an extension in demand as the price of cinema tickets falls from $21 to $16

ii a contraction in demand as the price of cinema tickets increases from $12 to $16.

Sample answer:

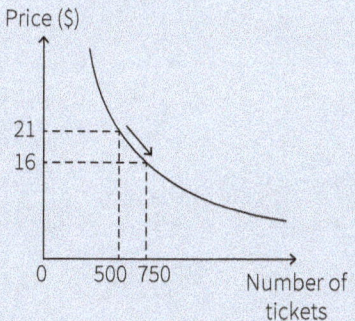

i An extension in demand for cinema tickets

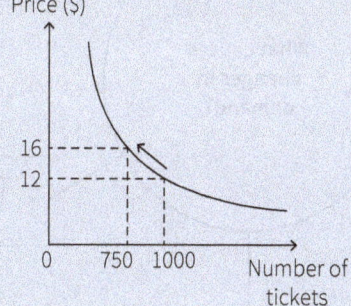

ii A contraction in demand for cinema tickets

SKILLS FOCUS

The arrows on the diagrams make it clear how the quantity demanded has changed. This is good practice and makes clear which movement you are explaining. Correctly drawn diagrams will help to enhance your answers.

7.4 Conditions of demand

A range of causes can bring about **changes in demand** – either more or less of a product being demanded.

> **TERM**
>
> **Changes in demand:** shifts in the demand curve.

> **TIP**
>
> Any change in demand will cause a shift in the *entire* demand curve as there is no change in the price of the product.

While price has an important effect on demand, it is not the only influence.

There are many reasons why consumers demand different quantities of a product, even though the price of the product has not changed – see Figure 7.2.

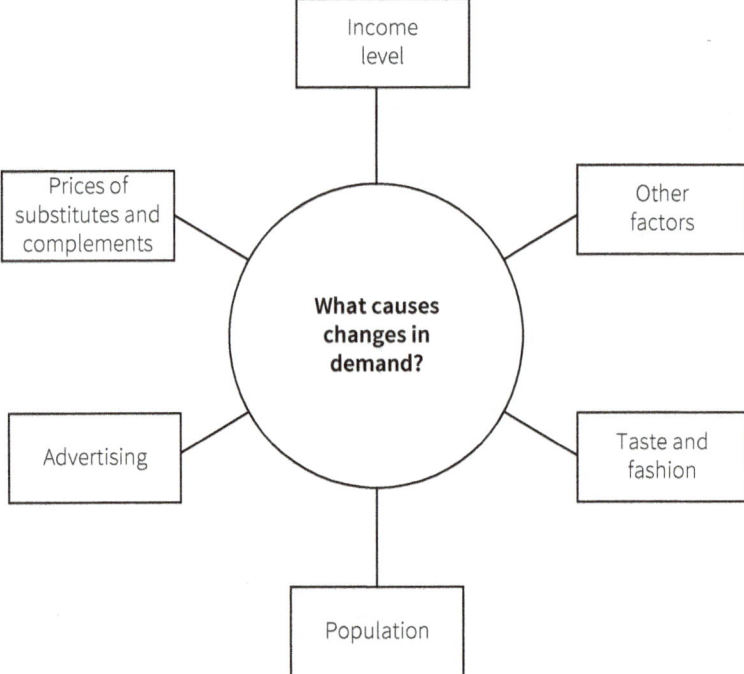

Figure 7.2 Causes of change in demand

It is not easy to prioritise these reasons but for many products, a change in income or a change in the prices of related products (known as **substitutes** and **complements**) can be very relevant.

TERMS

Substitute: a product that can be used in place of another.

Complement: a product that is used together with another product.

Normal goods: a product whose demand increases when income increases and decreases when income falls.

Inferior goods: a product whose demand decreases when income increases and increases when income falls.

TIP

Whether a good is **normal** or **inferior** depends on the income level of consumers.

TERMS

Increase in demand: a rise in demand at any given price, causing the demand curve to shift to the right.

Decrease in demand: a fall in demand at any given price, causing the demand curve to shift to the left.

Sample question

The sale of upmarket Range Rover Evoque vehicles in China increased by 19% in 2016. Explain **two** reasons for the **increase in demand** and how this affects the demand curve.

Sample answer:

Two possible reasons for the increase in demand could be an increase in disposable incomes of some Chinese consumers and a major advertising campaign for this upmarket vehicle. The increase in demand will lead to a shift to the right in the demand curve.

SKILLS FOCUS

The sample answer includes a reference to the stimulus material by noting the superior upmarket nature of the vehicle as a cause. This is good. Other possible causes for an increase in demand could have included an increase in the price of similar upmarket vehicles or the fashionable status attached to owning such a vehicle.

Sample question

Sambal is a popular sauce widely used in Indonesian home cooking. Suppose there has been a **decrease in demand** for sambal.

i State the effect on the demand curve for sambal.

ii Identify **two** reasons for the fall in demand.

Sample answer:

i The demand curve for sambal shifts to the left.

ii Reasons for fall in demand may include a fall in the price of similar cooking sauces, or an increase in the price of complements such as fish and vegetables.

SKILLS FOCUS

Other reasons might include a decrease in the price of takeaway food, or a change in food choices among young people. In theory, a shift to the left of the demand curve might have occurred because of a fall in consumer incomes. This is unlikely, though.

This is a good example of where the stem of the question is giving a prompt as to what might be a likely answer.

Progress check

Answer the following questions to check your understanding:

1 What is the usual relationship between demand and price?

2 Draw a typical straight line demand curve. On it, show:

   i a contraction in demand

   ii a decrease in demand.

   Explain what each means.

3 Give **three** reasons why the demand for chocolate is falling in many developed countries.

Revision checklist

You should know:

- Demand is the willingness and ability to buy a product.
- It can be represented by individual and market demand curves.
- A change in price leads to an increase or decrease in the quantity demanded.
- A change in demand occurs for various reasons and leads to a shift to the right or left of the entire demand curve.

STRUCTURED SKILLS PRACTICE

1. Explain the likely effects on the demand for a well-known brand of cola when

   i   its price increases

   ii there is an increase in the price of a substitute brand of cola.

   TIP
   Questions such as this can best be thought through with a diagram. The explanation should refer to the diagram, noting changes to both price and quantity.

2. Global sales of electric vehicles have increased by over 1000% since 2012. Explain **two** likely causes of this increase in demand.

Exam-style multiple choice questions

1. A new smart-phone has been launched, but its price is higher than expected. What will happen to a person's willingness and ability to purchase this product?

	Willingness	Ability
A	increases	increases
B	increases	decreases
C	decreases	decreases
D	decreases	increases

2. A retailer decreases the price of a poorly selling product. What will happen to the demand curve?

   A it will shift to the left

   B it will shift to the right

   C there will be a movement down the demand curve

   D there will be a movement up the demand curve

3. A government advertising campaign links the excessive consumption of fizzy drinks with type 2 diabetes. What will happen to the market demand curve for fizzy drinks?

   A it will shift to the left

   B it will shift to the right

   C there will be movement up or down

   D there will be no change

4. If sales of chicken and rice from local takeaway stalls have been falling when income levels have been increasing, what type of goods might chicken and rice be?

   A complementary goods

   B inferior goods

   C normal goods

   D substitute goods

Chapter 8: Supply

Learning summary

By the end of this chapter, you should understand:

- what is meant by supply and how to draw a supply curve
- the link between individual and market supply
- how to distinguish between extensions and contractions in supply
- the causes of shifts in the supply curve.

8.1 Definition of supply

When economists talk about **supply**, it refers to the willingness and ability of a producer to supply what the market requires at given prices. Supply is not the same as production, although it is influenced by the amount produced.

> **TERM**
>
> Supply: the willingness and ability to sell a product.

8.2 Supply and price

Supply and price are positively related. In other words, the supply of a product will increase or rise as the price rises and will decrease or fall as price falls.

8.3 Individual and market supply

Individual supply is the supply of one plant/firm, whereas **market supply** is the total supply of a product supplied by all the firms in the industry.

> **TERMS**
>
> Individual supply: supply from one firm.
>
> Market supply: total supply of a product.

The market supply for a product is arrived at by the aggregation of supply from all producers or firms. So, if ten firms produce a given product, the sum or aggregation of supply from each makes up the market supply.

A *supply schedule* is a table of data which shows how much of a product will be supplied at different prices. Table 8.1 shows an example for the monthly supply of rickshaw rides in an Indian city.

Table 8.1 A supply schedule showing monthly supply of rickshaw rides

Price per ride ($)	0.5	1	1.5	2	2.5
Quantity supplied (million)	50	140	220	300	375

The data can be plotted on a simple graph and joined up to give a *supply curve*. This is shown in Figure 8.1.

> **TIP**
>
> When drawing a supply curve, always make sure that price is on the vertical (y) axis and that quantity supplied is on the horizontal (x) axis. Check that you have labelled each correctly and remember to show the origin (0).

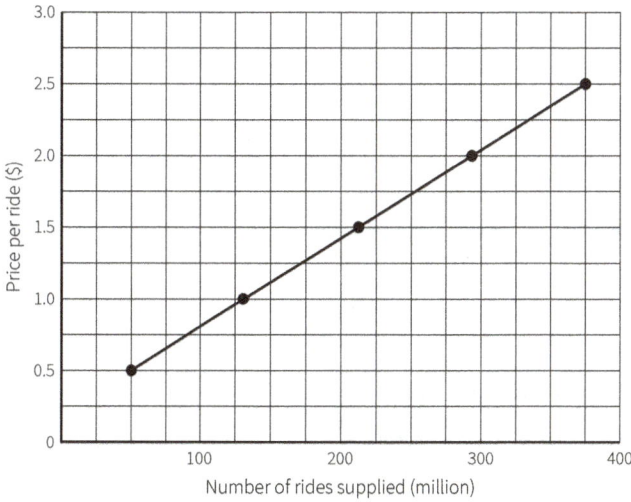

Figure 8.1 A supply curve showing monthly supply of rickshaw rides

> **TIP**
>
> The supply curve in Figure 8.1 is a straight line. It is still referred to as a supply curve.

The effect of a change in price on supply

A supply curve can be used to demonstrate how a change in the price of a product affects the quantity that is supplied. This is shown by a movement along the supply curve, up or down.

> **TERMS**
>
> **Extension in supply:** a rise in the quantity supplied caused by a rise in the price of the product itself.
>
> **Contraction in supply:** a fall in the quantity supplied caused by a fall in the price of the product itself.

 Both **extension in supply** and **contraction in supply** refer to 'quantity supplied'.

8.4 Conditions of supply

TERM

Changes in supply: changes in supply conditions causing shifts in the supply curve.

 Any **change in supply** will cause a shift in the *entire* supply curve as there is no change in the price of the product supplied.

While price has an important effect on what producers are willing to supply, it is not the only influence.

There are many reasons why producers find it necessary to supply different quantities, even though the price of the product has not changed. These reasons are complex and depend on what type of supply is involved. Figure 8.2 shows some of these reasons.

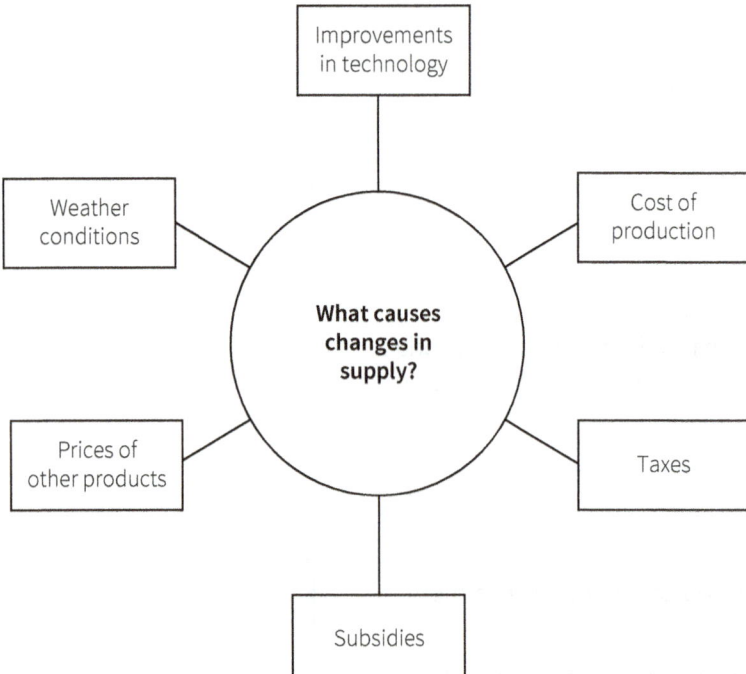

Figure 8.2 Causes of changes in supply

The importance of any factor affecting supply is invariably related to the nature of the product. Table 8.2 gives examples.

Table 8.2 How factors affecting supply differ in importance depending on the product

Agriculture	Industry	Service sector
The supply of crops, vegetables and fruit, and the health of livestock, may be affected by poor weather conditions. Excessive rainfall or lengthy drought can lower yields and hence supply. These problems are becoming more serious due to the effects of climate change in many parts of the world.	Changing costs of production and advances in technology affect the supply of almost everything that is produced. For example, an increase in wages will increase the costs of production, which in turn may be offset by technological improvements that lead to a rise in productivity.	Banks and large retailers have extended the use of IT in their businesses in order to cut costs and remain competitive.

TERMS

Increase in supply: a rise in supply at any given price, causing the supply curve to shift to the right.

Decrease in supply: a fall in supply at any given price, causing the supply curve to shift to the left.

Sample question

State whether the following would cause a **decrease in supply** or an **increase in supply** of tuna caught by fishing vessels from Mauritius:

i   an extended period of heavy rainfall and strong winds

ii a new infra-red camera that makes it easier to detect tuna

iii a rise in the price of other fish

iv new concerns over ethical fishing practices

v   research that shows the health benefits of eating tuna.

Sample answer:

i   a decrease in supply

ii an increase in supply

iii an increase in supply

iv a decrease in supply

v   an increase in supply

TIP Any change in the conditions of supply leads to a shift outwards or inwards of the supply curve. Be careful not to confuse with situations where there is a change in price, leading to a movement up or down the supply curve.

Sample question

Describe how subsidies and taxes might affect the ability of a small vegetable farmer in Pakistan and a small light-bulb manufacturer in China to supply.

Sample answer:

For the vegetable farmer, subsidies will reduce the price paid by consumers in local markets. The farmer's income will be likely to increase as she sells all that she is able to produce. Subsidies may prompt her to switch production to crops where subsidy is greatest. A change in taxation may have little or no effect because fresh food is not usually taxed.

For the light-bulb manufacturer, a new sales tax could lead to less supply in the domestic market. A tax on its profits could mean there are fewer funds available to invest in new equipment in the factory. Subsidies are unlikely to have any effect on supply, other than if export subsidies are given by the government.

SKILLS FOCUS

Farmers receive some income support directly from the government because market prices are less than they would be in an unsubsidised market. Small farmers do not pay income taxes. This contrasts with the Chinese manufacturer who may have to pay personal and corporate taxes. This is a good answer which clearly relates to both cases.

Progress check

Answer the following questions to check your understanding:

1. What is the usual relationship between supply and price?
2. Draw a typical supply curve. On it, show:
    i. an extension in supply
    ii. an increase in supply.

    Explain what each means.
3. Give **four** reasons why the global supply of coffee is increasing.

Revision checklist

You should know:

- ■ Supply is the willingness and ability to sell a product.
- ■ It can be represented by individual and market supply curves.
- ■ A change in price leads to an increase or decrease in the quantity supplied.
- ■ A change in supply occurs for various reasons and leads to a shift to the right or to the left of the entire supply curve.

STRUCTURED SKILLS PRACTICE

1. A garment manufacturer in Bangladesh supplies a number of wholesale customers in the US. It faces competition from garment manufacturers in China. Explain the likely effects on the supply of garments when:

   i its wholesale customers force down the prices they are willing to pay

   ii the Chinese government provides a new export subsidy for its garment manufacturers.

   TIP Use a diagram in your answer.

2. Global oil prices in 2017 stabilised at around $50 per barrel after reaching $150 per barrel in 2014. Discuss whether or not changes in supply or changes in demand have had a greater influence on price.

   TIP It is very unlikely with this type of question that the answer is one and not the other. Try to assess which is more important or if both have equal importance.

Exam-style multiple choice questions

1. Why is supply **not** the same as production?

   A production has to take place before supply

   B some goods produced may end up as warehouse stock

   C some products supplied may not be sold

   D when making products, suppliers do not know the market prices

2. What does a market supply curve show?

   A how much an individual firm will buy at various prices

   B how much a firm will sell at various prices

   C how much firms will sell at various prices

   D how much individuals will buy at various process

3. In 2017, drought conditions in France and Italy resulted in a reduction in olives harvested. Which shows the effect on the supply curve for olives?

   A a contraction of supply

   B an extension in supply

   C a shift to the left

   D a shift to the right

Chapter 9: Price determination

Learning summary

By the end of this chapter, you should understand:

- how demand and supply schedules and curves are used to establish equilibrium price and sales in a market
- how demand and supply schedules and curves are used to identify where there is disequilibrium in a market, in terms of shortages and surpluses.

9.1 How prices are determined

As shown in Chapters 7 and 8, consumers are willing to buy more of a product at low prices while producers are willing to supply more at high prices. Eventually, a price is determined. In street markets, this tends to be where the buyer and the seller agree on a price, often after much bargaining. In more developed markets, firms charge what they believe to be the **equilibrium price**, where demand and supply are equal.

> **TERM**
>
> Equilibrium price: the price where demand and supply are equal.

9.2 Market equilibrium

A market is in equilibrium where demand and supply are equal. This is often referred to as the market clearing price, giving an equilibrium price and an equilibrium quantity or sales.

Figure 9.1 shows such a situation where:

- P is the equilibrium price
- Q is the equilibrium quantity or sales.

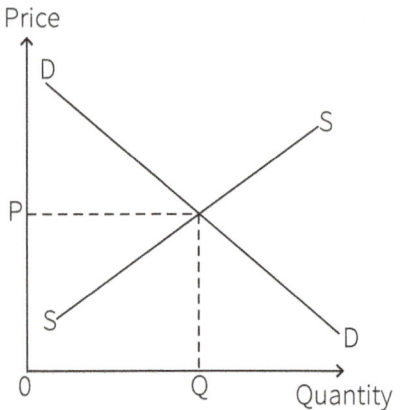

Figure 9.1 Market equilibrium

9.3 Market disequilibrium

A market is in **disequilibrium** when demand and supply are not equal. Disequilibrium occurs when there is excess supply or excess demand in a market.

> **TERM**
>
> Disequilibrium: a situation where demand and supply are not equal.

Sample question

In 2017, it was reported that the Ivory Coast, one of the main producers of cocoa beans, had produced a record crop resulting in a surplus of 400 000 tonnes.

i   Explain why this will result in disequilibrium in the market.

> **TIP**
>
> Remember that a good way of working out effects on supply is to use a diagram or diagrams.

ii Describe how the market is likely to return to equilibrium.

Sample answer:

i   The diagram shows that there will be excess supply in the market for cocoa beans.

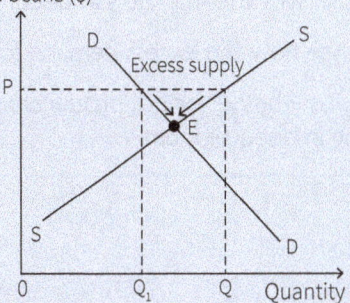

ii Where there is a surplus, producers will lower the price until the market clears with demand once again being equal to supply.

> **SKILLS FOCUS**
>
> The process of a market returning to equilibrium takes time. It is not quite as simple as this brief answer might imply. For example, producers may decide to destroy their supplies or perhaps store their excess cocoa beans in order to keep up prices.

Progress check

Answer the following questions to check your understanding:

1 When is a market in equilibrium?
2 Why does the market 'clear' when in equilibrium?
3 Explain excess demand and excess supply, and why these lead to disequilibrium in a market.

Revision checklist

You should know:

- [ ] Prices are determined where demand equals supply.
- [ ] A market is in disequilibrium where there are shortages and surpluses.
- [ ] Market forces restore a disequilibrium in a market to an equilibrium.

STRUCTURED SKILLS PRACTICE

1. The demand for chicken meat in China continues to increase faster than supply.

   i   Explain why the market is in disequilibrium.

   ii Analyse how the excess demand for chicken will be eliminated.

   iii Discuss whether or not producers or consumers benefit from the market being in disequilibrium.

   TIP Part (iii) is a question where you might assume that just one of them will benefit. Most answers will say that both will benefit, but will one benefit more than the other? This point should be made in your answer.

Exam-style multiple choice questions

1. When would a market clear?

   A when consumers have bought all that is available

   B when no more trading takes place

   C when suppliers have nothing to sell

   D when the amount consumers demand is equal to the amount that is supplied

2. A market is experiencing excess supply. What will happen to price and supply as the market moves back to equilibrium?

	Price	Supply
A	Decrease	Fall
B	Decrease	Rise
C	Increase	Fall
D	Increase	Rise

Price changes

Chapter 10

> **Learning summary**
>
> By the end of this chapter, you should understand:
>
> - how changes in market conditions cause price changes
> - how to use demand and supply diagrams to illustrate changes in market conditions and the consequences for equilibrium price and sales.

10.1 Causes of price changes

In most markets, prices are subject to change, whether this be daily, weekly, monthly or annually. Changing market conditions are the reason for price changes.

> ### Sample questions
>
> i Explain why food prices in most countries have continued to increase.
>
> ii Explain why the prices of mobile phones have continued to fall.
>
> **Sample answers:**
>
> i Food prices in most countries have continued to increase for two reasons. First, increases in population increase the total demand for food. Second, as income and living standards increase, the demand for some types of food also increases. An example of this is in China and India where increasing incomes have led to an increase in demand for some types of meat, especially poultry. Supply has found it difficult to keep up with increased demand and so prices have increased.
>
> ii The main reason for the falling prices of mobile phones is that production costs have been falling rapidly. Mobile phones are now mass produced, usually in economies with low labour costs. Manufacturers can reduce costs and hence prices through mass production. In turn, the fall in prices of mobile phones has increased their attractiveness to a high percentage of the world's population in all types of economy.
>
> **SKILLS FOCUS**
>
> Both answers give valid demand and supply reasons. This is good since most price changes occur for both reasons.

10.2 Consequences of price changes

Changing market conditions cause prices and sales to change. There are various likely consequences:

- an increase or decrease in demand
- an increase or decrease in supply
- a change in both demand and supply.

> **TIP** On demand and supply diagrams, the changes in market conditions are shown by a shift of the demand curve, the supply curve or both.

Figure 10.1 shows the effect on equilibrium price and sales of a decrease in the supply of olives due to storms and flooding. The equilibrium price has increased and sales have fallen.

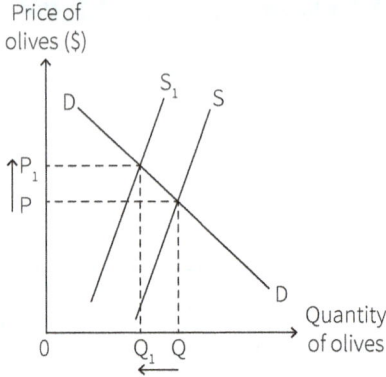

Figure 10.1 A decrease in the supply of olives

Progress check

Answer the following questions to check your understanding:

1. Why do prices change?
2. Draw a diagram to show the effect on equilibrium price and sales of:
   i. a decrease in demand
   ii. a decrease in supply.

Revision checklist

You should know:

- Prices and sales change due to changes in the market conditions of demand and supply.
- These changes can be illustrated on diagrams by shifts in demand curves and supply curves.
- Such shifts lead to changes in equilibrium prices and sales.

STRUCTURED SKILLS PRACTICE

1. The prices of mobile phones have continued to fall due to more efficient production methods and an increasing demand from consumers in all types of economy.

   i   Explain, using a demand and supply curve diagram, how prices have fallen in this way.

   ii Suppose the changes in conditions of demand and supply occurred at the same time. Explain, using a diagram, the consequences for equilibrium price and sales.

> **TIP** A common error is to draw the demand and supply curves the wrong way round. This makes any explanation meaningless.

Exam-style multiple choice questions

1. The supply of a product increases. What will happen as a result?

   A a movement along the demand curve and a fall in price

   B a movement along the demand curve and a rise in price

   C a movement along the supply curve and a fall in price

   D a movement along the supply curve and a rise in price

2. The demand for diesel vehicles in the UK fell in 2017 following concerns about air pollution. What happens as a result?

   A a movement along the demand curve and a fall in price

   B a movement along the demand curve and a rise in price

   C a movement along the supply curve and a fall in price

   D a movement along the supply curve and a rise in price

3. Following a change in demand and a change in supply, the equilibrium price has fallen and sales have increased. What does this indicate?

   A the change in demand occurred before the change in supply

   B the increase in supply is greater than the increase in demand

   C the increase in supply is less than the increase in demand

   D the increase in supply is the same as the increase in demand.

Chapter 11: Price elasticity of demand

Learning summary

By the end of this chapter, you should understand:

- what is meant by price elasticity of demand (PED) and how it is calculated
- how to interpret demand curve diagrams to show different PED
- whether and why demand is elastic or inelastic
- the relationship between PED and total spending on a product and revenue gained
- the implications for decision making by consumers, producers and government.

11.1 Definition and calculation of PED

$$\text{PED} = \frac{\text{Percentage change in quantity demanded}}{\text{Percentage change in price}}$$

TERM

Price elasticity of demand (PED): a measure of the responsiveness of the quantity demanded to a change in price.

TIP: PED measures the extent to which quantity demanded changes *following* a price change – not the reverse. The negative sign is usually ignored.

Sample question

The table below shows the weekly demand for air travel between two cities in Pakistan.

Price in $	Quantity of flights demanded ('000s)
40	10
35	15
30	25
25	35
20	40
15	45
10	48

i Calculate the PED when the price falls from $40 to $35.

ii Calculate the PED when the price falls from $20 to $15.

Sample answer:

i % change in quantity demanded is $\frac{5}{10} \times 100 = 50\%$

% change in price is $\frac{5}{40} \times 100 = 12.5\%$

Therefore PED is $\frac{50\%}{12.5\%} = 4$

ii % change in quantity demanded is $\frac{5}{40} \times 100 = 12.5\%$

% change in price is $\frac{5}{20} \times 100 = 25\%$

Therefore PED is $\frac{12.5\%}{25\%} = 0.5$

SKILLS FOCUS

Be careful when making this type of calculation. Common mistakes are to insert changes in the quantity demanded and changes in price the wrong way round. Another common error is to get the arithmetic wrong. Such errors make the answer meaningless. It is a good idea to think about the answer you have calculated and whether it makes sense.

11.2 Interpreting PED

TERMS

Elastic demand: when the quantity demanded changes by a greater percentage than the change in price.

Inelastic demand: when the quantity demanded changes by a smaller percentage than the change in price.

Figure 11.1 shows typical **elastic** and **inelastic demand** curves.

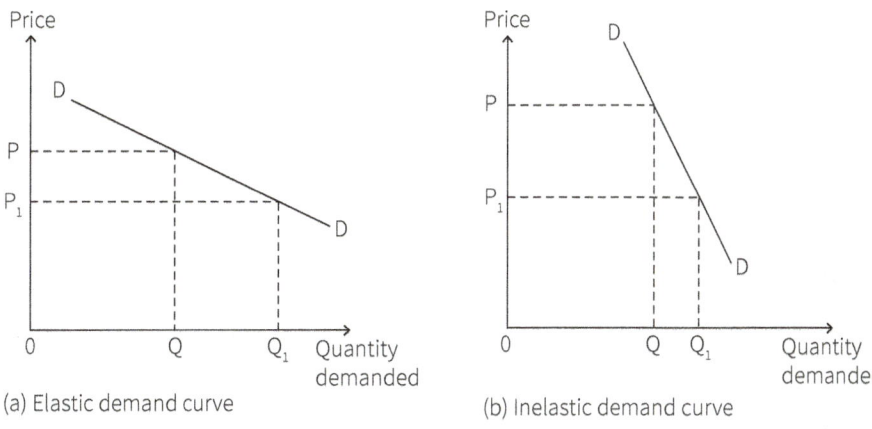

(a) Elastic demand curve   (b) Inelastic demand curve

Figure 11.1 Typical elastic and inelastic demand curves

TIP

When interpreting PED, remember that the sign (usually negative) and size provide you with important information.

In the sample question above on air travel in Pakistan:
- demand is elastic when price falls from $40 to $35
- demand is inelastic when price falls from $20 to $15.

In general:
- Elastic demand gives a PED figure of more than 1 but less than infinity – usually shown by a shallow demand curve.
- Inelastic demand gives a PED figure of less than 1 but greater than 0 – usually shown by a steep demand curve.

11.3 Determinants of PED

Various factors determine whether PED is elastic or inelastic. These are shown in Figure 11.2. The most important of these tends to be whether substitute products of a similar quality and price are available.

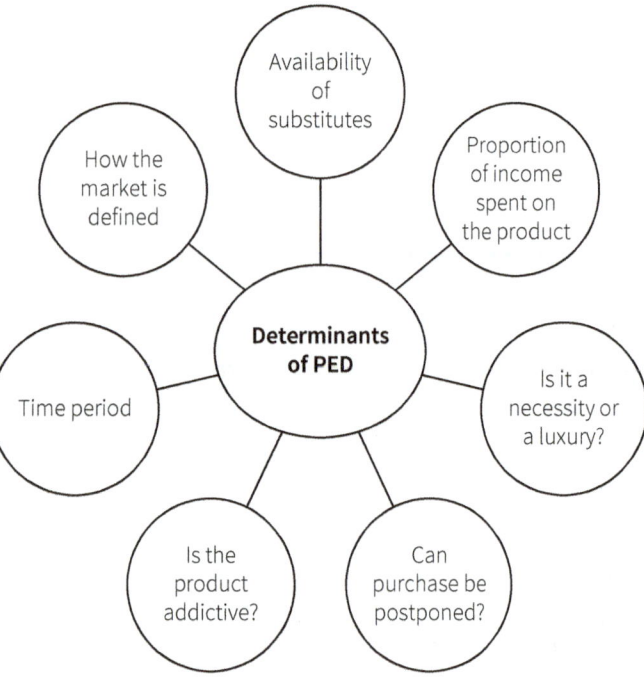

Figure 11.2 Determinants of PED

11.4 PED and total spending on a product and revenue gained

Remember that total spending by consumers is equal to price multiplied by the quantity demanded. It is the same as the revenue gained by producers.

The size of PED has an important influence on the change in spending and revenue arising from a change in the price of the product. This relationship is shown in Figure 11.3.

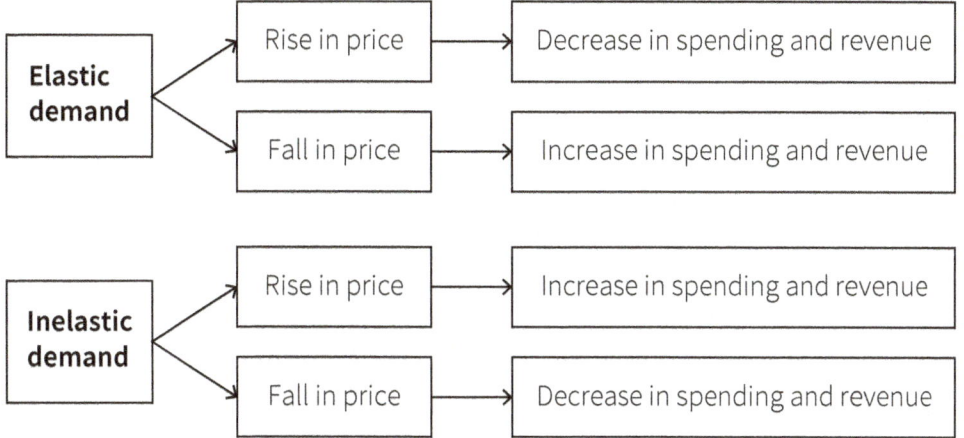

Figure 11.3 The relationship between PED and spending, and revenue

Progress check

Answer the following questions to check your understanding:

1 Refer to Figure 11.1. Explain why the two demand curves show elastic and inelastic demand.

2 Suppose that PED for a designer watch is 3. If the price falls by 10%, what will be the change in the quantity demanded?

3 With reference to PED, are there any circumstances when a producer should not increase the price of a product?

Revision checklist

You should know:

- [ ] PED measures by how much the quantity demanded for a product changes when there is a change in its price.
- [ ] The slope of the demand curve depends on the PED of a product.
- [ ] PED can be elastic or inelastic.
- [ ] There is a relationship between PED and total spending and total revenue.
- [ ] The value of PED affects decisions made by consumers, producers and government.

STRUCTURED SKILLS PRACTICE

1 Explain how a reduction in the price of a product with inelastic demand will increase sales but reduce revenue.

2 Refer back to the table showing weekly demand for air travel between two cities in Pakistan (in the sample question and answer part of Chapter 11.1). Explain how PED varies over a demand curve.

> **TIP** You will find it helpful to sketch the demand curve for this question.

3. It has been reported that the PED for gasoline in Mauritius is -0.21 in the short run and -0.44 in the long run. Explain why the figures differ.

> **TIP** In your answer to this question, remember to explain first what the figures mean in terms of both sign and size.

4. Discuss whether or not producers can use the PED of a product to determine whether they should change the price of their product.

> **TIP** A common error when answering this question is to copy the formula for PED. Remember that the percentage change in price is the denominator and the percentage change in quantity is the numerator. Before you answer the question, check that you know the formula for PED.

Exam-style multiple choice questions

1. How might the concept of price elasticity of demand be useful to the owner of a resort hotel in the Maldives?
   - A to determine the effect of a new advertising campaign
   - B to determine the effect of refurbishing the hotel
   - C to determine the effect on sales of reducing prices in low season
   - D to determine the hotel manager's salary

2. The price of guided tour holidays to India increased by 10% in 2017 and the quantity demanded fell by 4%. Which is true?
   - A the price elasticity of demand is 0.4 and elastic
   - B the price elasticity of demand is 0.4 and inelastic
   - C the price elasticity of demand is 2.5 and elastic
   - D the price elasticity of demand is 2.5 and inelastic

3. Which characteristic is **least** likely to make the demand for a product inelastic?
   - A it has close substitutes
   - B it is habit forming
   - C it is necessity
   - D it is relatively cheap

Price elasticity of supply

Chapter 12

Learning summary

By the end of this chapter, you should understand:

- what is meant by price elasticity of supply (PES) and how it is calculated
- how to interpret supply curve diagrams to show different PES
- whether and why supply is elastic or inelastic
- the implications for decision making by consumers, producers and government.

12.1 Definition and calculation of PES

TERM

Price elasticity of supply (PES): a measure of the responsiveness of the quantity supplied to a change in price.

$$PES = \frac{\text{Percentage change in quantity supplied}}{\text{Percentage change in price}}$$

TIP

PES measures the extent to which the quantity supplied changes *following* a price change – not the reverse. PES is usually positive as suppliers tend to be willing to supply more when price increases.

Sample question

The table below shows how many pairs of jeans two garment manufacturers in China are willing to supply each month depending on the market price.

Price in $	Producer A ('000s)	Producer B ('000s)
8	10	10
12	30	12
16	50	14
20	80	16
24	120	18

i Calculate the PES as price increases from $8 to $12 for each producer.

ii Identify which producer is likely to be able to respond more quickly to a large increase in orders for jeans.

Sample answers:

i % change in quantity supplied for Producer A is $\frac{20}{10} \times 100 = 200\%$

% change in quantity supplied for Producer B is $\frac{2}{10} \times 100 = 20\%$

% change in price is $\frac{4}{8} \times 100 = 50\%$

Therefore PES for Producer A is $\frac{200\%}{50\%} = 4$

And PES for Producer B is $\frac{20\%}{50\%} = 0.4$

ii Producer A is likely to be able to respond more quickly since PES is higher for all possible changes to price.

SKILLS FOCUS

PES is always a positive figure. Variations in its size have implications for supply.

12.2 Interpreting PES

TERMS

Elastic supply: when the quantity supplied changes by a greater percentage than the change in price.

Inelastic supply: when the quantity supplied changes by a smaller percentage than the change in price.

Figure 12.1 shows typical **elastic** and **inelastic supply** curves.

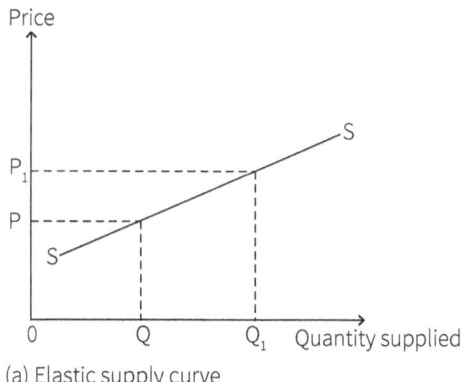
(a) Elastic supply curve

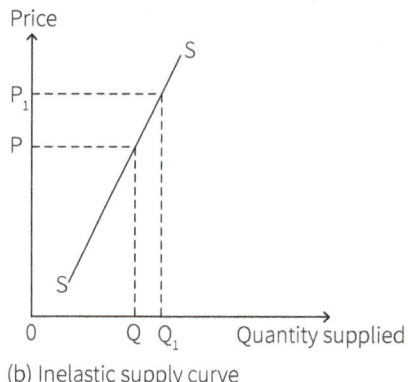
(b) Inelastic supply curve

Figure 12.1 Typical elastic and inelastic supply curves

In the sample question on the supply of jeans from manufacturers in China (see Chapter 12.1):

- supply from Producer A is elastic throughout
- supply from Producer B is inelastic throughout.

12.3 Determinants of PES

Various factors determine whether PES is elastic or inelastic. These are shown in Figure 12.2. The time taken to change supply is particularly important. For example, it is more difficult to increase the supply of most agricultural products compared to manufactured goods.

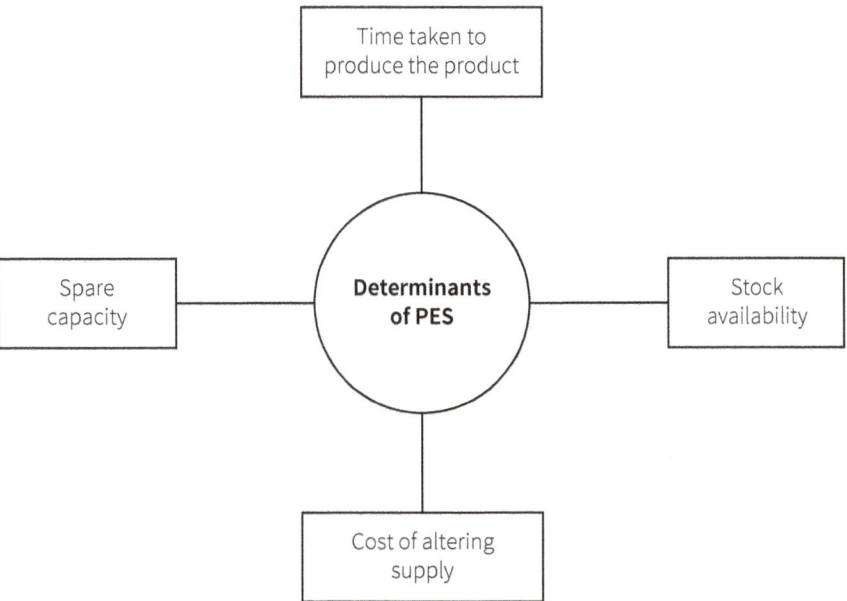

Figure 12.2 Determinants of PES

12.4 Implications of PES for decision making

Producers want supply to be as elastic as possible. This particularly applies in agriculture where producers hope to have some flexibility in the types of product and the volumes of product they put onto the market. For many farmers, though, the supply of what they grow is inelastic due to lengthy growing periods and a lack of suitable storage space.

Consumers also benefit from an elastic supply since this is responsive to changes in demand.

> ### Progress check
>
> Answer the following questions to check your understanding:
>
> 1 Refer to Figure 12.1. Explain why the two supply curves show elastic and inelastic supply.
> 2 Suppose the PES of increasing electricity generation from a power station is 0.3. If the price of electricity increases by 10%, what will be the change in the quantity supplied?

> ### Revision checklist
>
> You should know:
>
> - PES measures how the quantity supplied changes with a change in the price of a product.
> - The slope of the supply curve depends on the PES of the product.
> - Supply can be elastic or inelastic.
> - The value of PES affects decisions made by consumers, producers and government.

STRUCTURED SKILLS PRACTICE

1. Explain why manufactured goods tend to have a more elastic PES compared to most agricultural goods.

2. Discuss whether or not a producer should use PES when deciding whether to expand production in response to a large increase in the market price for the product.

3. In the last quarter of 2016, the supply of crude oil by OPEC (Organization of the Petroleum Exporting Countries) was deliberately cut by 4%. The price of oil continued to fall. Discuss whether or not this confirms that the PES of crude oil is inelastic.

TIP: Think also about what has happened to demand.

Exam-style multiple choice questions

1. How might the concept of price elasticity of supply (PES) be useful for an electric vehicle manufacturer?

   A to determine how long it takes to produce one vehicle

   B to determine how many more vehicles to supply when price falls by 5%

   C to determine how many vehicles will be sold when the price falls

   D to determine the market share of the manufacturer

2. The PES for a product is 1.5. If the price increases by 2%, which of these is correct for the percentage increase in the quantity supplied?

   A 0.5

   B 0.75

   C 3

   D 4

3. Which is likely to have the **most** elastic supply?

   A a farm growing fresh vegetables

   B a firm operating below full capacity

   C a firm which decides to spend $1 m on reorganising its production

   D a manufacturer of wide bodied jet aircraft

Market economic system

Learning summary

By the end of this chapter, you should understand:

- what is meant by a market economic system
- the difference between private and public sectors
- the advantages and disadvantages of the market economic system
- the role of market forces in different countries.

13.1 The market economic system

A market economic system is where most resources are owned and controlled by individuals and are allocated through market forces. The role of the government is confined to overseeing and enforcing the basic principles of demand and supply.

In reality, there is no example of an economic system that is entirely dependent upon market forces to allocate resources. The following economies are the closest to this ideal – Singapore, Hong Kong, the United States, New Zealand and Switzerland. All are developed economies.

Sample question

Identify which of the following may be found in a market economic system:

i   a US-owned manufacturer of fizzy drinks
ii local owners of market stalls
iii a state-owned steel producer
iv a former nationalised electricity provider
v   an airline owned by a local entrepreneur
vi a railway system that requires substantial subsidy.

Sample answer:

The businesses found in a market economic system are (i), (ii), (iv) and (v).

SKILLS FOCUS

The clue to the two answers that do not feature in a market economic system – (iii) and (vi) – is that both involve some form of government intervention. This is not true of the other four examples.

TERMS

Private sector: businesses owned by individuals or shareholders.

Public sector: the part of the economy controlled by the government.

When moving to a market economy, the government's policy is always to reduce the relative size of the **public sector** and increase the relative size of the **private sector**. This is often achieved through privatisation, whereby there is a sale of public sector assets to the private sector. Privatisation has been prevalent in many developing economies in recent years. Typical examples are China, India and Pakistan.

13.2 Advantages and disadvantages of the market economic system

Table 13.1 summarises the advantages and disadvantages of a market economic system.

Table 13.1 Advantages and disadvantages of a market economic system

Advantages	Disadvantages
It is responsive to changes in consumer demand.	Market failure occurs when market forces do not work well.
Price mechanism is an efficient way of allocating resources.	Environmental damage may result due to lack of government regulations.
Competition promotes efficiency and low prices.	Differences in income and wealth are likely to widen over time.
Quality is high and innovation is encouraged.	Social policies to protect the more vulnerable groups are likely to be limited.

Progress check

Answer the following questions to check your understanding:

1. From an economy you have studied, give an example of:
   i. a private sector business
   ii. a public sector business
   iii. a business that has recently been privatised.
2. Why does a market economic system not necessarily take into account:
   i. environmental problems generated by private firms
   ii. a need to reduce inequality?

Revision checklist

You should know:

- [ ] The strength of the market system depends on the relative importance of the market mechanism and the government in the affairs of the economy.

- [ ] Market economic systems have many advantages drawn from economic theory – they also have many disadvantages arising from market failure.

STRUCTURED SKILLS PRACTICE

1. In 2015, the International Monetary Fund classified Pakistan as an 'emerging market economy'. Explain why this is so.

2. Discuss whether or not a market economic system is the best form of organisation for a developing economy.

> **TIP**
>
> The 'discuss' command word gives a strong indication that other types of economic system might be appropriate. Think also about the few market economies known to you. Singapore, the USA and possibly Hong Kong are examples that are usually recognised as market economies. Most others tend to be mixed, albeit with a varying degree of market economy.

Exam-style multiple choice questions

1. Singapore is a very good example of a market economic system. What is the **most** likely reason for this?

   A its government has considerable control over the private sector

   B it has a highly educated working population

   C it has few natural resources

   D over 85% of its economy is owned by the private sector

2. Which is **not** a characteristic of a market economic system?

   A business and individuals can make high incomes

   B consumers have a wide choice of government services

   C prices are determined by demand and supply

   D the price of some food products is fixed by the government

Chapter 14

Market failure

Learning summary

By the end of this chapter, you should understand:

- what is meant by market failure
- the differences among private, external and social costs and benefits
- why external costs and benefits cause market failure
- what is meant by merit and demerit goods, and why they result in market failure
- the difference between private and public goods, and why public goods cause market failure
- why monopoly power and factor immobility result in market failure
- the consequences of market failure.

14.1 The nature of market failure

Market failure occurs when the market mechanism results in a misallocation of resources. There are many examples of market failure in all economies.

TERM

Market failure: market forces resulting in an inefficient allocation of resources.

Sample question

Decide which of the following are examples of market failure:

i   a supermarket that runs out of its stock of rice
ii excessive pollution from a fish canning factory
iii a situation where poor people cannot afford to get medical treatment
iv a supplier charging high prices when there is a shortage of supply
v   emissions from vehicles that lead to respiratory diseases amongst pedestrians
vi a shortage of textbooks in secondary schools.

Sample answer:

The examples of market failure are (ii), (iii), (v) and (vi).

SKILLS FOCUS

In (i) and (iv), although the market is not working effectively, the circumstances can be resolved through market forces. In all other cases, the market is not providing an efficient allocation of resources, hence market failure.

14.2 Costs and benefits

> **TERMS**
>
> **Private costs:** costs borne by those directly consuming or producing a product.
>
> **External costs:** costs imposed on those who are not directly involved in the consumption and production activities of others.
>
> **Social costs:** the total costs to a society of an economic activity.
>
> **Private benefits:** benefits received by those directly consuming or producing a product.
>
> **External benefits:** benefits enjoyed by those who are not directly involved in the consumption and production activities of others.
>
> **Social benefits:** the total benefits to a society of an economic activity.
>
> **Third parties:** those not directly involved in producing or consuming a product.

> **TIP**
>
> The terms in this section are very important for understanding market failure. Do not confuse **external costs** with **social costs** or **external benefits** with **social benefits**.

Market failure arises when not all of the costs and benefits of an activity are taken into account. Costs to other people (**third parties**) result in *over-production*. Benefits to other people lead to *under-consumption*. Two examples are given in Table 14.1.

Table 14.1 Examples of external costs and benefits

	Over-production	Under-consumption
	Figure 14.1 (a) Over-production $(0Q - 0Q_x)$	Figure 14.1 (b) Under-consumption $(0Q_x - 0Q)$
Market failure	External costs	External benefits
Example	Environmental problems arising from vehicle use in congested cities	Infant vaccination programmes
Outcome	Greater use of vehicles since only private costs are considered	Fewer vaccinations and more likelihood of spread of diseases

14.3 Merit goods and demerit goods and information failure

Merit goods are more beneficial to consumers than they themselves realise and they have benefits for those who are not directly involved in their consumption, that is, external benefits.

Demerit goods are the opposite of merit goods – they are more harmful to consumers than they realise and they generate external costs.

> ### TERMS
>
> **Merit goods:** products which the government considers consumers do not fully appreciate how beneficial they are and which will therefore be under-consumed if left to market forces. Such goods generate positive externalities.
>
> **Demerit goods:** products which the government considers are not fully appreciated by consumers in terms of how harmful they are and which will therefore be over-consumed if left to market forces. Such goods generate negative externalities.

Where there is information failure, as shown in Table 14.2, consumers are not fully aware of the benefits or costs of consumption. If they were, consumption habits would change.

Table 14.2 Examples of merit and demerit goods, and information failure

	Merit good	Demerit good
Example	Compulsory secondary education	Junk food
Why market failure?	Information failure as the benefits are not understood	Information failure as the costs are not recognised by smokers
What can be done?	Government can provide information, subsidise cost or provide education free of charge	Government can impose high taxes on junk food and ensure healthcare information is provided in the media

14.4 Public goods and private goods

> ### TERMS
>
> **Public good:** a product which is non-rival and non-excludable and hence needs to be financed by taxation.
>
> **Private good:** a product which is both rival and excludable.

Table 14.3 summarises the characteristics of **public** and **private goods**.

Table 14.3 Characteristics of public and private goods

Public good	Private good
Examples: Flood defence system, street lighting	*Examples:* Mobile phone, takeaway food
• Private firms will not provide as they are difficult to charge for. • Non-excludable – cannot exclude non-payers from benefits. • Non-rival – consumption by one person does not reduce consumption by others.	• Market price is paid by consumers. • Excludable – non-payers do not get benefits of consumption. • Rival – no one else can consume.

14.5 Other causes of market failure

- *Abuse of monopoly power.* If a firm dominates a market and controls the supply, it will not be efficient and will charge high prices to consumers. The product may also be of poor quality. Governments can use their powers to increase competition in markets where producers have excessive market power.
- *Factor immobility.* As noted in Chapter 2, this is a problem for all factors of production, especially labour. Governments can aid labour mobility by providing resources to re-train workers and aid geographical mobility by enabling workers to relocate to where there are jobs.

Progress check

Answer the following questions to check your understanding:

1. Consider the following cases:
    i   a tuna processing factory in Mauritius
    ii a scheme to fund more university places for students from poor families.

   For each, make a list of the likely private costs, private benefits, external costs and external benefits that might occur.

2. Explain why:
    i   free dental care is a merit good
    ii junk food is a demerit good.

3. Explain why:
    i   a local fire protection service is a public good
    ii a new moped is a private good.

Revision checklist

You should know:

- Markets fail to produce the best allocation of resources for many reasons.
- Market failure can be described in terms of private, external and social costs, and private, external and social benefits.
- Merit goods and demerit goods are usually so classified on account of information failure.
- Public goods have the characteristics of non-rivalry and non-excludability. This is not true of private goods.
- The consequence of market failure is a misallocation of resources.

STRUCTURED SKILLS PRACTICE

1.
   i Explain **two** external benefits associated with the use of mass transit in cities.

   ii Analyse why this can lead to a situation of over-consumption.

TIP Remember that external benefits apply to so-called third parties. A common error is to think that they are the same as the externality.

Exam-style multiple choice questions

1. What are the social costs of an activity?
   - A the private costs minus the external costs
   - B the private costs plus the external costs
   - C the social benefits minus the external costs
   - D the social benefits plus the external costs

2. A government increases its spending on secondary education. What is the **most** likely outcome?
   - A external benefits for the economy
   - B external benefits for those now attending secondary schools
   - C social benefits through increased incomes
   - D social benefits through reduced unemployment

3. Which is a characteristic of a demerit good?
   - A it has external costs in its consumption
   - B it has higher social costs than its consumers realise
   - C it imposes costs on those not involved in its consumption
   - D it is non excludable

4. Why is a public good non-rival?
   - A consumption by one more person does not reduce someone else's consumption
   - B it is provided free of charge
   - C there is a limit to its consumption
   - D there is only one type of public good in any place

Chapter 15: Mixed economic system

Learning summary

By the end of this chapter, you should understand:

- what is meant by a mixed economic system
- the effects of imposing maximum and minimum prices in product and labour markets
- the policies that may be used to correct market failure including indirect taxation and subsidies
- the meaning of regulation, privatisation, nationalisation and direct provision of goods
- the effectiveness of government intervention in overcoming the drawbacks of a market economic system.

15.1 A mixed economic system

This is the typical economic system in most types of economy, developed and developing. In principle, a **mixed economic system** combines the features and benefits of a planned system and a market economic system.

> **TERM**
>
> Mixed economic system: an economy in which both the private and public sectors play an important role.

Sample question

Give **two** advantages and **two** disadvantages of a mixed economy.

Sample answer:

Two advantages of a mixed economy are that public goods and merit goods are provided by the government, and the government can seek to achieve a more even distribution of income through the use of taxation and subsidies.

Two disadvantages are that there are many examples of market failure and, if there is too much government intervention, private firms may be discouraged from expanding because of too many regulations and red tape.

> **SKILLS FOCUS**
>
> The question asks for two advantages and two disadvantages. There is no need to give more. The answer could be enhanced by referring to examples from a mixed economy that you have studied.

15.2 Maximum and minimum prices

A government may decide to set a price ceiling, or a price floor, in a market as a means of limiting a firm's ability to set its own prices.

The differences are shown in Table 15.1.

Table 15.1 Differences between a price ceiling (maximum price) and a price floor (minimum price)

Price control	Above or below equilibrium price	Effects on market	Where used
Maximum price	Below	Shortage Rationing	Wheat Cooking oil Flour Sugar Fuel
Minimum price	Above	Excess supply	Agricultural products Demerit goods Wages of unskilled labour

15.3 Subsidies and indirect taxation

A government may **subsidise** a number of its country's firms. In contrast, it taxes firms' profits, which has an impact on firms' ability and willingness to invest. **Indirect taxes** raise firms' costs of production, while income tax lowers consumers' disposable income, leading to lower demand for firms' products. See Table 15.2 for more information.

> **TERMS**
>
> Subsidy: a payment by a government to encourage the production or consumption of a product.
>
> Indirect taxes: taxes on goods and services.

Table 15.2 Information on subsidies and indirect taxes

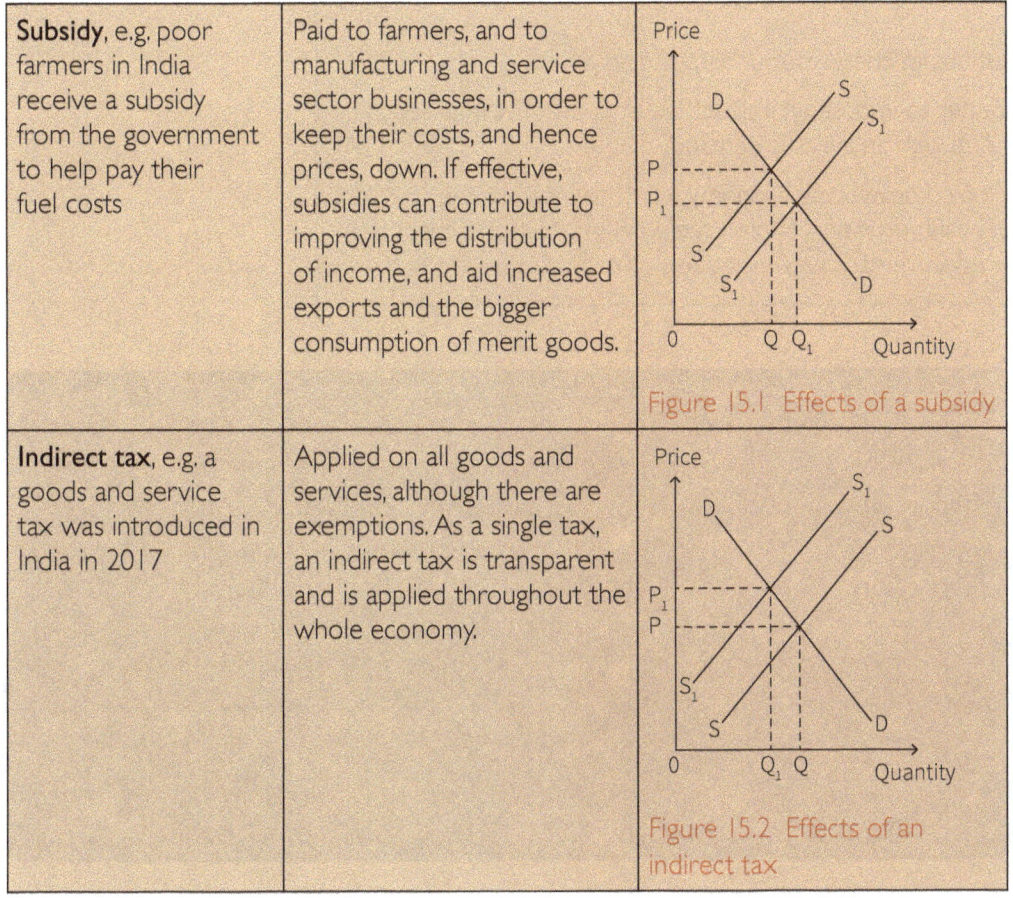

Subsidy, e.g. poor farmers in India receive a subsidy from the government to help pay their fuel costs	Paid to farmers, and to manufacturing and service sector businesses, in order to keep their costs, and hence prices, down. If effective, subsidies can contribute to improving the distribution of income, and aid increased exports and the bigger consumption of merit goods.	Figure 15.1 Effects of a subsidy
Indirect tax, e.g. a goods and service tax was introduced in India in 2017	Applied on all goods and services, although there are exemptions. As a single tax, an indirect tax is transparent and is applied throughout the whole economy.	Figure 15.2 Effects of an indirect tax

The impact of a subsidy or indirect tax depends on the size of the subsidy or indirect tax and the price elasticity of demand.

> **TIP**
> Imposing a subsidy shifts the supply curve to the right. Imposing an indirect tax shifts the supply curve to the left – see Chapter 8.

15.4 Other forms of government intervention to address market failure

> **TERMS**
>
> Regulation: various means by which governments seek to control production and consumption.
>
> Privatisation: the sale of public sector assets to the private sector.
>
> Nationalisation: moving the ownership and control of an industry from the private sector to the government.
>
> Direct provision: where a government provides essential goods and services.

Progress check

Answer the following questions to check your understanding:

1. Explain whether it is better to impose an indirect tax on a product that has an elastic demand or on one with an inelastic demand.
2. The government of a mixed developing economy wants to increase the quantity and quality of health provision. Explain the ways in which this might be done and discuss how effective each way might be.

Revision checklist

You should know:

- A mixed economic system has both private and public sectors.
- Imposing a maximum price can lead to shortages, while imposing a minimum price can lead to excess supply.
- Subsidies and indirect taxation can be used to correct market failure.
- Regulations, privatisation, nationalisation and direct provision are features of a mixed economic system.
- Government intervention seeks to overcome some of the drawbacks of a mixed economic system.

STRUCTURED SKILLS PRACTICE

1. The government of Venezuela imposes maximum prices on a wide range of staple goods and consumer products.
    i. Explain how maximum price control is likely to generate a shortage in a competitive market.
    ii. Explain any circumstances when a shortage may not develop.
2. Some governments have fixed minimum prices paid to farmers for agricultural crops.
    i. Explain how minimum price control is likely to generate surpluses in a competitive market.
    ii. Explain how a government might avoid such a situation.

> **TIP**
> It will help you to use diagrams in your answers to part (i) of each question.

Exam-style multiple choice questions

1. A government has imposed a maximum price on wheat flour. What will happen in the market as a result?

	Price	Effect on market
A	Above equilibrium	Excess supply
B	Above equilibrium	Shortage of supply
C	Below equilibrium	Excess supply
D	Below equilibrium	Shortage of supply

2. Assuming each is the same price, which is **most** likely to generate most revenue from an increase in a goods and services tax?

   A chicken meat

   B petrol

   C cinema tickets

   D restaurant meals

3. Which is **not** a reason for subsidising cooking oil?

   A cooking oil is an essential private good

   B cooking oil is made from locally farmed grain products

   C cooking oil prices continue to rise

   D cooking oil is widely used by all families

Exam-style structured questions for Section 2

Data response question

Read the source material carefully before answering the question.

> **Source material: China's increasing demand for passenger vehicles**
>
> China is the world's largest auto market. Annual production increased by around 28 million vehicles in 2016, giving an overall total of over 300 million passenger vehicles. There are heavy concentrations of ownership in mega cities such as Beijing, Guangzhou, Shanghai and Shenzhen but with much lower ownership in poorer rural areas. Overall, vehicle ownership remains low at around 270 vehicles per thousand population.
>
> What once seemed to be unstoppable growth in the market stalled in 2017. The rate of growth of car sales fell, in part, as a result of an increase in the tax on small vehicles. This was a reversal of tax cuts made in 2016 in a bid to increase demand.
>
> Figure S2.1 shows the trend in car sales from 2008 to 2017.
>
> China also has the biggest number of new energy vehicles (NEVs), the term given to part or fully electric vehicles. In 2016, 500 000 were sold, more than the rest of the world together. Many producers of these vehicles have received massive subsidies from the government. In 2017, though, the government announced that it was removing all such subsidies by 2020 as it was concerned that money was being wasted on 200 or so small producers, many of whom have taken the subsidies but not made any cars. There is little indication that NEVs from Chinese manufacturers are yet to be commercially viable, unlike similar vehicles from elsewhere.
>
> China has some of the worst atmospheric pollution and traffic congestion in Asia. In Beijing, there has been a rapid increase in the number of young people with respiratory problems and the continuous noise from traffic increases strain and stress for many inhabitants. Traffic accidents involving cyclists and motor cyclists have also increased. The use of NEVs may be a positive move to counteract these problems. The reality, though, is that petrol and diesel vehicles will continue to fuel China's ever-increasing thirst for more cars.

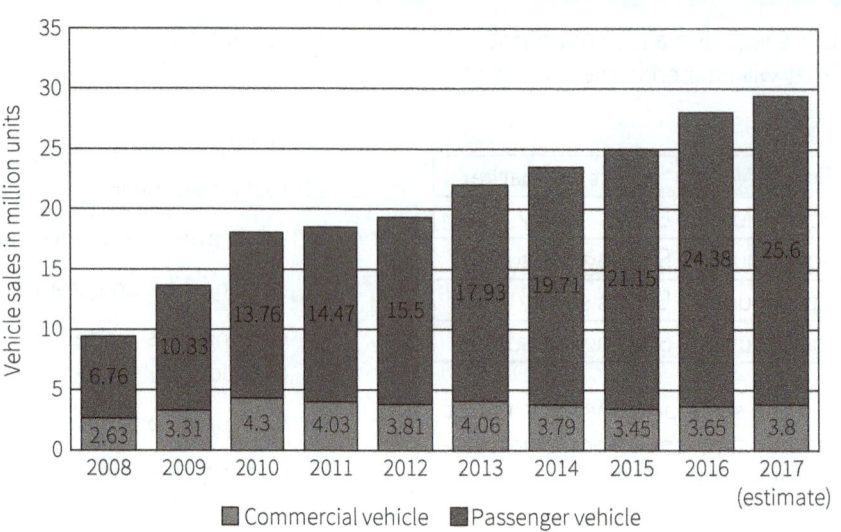

Figure S2.1 Car sales (passenger and commercial vehicles) in China, 2008–2017 (in millions of units)

Source: Statista, 2017.

Answer all parts of this question. Refer to the source material in your answers.

a   Define 'market failure'. [1]

b   Describe the trend in car sales in China from 2008 to 2017. [2]

c   State **two** possible reasons for the increase in demand for cars in China from 2016 to 2017. [2]

d   Explain how the cut in taxation on small-engine vehicles in 2016 should increase vehicle sales. [4]

e   Explain **two** external costs arising from the increasing use of vehicles in Beijing. [4]

f   Analyse why the consequence of external costs is a misallocation of resources. [5]

g   Discuss whether or not there are likely to be any external benefits from the use of NEVs in Chinese cities. [6]

h   Discuss whether or not subsidies paid to Chinese producers of NEVs are justified. [6]

Four-part question

This question is introduced by stimulus material. In your answer, you may refer to this material and/or to other examples that you have studied.

The price elasticity of supply for most agricultural goods is inelastic. In 2016, the harvest of cashew nuts in Vietnam, a major producer, was down by 11% due to prolonged drought. At the same time, there was rising demand for cashew nuts from China and the USA. The market was in disequilibrium, with demand exceeding supply.

a   Define 'price elasticity of supply'. [2]

b   Explain why the price elasticity of supply for cashew nuts is inelastic. [4]

c   Analyse the effects on the cashew nut market of the supply and demand changes. [6]

d   Discuss whether or not producers of cashew nuts might be able to respond to the supply problems faced by Vietnamese producers in 2016. [8]

Section 3: MICROECONOMIC DECISION MAKERS

Chapter 16: Money and banking

Learning summary

By the end of this chapter, you should understand:

- what is meant by money, its functions and characteristics
- the role and importance of commercial banks
- the role and importance of central banks.

16.1 Money: functions and characteristics

> **TERM**
>
> **Money:** any item which is generally acceptable as a means of payment.

The functions of **money**, along with what they signify and its characteristics, are summarised in Table 16.1.

Table 16.1 Functions and characteristics of money

Function	Meaning	Characteristics
Medium of exchange	Is acceptable to buyers and sellers	• Limited in supply
Store of value	Has a value over time	• Acceptable as a means of payment
Unit of account	Allows prices to be established	
Standard of deferred payments	Enables some payments to be made later	• Durable • Portable • Divisible • Easily recognised

Sample question

A developing economy is experiencing an annual rate of inflation of 20%. Explain the functions of money which are likely to be most affected.

Sample answer:

Money has four roles or functions within the economy. The most obvious one to be affected is its function as a store of value. Any money held as notes or deposited in a commercial bank will be losing value. There are also problems with money's function as a standard of deferred payment, because those owed money are likely to want their bills paid as soon as possible and those owing money are more likely to hold back payment.

The functions of medium of exchange and unit of account are unlikely to be affected.

An annual rate of inflation of 20% is serious. Two of the functions of money are already under threat and, if the rate is not controlled and reduced, the economy is likely to go into recession.

SKILLS FOCUS

A good feature of this answer is that it not only considers each of the four functions of money but also makes an important point about the severity of the current rate of inflation and its likely impact on these functions. There is a potential danger that money's function as a medium of exchange could be threatened if this annual rate increases further.

> **TIP**
> Do not confuse the *functions* of money with the *characteristics* of money. Money's functions refer to the roles money has in the economy.

16.2 Banking

TERMS

Commercial banks: banks which aim to make a profit by providing a range of banking services to households and firms.

Central bank: a government-owned bank which provides banking services to the government and commercial banks and operates monetary policy.

The roles of **commercial banks** and **central banks** are shown in Table 16.2.

Table 16.2 What commercial banks and central banks do

Commercial banks	Central banks
• accept deposits from customers	• act as banker to government
• lend money to customers	• act as banker to commercial banks
• enable customers to make payments and withdraw money from accounts	• manage national debt
• provide other services such as foreign currency exchange and storage of valuables	• issue notes and coins
	• implement (government) monetary policy
	• hold reserves of gold and foreign currencies

> **TIP**
> The role of the central bank varies. For example, the European Central Bank determines the rate of interest for all members of the euro area.

Progress check

Answer the following questions to check your understanding:

1. Which is the most important function of money?
2. Why was salt sometimes a form of money?
3. How do consumers and producers interact with commercial banks?
4. Why do most governments rely heavily on their central banks?

Revision checklist

You should know:

- ☐ Money is anything that is acceptable as a means of payment.
- ☐ Money has four functions and certain characteristics.
- ☐ Commercial banks and central banks have important yet different roles in an economy.

STRUCTURED SKILLS PRACTICE

1.
   i. Explain how commercial banks support consumers and producers in most types of economy.
   ii. Explain how a central bank supports the government in a market economic system.

    TIP You could enhance your answer by drawing upon information from an economy you have studied.

Exam-style multiple choice questions

1. What is **least** likely to be a form of money in a market economic system?

   A bank deposits
   B camels
   C debit cards
   D foreign currency

2. In parts of China, tea is sometimes used as a form of money. Which function of money is tea **least** likely to match?

   A medium of exchange
   B standard of deferred payments
   C store of value
   D unit of account

3. What is the main function of a central bank?

   A it controls the supply of coins and notes
   B it facilitates the deposit and withdrawal of cash for a person
   C it offers overdrafts to personal customers
   D it provides banking services to very rich customers

Households

> **Learning summary**
>
> By the end of this chapter, you should understand:
> - the influences on the spending of households
> - the influences on the saving of households
> - the influences on the borrowing of households.

17.1 Influences on spending

People spend in order to buy goods and services, and to maintain a given standard of living. The main influence on the amount spent by a person or household is **disposable income**. As income rises, people usually spend more in total, but less as a percentage of their income.

> **TERM**
>
> Disposable income: income after income tax has been deducted and state benefits received.

Figure 17.1 shows the main influences on spending.

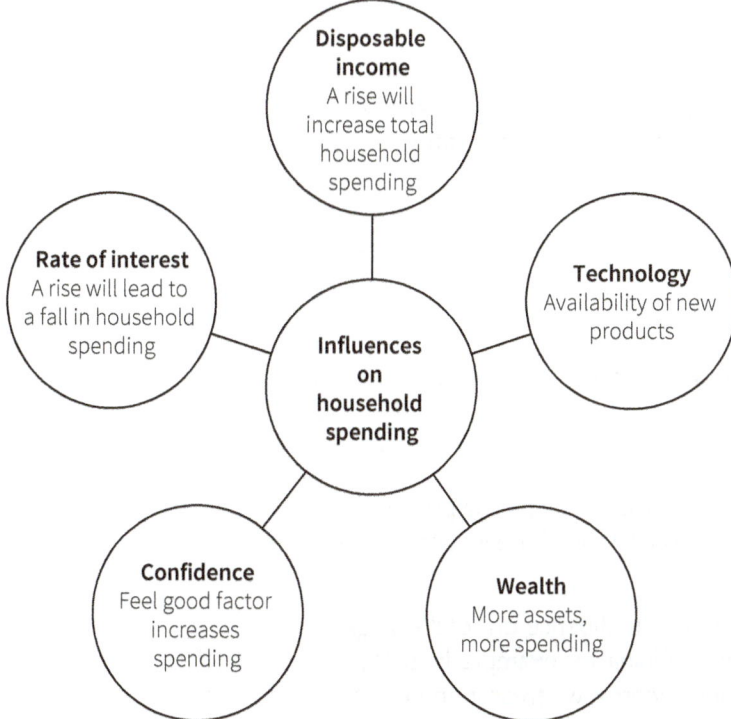

Figure 17.1 The main influences on household spending

> **TIP**
> Remember that income and wealth are different. Wealth refers to the stock of assets, while income is a regular flow of money for households. A common error is to confuse the terms. Questions more usually require you to consider income rather than wealth.

Sample question

After years of negative growth of household spending, in 2017 it was reported that, in Japan, spending by households had started to increase by 1% or 2% per year. Explain **two** reasons why this increase may have occurred.

Sample answer:

The most likely explanation for the increase in household spending relates to confidence – Japanese consumers are now feeling more optimistic about future economic prospects, and their own incomes and employment. Household spending increases marginally as a consequence.

A second factor is the rate of interest in Japan – this has been negative, discouraging people from saving but encouraging them to spend as any savings will be reducing in value.

SKILLS FOCUS

The sample answer indicates some background knowledge of problems that the Japanese economy has been experiencing. This improves its quality. Alternatively, you could write a more theoretical answer based on Figure 17.1.

17.2 Influences on saving

As with consumption, the main influence on saving is disposable income. As disposable income rises, the total amount saved and the proportion saved (the **savings ratio**) increase.

> **TERM**
>
> Savings ratio: the proportion of household disposable income that is saved.

Saving can take many forms such as putting money in a bank account, buying property or investing in a workplace pension. Saving mainly depends on four of the influences that determine household spending, as shown in Table 17.1.

In addition, the attitude of households can have an important influence on total savings and the proportion of disposable income that is saved. In China, for example, in 2015, household savings accounted for over 30% of disposable income, whereas in the UK it was just 0.5%.

Table 17.1 How influences on household spending affect saving

Influences on household spending	Effects on saving
Disposable income	As this rises, households are likely to increase the total amount saved and the proportion saved increases.
Rate of interest	A rise is likely to increase savings because the cost of borrowing to fund spending increases, so reducing spending.
Wealth	Wealthier people are likely to save more than those from poor households.
Confidence	Households will save more if economic prospects are uncertain.

17.3 Borrowing

Households invariably find that there is a need to borrow money. When this occurs, household income increases. There are various reasons why households may wish to borrow such as to purchase an apartment or car, or to fund education. The main influences on borrowing are shown in Figure 17.2.

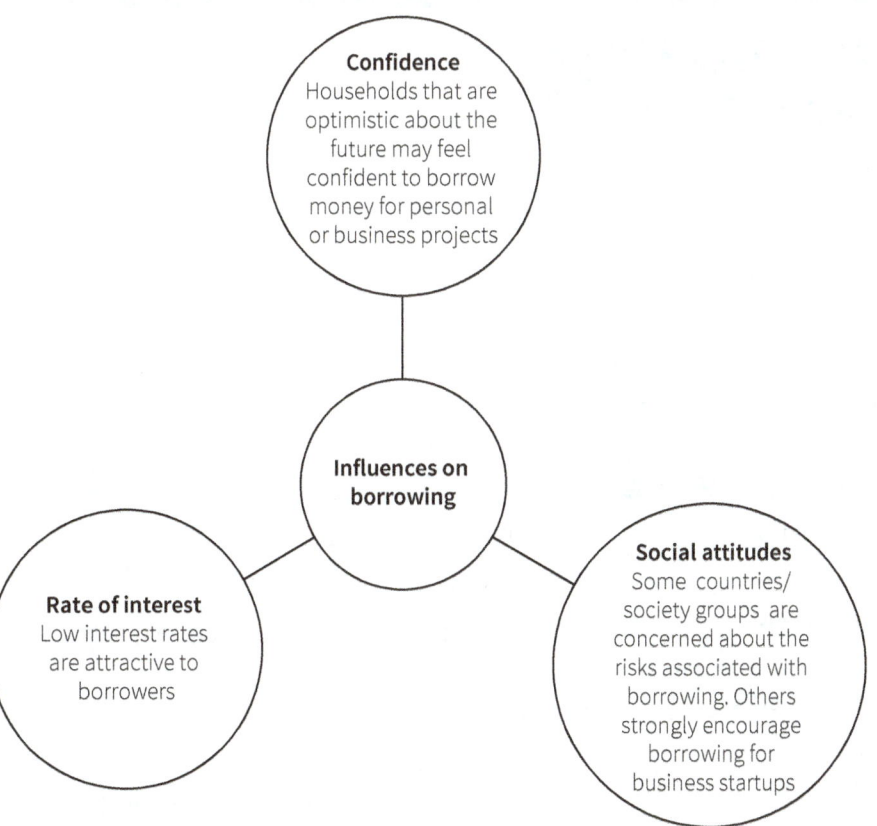

Figure 17.2 The main influences on borrowing

Progress check

Answer the following questions to check your understanding:

1. Why is disposable income the most important influence on household spending?
2. Why do households in some countries save more of their disposable income than households in other countries?
3. Explain the difference between saving and borrowing.

Revision checklist

You should know:

- There are many factors that influence household spending – disposable income is the most important for the majority of households.
- Household saving also depends on many factors, including disposable income.
- Borrowing by households can depend on the rate of interest, although, in some countries, social attitudes may not be in favour of borrowing.

STRUCTURED SKILLS PRACTICE

1. Analyse why households in China save a high percentage of disposable income.

TIP: A good way to answer this question is to think about what determines the savings ratio and what savings are used for. You do not require any specific knowledge of China.

Exam-style multiple choice questions

1. What happens as disposable household income falls?

   A the proportion of income that is saved increases

   B the proportion of income that is saved is unchanged

   C the proportion of income that is spent decreases

   D the proportion of income that is spent increases

2. In 2015, the ratio of savings to disposable household income in Latvia was −12%. What might have happened as a result?

   A disposable incomes have fallen

   B fewer people want to save

   C reduced interest rates encourage greater household spending

   D spending was greater than disposable income

3. Interest rates fall. What is **most** likely to happen to household expenditure and borrowing?

	Expenditure	Borrowing
A	rise	rise
B	rise	fall
C	fall	rise
D	fall	fall

Workers

Chapter 18

> **Learning summary**
>
> By the end of this chapter, you should understand:
>
> - the wage and non-wage factors that influence an individual's choice of occupation
> - how wages are determined
> - reasons for differences in earnings
> - the advantages and disadvantages of the division of labour/specialisation for workers, firms and the economy.

18.1 Factors that influence an individual's choice of occupation

> **TERMS**
>
> **Earnings:** the total pay received by a worker.
>
> **Wage rate:** a payment which an employer contracts to pay a worker – the basic wage a worker receives per unit of time (e.g. an hour) or unit of output.

> **TIP**
>
> Make sure you understand the difference between **earnings** and **wage rates**. Most of the economic theory about labour markets is in terms of wage rates.

Wage and non-wage factors influence the decision that a worker makes when deciding whether to take a particular job. There are many non-wage factors.

Figure 18.1 identifies some of these wage and non-wage influences.

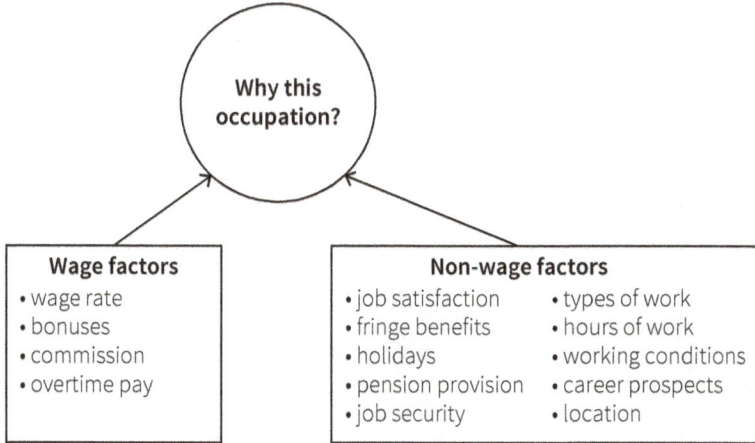

Figure 18.1 Wage and non-wage factors

Sample question

A person has trained to be an accountant but decides to take a job as a community support worker on greatly reduced earnings.

Explain **two** possible non-work factors that might have influenced this decision.

Sample answer:

A person may decide that they will gain more job satisfaction as a community worker than as an accountant. They may feel good to be giving something back to society.

They may also require more flexible hours of work. An accountant may have to work regular office hours, whereas a community worker may have the flexibility to work at different times. This may suit the person's lifestyle better.

Another factor could be the type of work. A community worker is likely to come across all sorts of different problems and issues while an accountant's job may be more routine.

SKILLS FOCUS

The factors outlined in the sample answer are very likely, although there are others that could apply. In many respects, the reasons depend on the attitude and performance of the individual worker. The answer could be improved by making reference to the accountant's loss of earnings when becoming a community worker.

18.2 Wage determination

The wage rate in a labour market is determined by the interaction of the demand and supply of labour. The equilibrium wage is where the demand and supply of labour are equal.

> **TIP**
> The wage rate is an example of a price. The general principles introduced in Chapters 9 and 10 also apply to the labour market.

The demand for labour and the supply of labour are key factors that determine the wages received by a worker or group of workers. Figure 18.2 shows the nature of demand and supply for hotel managers and cleaning staff.

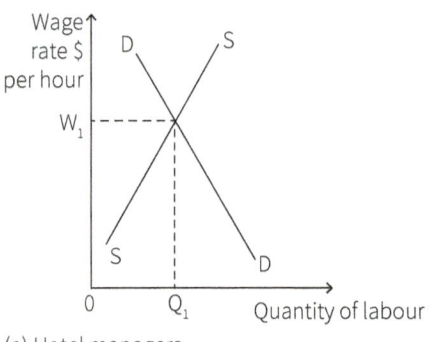
(a) Hotel managers

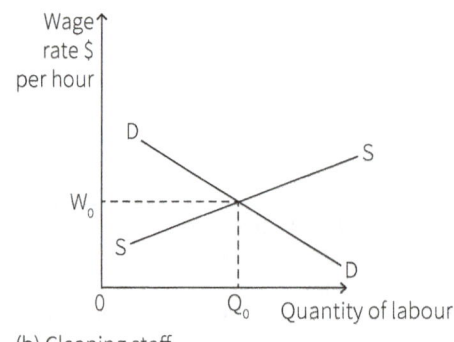
(b) Cleaning staff

Figure 18.2 Wage determination: the market for hotel managers and cleaning staff

The reasons for the differences in wages between hotel managers and cleaning staff include:

- low supply of hotel managers, relative to demand
- hotel managers require training and experience
- high supply of cleaners relative to demand
- cleaners require few skills.

Other influences include:

- the relative bargaining power of employers and workers
- where a national minimum wage is applied
- where a group of workers are treated unfairly, for example different wage rates for male and female staff doing the same job.

18.3 Reasons for difference in earnings

Like any market, the labour market is subject to change over time. Changes in demand and supply can lead to a change in wage rates.

Sample question

Many developed countries have ageing populations. This means that the demand for workers in care homes is increasing. To meet this increase in demand, it is necessary for more care home staff to be recruited from developing economies.

Analyse the effects of these changes on the wage rates of care home staff.

Sample answer:

The diagram shows that an increase in demand for care home workers leads to a shift to the right of the demand curve. This results in an increase in wage rates.

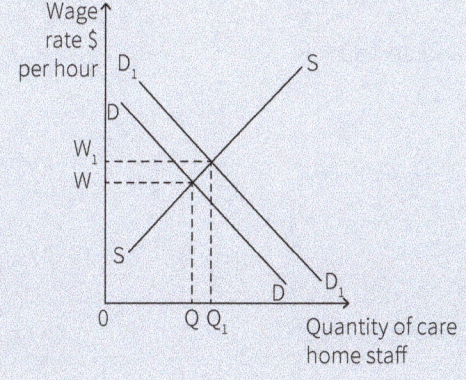

The increase in supply of workers leads to a shift to the right of the supply curve, which is likely to result in a fall in wage rates. This is shown in the diagram below.

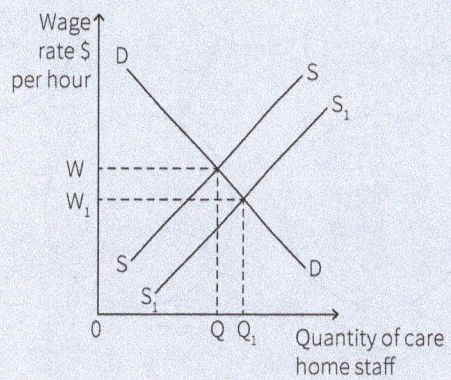

SKILLS FOCUS

This sample analysis question has a clear emphasis on producing correct diagrams. Very little explanation is required. The answer is in terms of a change in demand and a change in supply. The diagrams provide an effective way of responding to the question as it is highly unlikely that the two changes would happen simultaneously.

There are many other reasons for differences in earnings. Some of the more important ones are shown in Figure 18.3.

Figure 18.3 Factors influencing differences in earnings

The size of the change in the wage rate depends on the elasticities of demand and supply of labour.

> **TIP**
> Remember that the demand and supply of some types of labour is relatively inelastic – such workers will usually earn higher earnings than where demand and supply are more elastic.

18.4 Specialisation and division of labour

> **TERMS**
>
> Specialisation: the concentration on particular products or tasks.
>
> Division of labour: workers specialising in particular tasks.

Table 18.1 shows some advantages and disadvantages of **specialisation** and the **division of labour**.

Table 18.1 Specialisation and division of labour: advantages and disadvantages

Advantages	Disadvantages
• Lower cost per unit produced. • Increased output per worker. • Lower training costs. • Improved competitiveness.	• Workers may get bored (may result in higher unit costs). • Reduced quality of product. • Increased sickness and days off work. • Difficult to cover absences. • Occupational immobility.

> **Progress check**
>
> Answer the following questions to check your understanding:
>
> 1. What is the difference between earnings and a wage rate?
> 2. Why might a worker move to a job that pays less?
> 3. Refer to Figure 18.2. How might differences in demand and supply elasticities be used to explain the differences in wage rates between hotel managers and cleaning staff?
> 4. Give **two** reasons for:
>   i. a fall in demand for workers in the motor vehicle assembly industry
>   ii. an increase in demand for workers in call centres.

Revision checklist

You should know:

- [ ] An individual's choice of occupation is determined by many factors that include both wage and non-wage considerations.
- [ ] Wages are invariably determined by the demand and supply of labour.
- [ ] There are other factors that determine earnings, particularly the elasticities of demand and supply of labour.
- [ ] Specialisation and the division of labour can provide advantages for workers, firms and the economy.

STRUCTURED SKILLS PRACTICE

1. Explain the likely effects on the labour market when a new minimum wage is introduced.

2. Analyse what would happen to the wage rate and the number of nurses employed if there was an increase in demand and an increase in supply occurring at the same time.

> **TIP**
> Remember that wage rate is the price of labour. This question is best answered by means of a diagram followed by an analysis of the respective shifts in the demand and supply curves.

Exam-style multiple choice questions

1. Which is **not** a non-wage factor that may influence a person's choice of occupation?

   A fringe benefits
   B hours of work
   C job satisfaction
   D overtime pay

2. In India, there has been a big increase in the number of jobs in IT. What is the **least** likely reason for this?

   A IT is essential in many types of business
   B IT workers are well paid
   C there are more graduates qualified in IT
   D working in IT is boring

3. A garment manufacturer in Bangladesh decides to split the production process into various tasks, rather than have one machinist make the full garment. What is the **most** likely reason for this?

   A machinists have gone on strike for more pay
   B machinists will now work longer hours
   C output per worker will increase
   D there is a shortage of machinists

Trade unions

Chapter 19

Learning summary

By the end of this chapter, you should understand:

- what is meant by a trade union
- the role of trade unions in the economy
- what influences the strength of trade unions
- the advantages and disadvantages of trade union membership.

19.1 Trade unions and their role in the economy

TERMS

Trade union: an association which represents the interests of a group of workers.

Collective bargaining: representatives of workers negotiating with employers' associations.

Trade unions aim to protect the interests of their members through **collective bargaining**. This gives them more influence compared to a worker negotiating individually with their employer. Negotiations cover issues such as wage rates, hours of work, working conditions and other matters relating to employment.

In some countries, trade unions can influence government policy on matters relating to the legal employment of labour, such as holiday entitlements and a minimum wage.

> **TIP**
>
> Trade unions exist to benefit their members who pay a subscription. They may often do this at the expense of other employees who are not a member of the trade union or who belong to a different union.

Trade unions are often less strong in developing economies than in developed countries. Their strength also depends on the type of business, whether small or large, and what sector it is in – see Figure 19.1.

Trade unions seek to increase wages by restricting the supply of labour in the market or by requiring all workers in a firm to be union members.

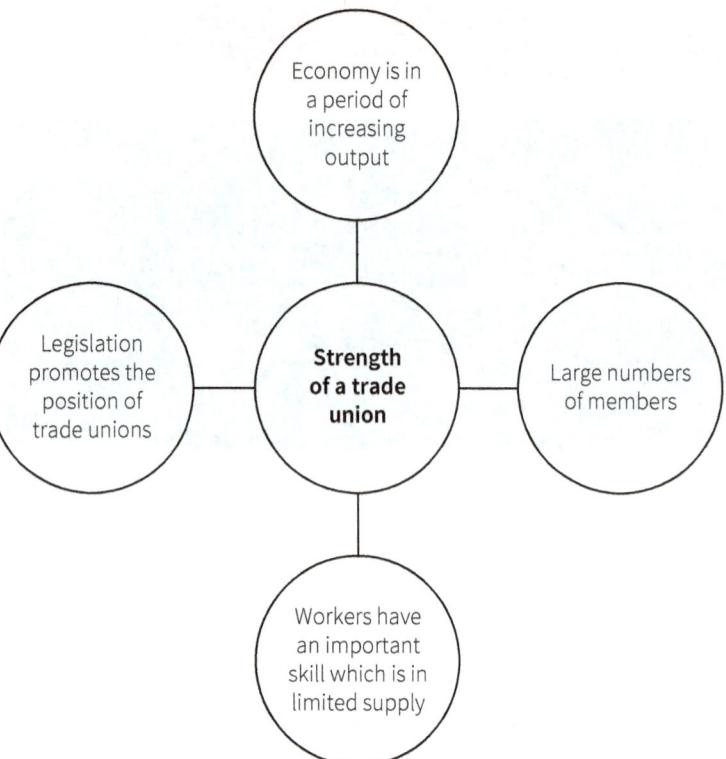

Figure 19.1 Factors likely to increase the strength of a trade union

Sample question

Analyse how, by restricting the supply of labour, a trade union may cause unemployment among its members.

Sample answer:

When a trade union is seeking to increase the wages of its members, it can do so by decreasing the supply of workers. This can only be achieved if the supply is inelastic. The result is a fall in employment of union members from Q_0 to Q_1, although the wage rate for those employed will increase from W_0 to W_1. Employers understandably reduce their demand for labour at the higher wage level. This is shown in the diagram.

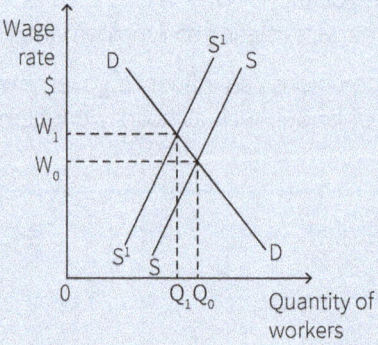

SKILLS FOCUS

If the supply of labour is elastic, then an employer is likely to resist any attempt by a trade union to increase wages. Make sure that the supply curves in the diagram are inelastic and the reduction in unemployment is clear.

19.2 Advantages and disadvantages of trade union membership

The advantages and disadvantages of trade union membership are shown in Table 19.1.

Table 19.1 Trade union membership advantages and disadvantages

Advantages	Disadvantages
• Can negotiate with employers for better pay and working conditions. • Can provide greater strength in negotiations compared to individual workers. • Protects against discrimination. • Provides additional support for members.	• Could cause unemployment among its members. • Could disrupt production through strikes. • Could increase labour costs for firms. • Could reduce labour flexibility for firms.

> **TIP**
> The power of trade unions depends on many factors and is often weak in developing economies where there is an abundant supply of labour.

Progress check

Answer the following questions to check your understanding:
1. Describe the role of trade unions in collective bargaining with employers.
2. Why might some trade unions have weak bargaining power?

Revision checklist

You should know:

- [ ] A trade union is an organisation that represents workers and undertakes collective bargaining with employers.
- [ ] Collective bargaining covers a wide range of topics relating to the employment of trade union members.
- [ ] Some activities undertaken by trade unions may not always be in the best interests of members, firms and the government.

STRUCTURED SKILLS PRACTICE

1 Discuss whether or not it is possible for a trade union to increase the wages for its members while protecting the number of members employed by a firm.

TIP This question is about what might be regarded as the classic dilemma facing a trade union. A good way of starting the answer is to show a shift to the left of the supply curve for labour. Remember that trade unions usually only protect the interests of their members, not labour in general.

Exam-style multiple choice questions

1 Which issue is **least** likely to be discussed by a trade union in collective bargaining with an employer?

   A an increase in overtime pay

   B a reduction in working hours

   C financial help from a trade union when a member is ill

   D procedures for redundancy

2 Introducing a minimum wage is favoured by trade unions. What happens as a result?

   A it has no effect on earnings

   B it increases the pay of many workers

   C it increases the pay of union members

   D it reduces inflation

Firms

Chapter 20

Learning summary

By the end of this chapter, you should understand:

- how firms can be classified
- why small firms exist and their advantages and disadvantages
- why firms grow
- the advantages and disadvantages of mergers
- how internal and external economies, and diseconomies of scale can affect a firm/industry as the scale of production changes.

20.1 Classification of firms

A firm is any business that hires factors of production to produce goods and services. Firms producing the same type of product make up an **industry**.

TERM

Industry: a group of firms producing the same product.

TIP

A firm is the same as the industry when there is just one firm producing a particular product.

Firms can be classified in various ways, as shown in Figure 20.1.

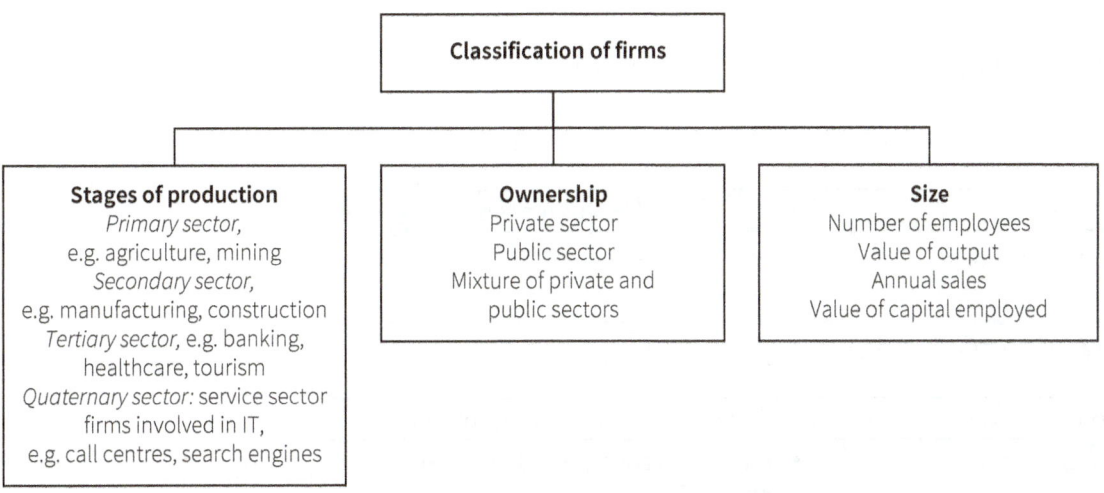

Figure 20.1 Classification of firms

20.2 Small firms

In all types of economy, especially developing economies, a large proportion of firms are small. In India and Pakistan, for example, it is believed that at least 99% of all firms are small.

> **TIP** It is difficult to define 'small'. It depends on the type of business. A general rule is that any firm with fewer than 50 employees is small.

Figure 20.2 shows some of the reasons why the typical firm is small.

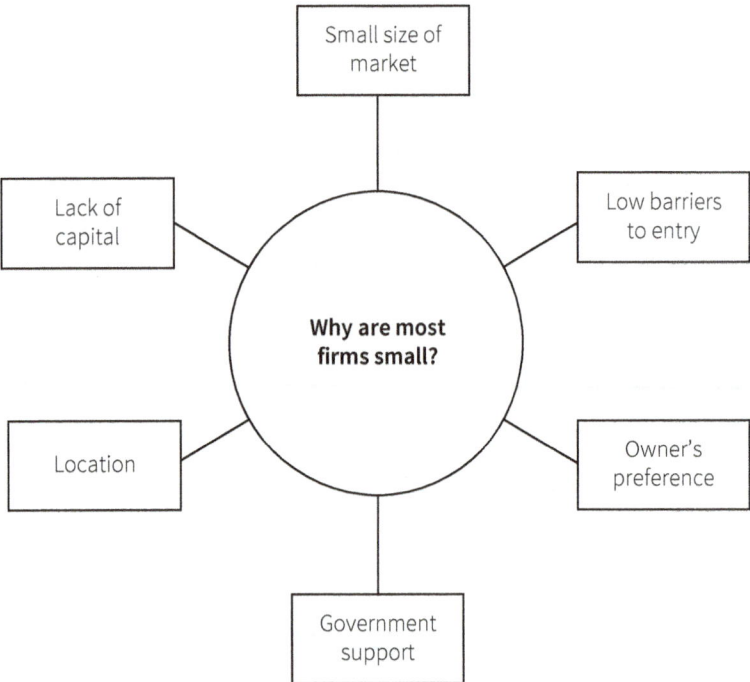

Figure 20.2 Reasons why most firms are small

The advantages and disadvantages of small firms are shown in Table 20.1.

Table 20.1 Small firms: advantages and disadvantages

Advantages	Disadvantages
• can quickly adapt to change	• have limited resources when trading is difficult
• have direct contact between owners and customers	• have a high failure rate
• are prepared to be innovative	• find it difficult to get external funding
• are prepared to take risks	• may pay higher costs than larger competitors
• have owners who are in touch with employees	• are vulnerable to takeovers

Sample question

In Malaysia, businesses that provide takeaway food and cheap restaurant meals are predominantly small firms. Explain **two** reasons for this.

Sample answer:

There may be a limited local market for the business, particularly in an area where there is lots of competition from other restaurants also offering cheap takeaway food and meals.

A second reason might be that the owner is unable to expand through lack of financial capital. They may be unable to obtain the funding required to grow the business.

SKILLS FOCUS

The answer focuses on two main reasons. Other suggested reasons include:

- a new business can start up with limited funding
- owners may prefer to remain small, particularly if they can obtain a reasonable living
- 'start up' funding may be available.

The same could apply to similar businesses in most other developing economies. The provision of food is one of the few parts of the economy where there is scope for entrepreneurial activity, yet the opportunities for growth are very limited for most firms.

TIP

A question may ask you to explain or identify a number of reasons related to the topic. The number will be shown in bold type, e.g. **two**. You may find it helpful to highlight or circle the number of reasons to remind you how many to write about. Always write about the two reasons you feel most confident about. Don't spend valuable time identifying or explaining more than the number of reasons requested by the question as you will not receive credit for this.

20.3 Causes of the growth of firms

Firms grow in two ways:

- *Internal* or *organic growth* through increasing output and market share. An example is the growth of Costa Coffee in China.
- *External growth* through a **merger** or takeover. An example is the takeover by Mobilink of Warid Telecom in Pakistan in 2015.

TERM

Merger: where two or more firms join together to form one new firm.

There are three types of merger. These are shown in Figure 20.3.

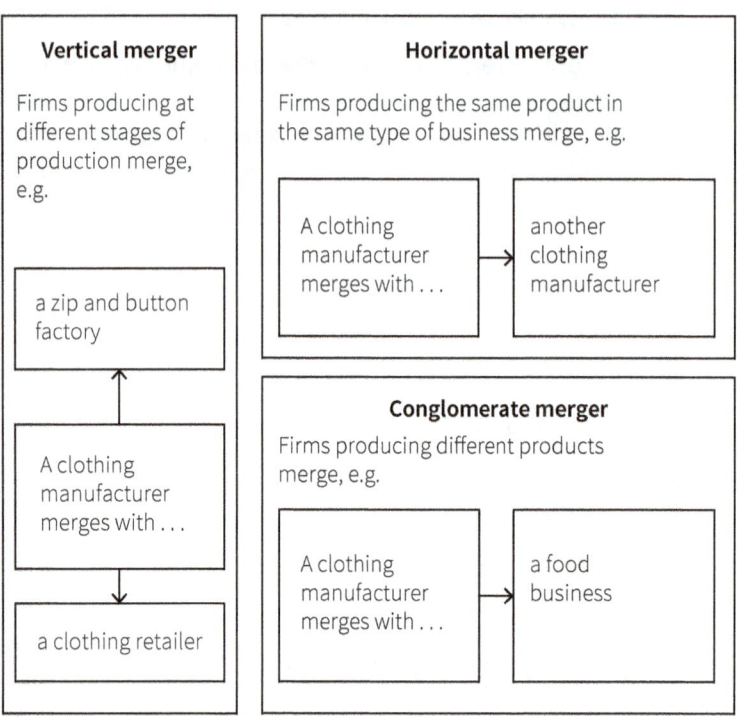

Figure 20.3 Types of merger

20.4 Economies and diseconomies of scale

Economies of scale are the benefits that can be gained when a firm produces on a larger scale. These benefits are shown through lower long run average costs.

> **TERMS**
>
> Economies of scale: lower long run average costs resulting from a firm or industry growing in size.
>
> Diseconomies of scale: higher long run average costs arising from a firm or industry growing in size.

Economies of scale can be:

- internal, to a firm
- external, to an industry.

> **TIP**
>
> Economies and **diseconomies of scale** can apply to any firm producing on a larger scale, not just large firms.

Figure 20.4 shows how these can be represented in a firm.

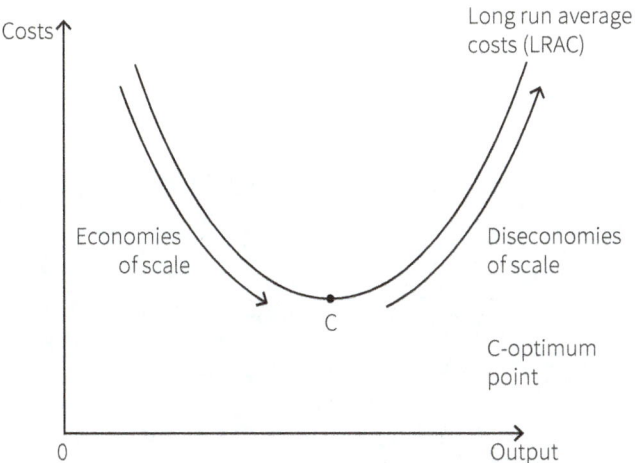

Figure 20.4 Internal economies and diseconomies of scale

Some typical examples of internal economies and diseconomies of scale are identified in Table 20.2.

Table 20.2 Examples of internal economies and diseconomies of scale

Internal economies of scale and examples of benefits	Internal diseconomies of scale and examples of rising costs
buying economies, e.g. discounts when buying supplies and raw materials	communication problems, e.g. difficulty of keeping everyone informed in large firms
technical economies, e.g. large factories using more efficient, advanced machinery	control problems, e.g. difficulty of managing large, complex businesses
managerial economies, e.g. specialist managers increasing a firm's efficiency	labour relations, e.g. workers feeling neglected and not fully motivated in large firms
financial economies, e.g. larger firms usually accessing cheaper loans from banks	
risk-bearing economies, e.g. larger firms usually producing a wider range of products to spread risk	

External economies and diseconomies of scale are the lower and higher long run average costs that can apply to an industry as distinct from a single firm. A good example is in Shenzhen, known as the 'lighting capital of China'. Here, there are thousands of skilled workers, parts suppliers and specialist services which make this the obvious choice of location for lighting manufacturers.

Progress check

Answer the following questions to check your understanding:
1. As well as by number of employees, how can firms be classified?
2. How do firms grow?

3 What is the difference between:
   i   internal and external economies of scale?
   ii economies of scale and diseconomies of scale?

Revision checklist

You should know:

- Firms can be classified in various ways.
- Small firms are typical in all economies – they have various advantages, yet some disadvantages.
- Firms grow through internal expansion or externally through merger and acquisitions.
- Economies of scale are either internal to a business or external to an industry. They accrue in the form of falling long run average costs as the scale of output increases.
- Internal and external diseconomies of scale can also apply to a firm as the scale of output increases.

STRUCTURED SKILLS PRACTICE

1 Explain why small firms are unlikely to be involved in the manufacture of steel.
2 The Airbus A380 aeroplane can carry almost 600 passengers, whereas other long-haul aircraft carry fewer than 400 passengers. Analyse the likely economies and diseconomies of scale that might apply to airlines that use A380s.

TIP: Make sure you give a balanced answer. When analysing selected economies of scale, apply the general principles to the point of the question, in this case aircraft operations.

Exam-style multiple choice questions

1 A pharmacy is an example of a firm in which sector?
   A primary sector
   B quaternary sector
   C secondary sector
   D tertiary sector

2 In 2017, Starwood and Marriott merged to form the largest hotel chain in India. What is this an example of?
   A a monopoly
   B conglomerate merger
   C horizontal merger
   D vertical merger

3 Why does a large supermarket benefit from economies of scale?
   A it can negotiate bulk discounts from suppliers
   B it is open for business every day
   C it sells products at a discount
   D it stocks a wide range of products

Firms and production

Chapter 21

Learning summary

By the end of this chapter, you should understand:

- what influences the demand for factors of production
- the reasons for adopting labour-intensive or capital-intensive production
- the difference between productivity and production.

21.1 Demand for factors of production

TIP

Refer to Chapter 2 for details of the factors of production.

TERMS

Production: total output.

Productivity: the output per factor of production in an hour.

TIP

A common error is to think that **production** and **productivity** are the same thing. Make sure you understand the difference between these two terms.

The demand for factors of production is derived from their use in enabling production to take place.

If a firm needs to increase or decrease its output, it can do this by altering the factors of production it uses. In the short run, this can often be done through changing the amount of labour employed, especially if it has spare capacity. Here, labour is a variable factor of production. Fixed factors of production do not change as the quantity of output changes.

The demand for factors of production depends upon many things – see, for example, Figure 21.1.

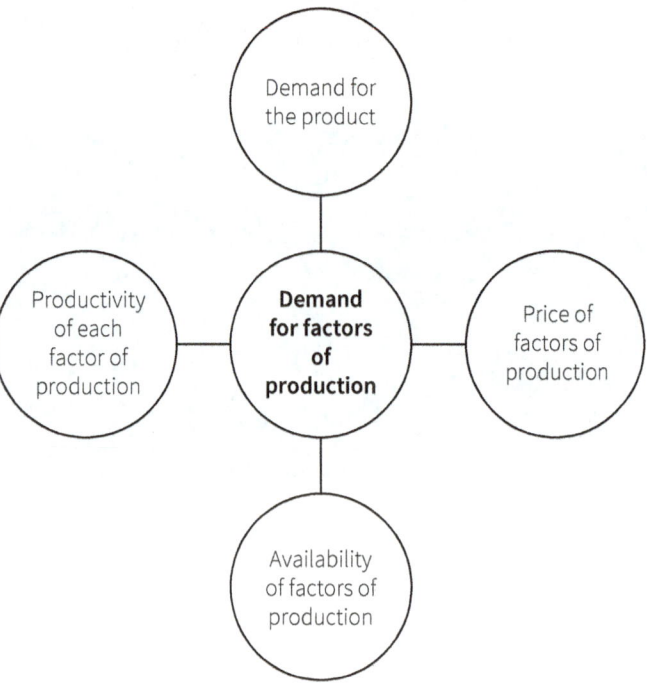

Figure 21.1 Examples of demands for factors of production

Sample question

In hot climates, the production of vegetables in a field can be increased by watering the vegetable crops. The table shows the effect of this.

No. of waterings per month	Output of vegetables (units)
0	20
1	30
2	80
3	150
4	180
5	200

i   Identify which factor of production is fixed and which is variable.

ii Explain which level of watering gives the highest productivity.

Sample answer:

i   The field is a fixed factor of production. The watering is variable.

ii Productivity is calculated by dividing the output of vegetables by the number of waterings. This indicates that 3 waterings per month gives the highest productivity.

SKILLS FOCUS

Remember that productivity is output per unit of input. The usual examples are in the case of manufacturers where the output is the goods produced and the input is the number of workers.

21.2 Labour-intensive and capital-intensive production

Table 21.1 provides some features of these two methods.

Table 21.1 Features of capital-intensive and labour-intensive production

Capital-intensive production	Labour-intensive production
• huge amounts of capital • small amounts of labour e.g. aircraft production where billions of dollars are needed to produce new planes such as the Airbus A380 or the Boeing 787 Dreamliner	• output depends most on employment of labour compared to other factors of production e.g. most service activities such as small grocery stores, takeaway food stalls, activities which require skilled workers to produce output, or where it is difficult to use machinery such as in flower cultivation

21.3 Production and productivity

It can be expected that:

- if productivity (output per person) increases with no change in working hours, production will increase
- production and productivity are likely to continue to increase due to technological advances and improvements in education.

Progress check

Answer the following questions to check your understanding:
1. What is the difference between production and productivity?
2. Why are some factors of production fixed and others variable in the short run?
3. Give **two** examples of capital-intensive and labour-intensive industries.

Revision checklist

You should know:
- ☐ Production is total output. Productivity is output per worker or factor of production.
- ☐ In the short run, there is at least one fixed factor of production.
- ☐ Labour-intensive production occurs when there is a high supply of low-wage labour or when labour forms a large part of the production process.
- ☐ Capital-intensive production can result in higher output at lower cost.

STRUCTURED SKILLS PRACTICE

1. A shoe manufacturer in Indonesia wishes to increase both production and productivity. Explain **one** way in which it could do each of these.

> **TIP**
> If in any doubt, go back to the second tip in Chapter 21.1. If there is any confusion, your answer will be meaningless.

Exam-style multiple choice questions

1. A garment manufacturer may reduce demand for labour and increase demand for capital equipment. What does this indicate?

   A the factory is too small for production to increase

   B the machinery for producing garments keeps breaking down

   C the rate of interest for borrowing loans has increased

   D workers in the factory have demanded a pay rise

2. Which is the most likely explanation for using more robots rather than more workers in the assembly of motor vehicles in developing economies?

   A robots are more productive than labour

   B the demand for motor vehicles is increasing

   C there is a large pool of unskilled labour available

   D vehicle parts are now sourced locally

Firms' costs, revenue and objectives

Chapter 22

Learning summary

By the end of this chapter, you should understand:

- how to define and calculate total cost, average total cost, fixed cost, variable cost, average fixed cost and average variable cost
- how to draw and interpret diagrams that show how changes in output can affect costs of production
- how to define total revenue and average revenue
- how sales affect revenue
- the objectives of firms including survival, social welfare, profit maximisation and growth.

22.1 Costs of production

Several costs are involved in production – **total cost** and **average total cost**, **fixed costs** and **average fixed cost**, **variable costs** and **average variable cost**.

TERMS

Total cost: the total cost of production.

Average total cost: total cost divided by output.

Fixed costs: costs which do not change with output in the short run.

Average fixed cost: total fixed cost divided by output.

Variable costs: costs that change as output changes.

Average variable cost: total variable cost divided by output.

Sample question

The table shows the relationship between output and costs for a factory producing farm machinery.

i Calculate the missing costs.
ii Explain the effect on costs as the factory's output increases.

Output (units)	Total cost (TC) ($)	Total fixed cost (TFC) ($)	Total variable cost (TVC) ($)	Average cost (AC) ($)	Average fixed cost (AFC) ($)	Average variable cost (AVC) ($)
1	2200	1200				
2		1200		1480		
3		1200		1190		
4		1200				790
5		1200	4250		240	
6	6990	1200			200	

Sample answer:

i

Output (units)	Total cost (TC) ($)	Total fixed cost (TFC) ($)	Total variable cost (TVC) ($)	Average cost (AC) ($)	Average fixed cost (AFC) ($)	Average variable cost (AVC) ($)
1	2200	1200	1000	2200	1200	1000
2	2960	1200	1760	1480	600	880
3	3570	1200	2370	1190	400	790
4	4360	1200	3160	1090	300	790
5	5450	1200	4250	1090	240	850
6	6990	1200	5790	1165	200	965

ii As output increases, total fixed cost is unchanged, while total cost increases. Average cost falls, is the same and then increases. Average fixed cost falls as output increases, while average variable cost falls, is the same and then increases with the increase in output.

SKILLS FOCUS

The data in the table is consistent with the usual diagrams that are drawn to show how costs vary with output. These are shown in Figure 22.1. Manipulating data is a good way of helping you understand each of the different cost concepts.

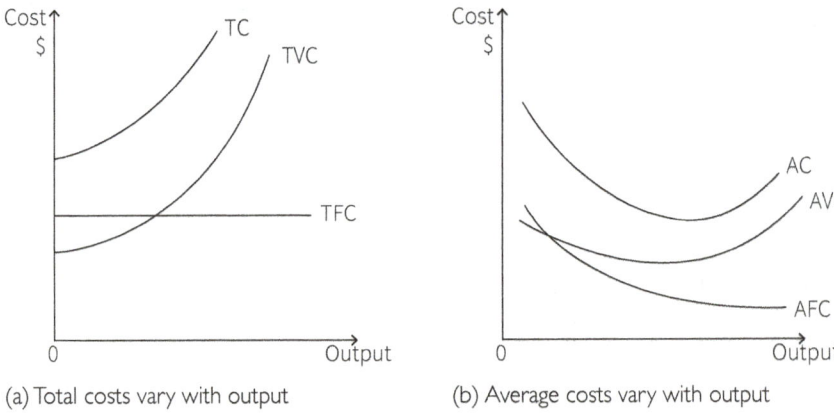

(a) Total costs vary with output

(b) Average costs vary with output

Figure 22.1 Total cost and average cost

22.2 Revenue

TERMS

Total revenue: the total amount of money received from selling a product.

Average revenue: the total revenue divided by the quantity sold, which is the same as price.

It is also useful at this point to understand what is meant by profit. This is what is left after total cost is deducted from **total revenue**.

> profit = revenue − cost

Sample question

The table shows sales information for three Chinese manufacturers of light fittings. Calculate:

i   Which firm earns most revenue?

ii Which firm makes most profit?

	Price per unit ($)	Number of units sold	Total cost ($)
Firm A	15	350	3000
Firm B	18	300	4050
Firm C	20	250	3600

Sample answer:

i   Total revenue = price per unit × number of units sold

Firm A: 15 × 350 = $5250

Firm B: 18 × 300 = $5400

Firm C: 20 × 250 = $5000

Therefore, Firm B earns most revenue.

ii Profit = total revenue − total cost

Firm A: $5250 − $3000 = $2250

Firm B: $5400 − $4050 = $1350

Firm C: $5000 − $3600 = $1400

Therefore, Firm A makes most profit.

22.3 Objectives of firms

Firms have various objectives – see Figure 22.2. These apply for all firms, small as well as large.

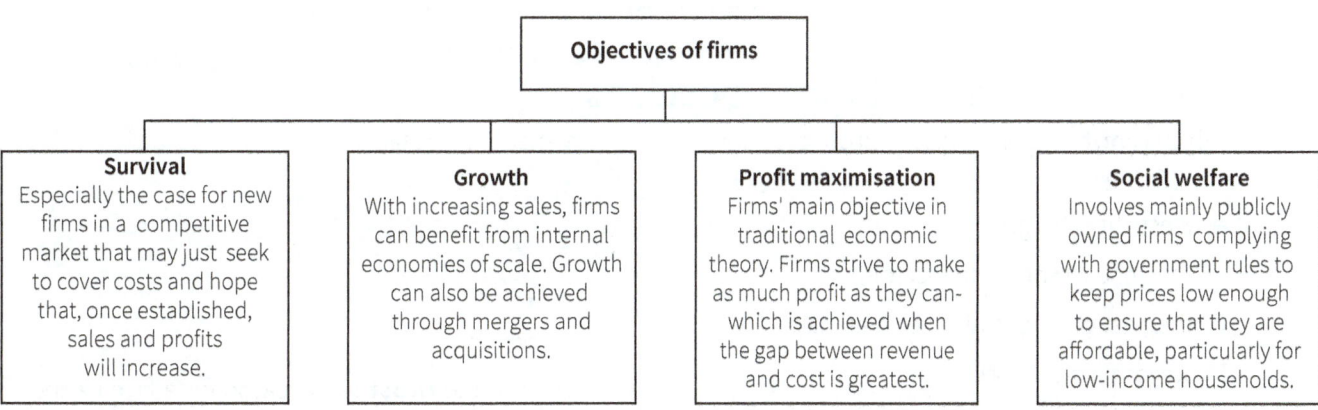

Figure 22.2 The main objectives of firms

Progress check

Answer the following questions to check your understanding:

1. How is average total cost calculated?
2. Describe the shape of the average cost curve as output increases.
3. What is profit?
4. Explain the profit maximisation objective of a firm.

Revision checklist

You should know:

- The costs of production of a firm consist of fixed costs and variable costs which, when combined, give total costs.
- The average revenue of a firm is the price it receives for its product.
- Profit is the difference between revenue and cost.
- Firms pursue a range of objectives including profit maximisation.

STRUCTURED SKILLS PRACTICE

1. Economic theory suggests that firms have just one objective – profit maximisation. Discuss whether or not this is correct.

   TIP Remember that profit maximisation is an assumption made in economic theory. Firms have other realistic objectives.

Exam-style multiple choice questions

1. Which is **not** a variable cost of production for a firm that manufactures agricultural machinery?

   A electricity charges
   B the annual rent for the factory
   C the cost of steel and other materials
   D wages paid to workers

2. The table below is for a shoe manufacturer in the Philippines:

Output	100 units
Total fixed cost	$100
Total variable cost	$300
Price per unit	$5

   What is the total profit?

   A $100
   B $200
   C $300
   D $400

3. What is the **most** likely reason for a firm having a survival objective?

   A it doesn't know its costs
   B it fears competition from bigger firms
   C it hopes to stay in the market and then grow
   D its product is not wanted by consumers

Market structure

Chapter 23

Learning summary

By the end of this chapter, you should understand:

- the effect of having a high number of firms on price, quantity, choice and profit
- the characteristics of monopoly
- the advantages and disadvantages of monopoly.

23.1 Competitive markets

TERMS

Market structure: the conditions which exist in a market including the number of firms.

Competitive market: a market with a number of firms that compete with each other.

Market structures vary from being very competitive in terms of there being a large number of firms – to monopoly where there is just one firm. The features of a **competitive market** are shown in Figure 23.1.

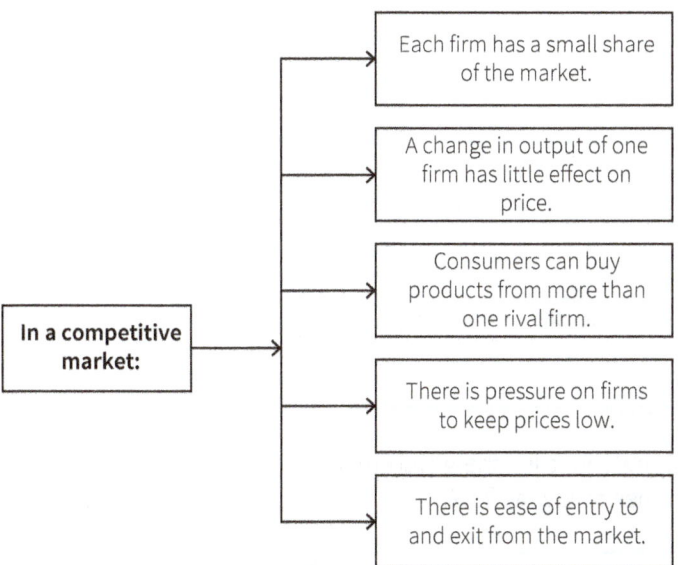

Figure 23.1 Features of a competitive market

This last characteristic (ease of entry) has a link with the profits that can be earned by a firm. A firm will remain in a market if it earns what is known as *normal profit*. If profits above this level, known as *supernormal* or *abnormal profits*, are earned, then this will attract new firms into the market. Their entry will reduce profits back to normal.

> **TIP**
> The number of firms in a market is usually the best indication of how competitive that market is.

Sample question

In many countries, local markets provide a vibrant competitive market for food and other items. Explain why such markets continue to thrive.

Sample answer:

Any competitive market can be expected to promote efficiency, otherwise firms would be forced out of business. Local markets are very competitive with prices at lowest possible cost. Stalls that sell the same product at a higher price compared to others will not survive. A further reason for their survival is that traders know the local market in terms of quality and what customers like. If it is seen that excessive profits are being earned, then new businesses will enter the market as there are no barriers to entry.

SKILLS FOCUS

The sample answer draws upon relevant economic concepts and terms. It could be improved by relating your own local experience of these concepts, with a final statement saying whether a local market really is as competitive as the theory indicates.

23.2 Monopoly markets

TERMS

Monopoly: a market with a sole supplier.

Barrier to entry: anything that makes it difficult for a firm to start producing a product.

In theory, a **monopoly** has 100% share of the market. In some countries, the government defines a monopoly as having far less market share, sometimes as low as 25%.

> **TIP**
> Very few monopolies with 100% of the market exist. Many are publicly owned firms, such as railways or mass transit systems, and are termed 'natural monopolies' as it does not make sense for there to be competition.

Monopolies often exist through:

- ownership of a particular resource
- a patent or licence that stops other firms producing
- being able to cut costs and prices, and force competitors out of the market.

Figure 23.2 shows the main characteristics of a monopoly.

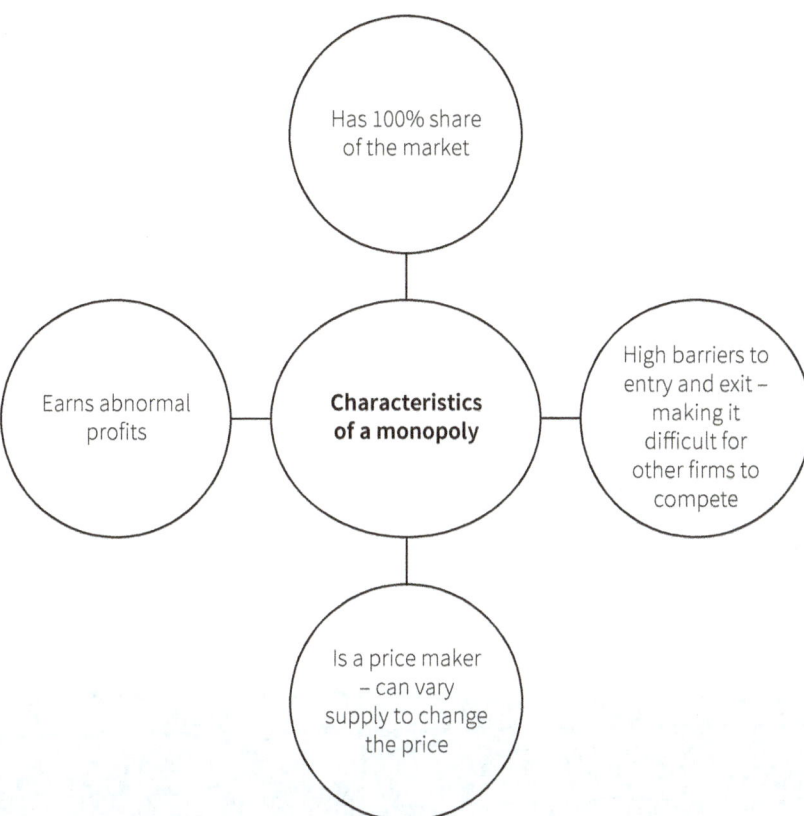

Figure 23.2 The main characteristics of a monopoly

McDonald's has recently opened its first restaurant in Aurangabad, India. It has a monopoly for the sale of its American food. The typical local food outlet is small and privately owned and there are hundreds of them in the city. Table 23.1 describes the contrasting characteristics of these two markets.

Table 23.1 Comparing two markets

	McDonald's	Small food outlet
Number of firms	One	Hundreds
Share of market	100%	Very little
Influence on price	Complete	Little
Consumer choice	None	Substantial
Low prices	Unlikely	Yes
Ease of entry	Very difficult	Easy
Level of profit in the long run	Abnormal	Normal

There are arguments for and against monopolies, as shown in Table 23.2.

Table 23.2 Advantages and disadvantages of monopolies

Case against monopolies	Case for monopolies
• Inefficient due to lack of competition.	• Large-scale production means greater efficiency and lower prices.
• High prices due to restricting supply.	• Prevent wasteful duplication.
• Poor quality product as consumers have no alternative.	• High profits fund expenditure on research and development.
• Slow to respond to change.	

Progress check

Answer the following questions to check your understanding:

1. Describe the characteristics of a competitive market.
2. What is the difference between normal profit and abnormal profit?
3. Suggest **two** examples of a monopoly and justify your choice.

Revision checklist

You should know:

- [ ] The number of firms in a market is a good guide to whether that market is competitive.
- [ ] A monopoly has 100% share of a market in theory.
- [ ] The strength of barriers to entry has a direct bearing on the competitiveness of a market.
- [ ] Strong barriers to entry allow abnormal profits to be earned in the long run.

STRUCTURED SKILLS PRACTICE

1. Discuss whether or not a monopoly can ever operate in the best interests of consumers.

Exam-style multiple choice questions

1. The taxi market in Lahore is very competitive. What is the **least** likely reason for this?

    A drivers are prepared to work long hours

    B other forms of transport are available

    C petrol is very expensive

    D taxi fares are low

2. Which is **most** likely to be a barrier to entry for a new firm seeking to enter a competitive market?

    A all firms are earning abnormal profits

    B many firms are making losses

    C the cost of entry into the market is low

    D the firm's brand is unknown to consumers

Exam-style structured questions for Section 3

Data response question

Read the source material carefully before answering the question.

> **Source material: Indian government set to end steel monopoly in rail tracks**
>
> The government-owned Indian Railways is the fourth largest rail network in the world. It has around 8000 locomotives and runs 7000 passenger and 4000 freight trains daily. With 1.5 million employees, it is one of the largest employers in India.
>
> Indian Railways receives a substantial government subsidy in recognition of the vital services it provides, particularly outside of the main cities and through its freight services. Suburban rail services are also essential for workers in big cities such as Chennai, Delhi and Mumbai to get to work.
>
> Indian Railways is progressing a much needed modernisation programme which aims to reduce journey times and improve rail safety. Massive supplies of new steel rails are needed to implement this programme. The rails are supplied by another public sector firm, Steel Authority of India Ltd (SAIL), which has a legal monopoly to supply. A major problem is that SAIL has failed to produce its contractual target in eight out of the past ten years. This year, the shortfall is 250 000 tonnes out of a target of 850 000 tonnes. It is due to open a new long-delayed rolling mill in Bhilal later this year in order to increase production. The high fixed costs involved in steel production mean that it is essential that SAIL retains the Indian Railways contract.
>
> The shortfall of steel rails has slowed the government's plans to modernise the rail network. Indian Railways is now looking to see how it can engage with other suppliers such as the privately owned Jindall Steel, which is very keen to supply.
>
> - The Economic Times, 24 March 2017 (adapted).

Table S3.1 Crude steel production in India, 2011/12–2015/16

Year	Crude steel production (million tonnes)
2011–2012	74.29
2012–2013	78.42
2013–2014	81.69
2014–2015	89.98
2015–2016	89.79

Source: Government of India, Ministry of Steel Annual Report, 2016–17.

Answer all parts of the question. Refer to the source material in your answers.

a Define a 'monopoly'. [1]

b Describe what is meant by a 'public sector firm' such as Indian Railways. [2]

c Describe how the production of crude steel in India has changed from 2011 to 2016. [2]

d Steel production has a high percentage of fixed costs to total cost. Explain what this means. [4]

e Explain **two** possible advantages of SAIL's monopoly. [4]

f Analyse how SAIL is likely to benefit from economies of scale. [5]

g Discuss whether or not Indian Railways might gain from a more competitive market for steel rails. [6]

h Discuss whether or not Indian Railways should receive more subsidy from the government. [6]

Four-part question

This question is introduced by stimulus material. In your answer, you may refer to this material and/or to other examples that you have studied.

The nature of the labour market in most countries is that employers are in a much stronger position than the workers they employ. This is particularly the case in many developing economies where labour is in plentiful supply and where there may be few trade unions.

a Define 'trade union'. [2]

b Explain how wages are determined in a competitive market. [4]

c Analyse why skilled workers earn more than unskilled workers. [6]

d Discuss whether or not the trade unions and the government can do anything to increase the earnings of unskilled workers. [8]

Section 4:
GOVERNMENT AND THE MACROECONOMY

Chapter 24: The role of government

Learning summary

By the end of this chapter you should understand:

- the role of government, locally, nationally and internationally.

24.1 The role of government

Government plays a larger role in a mixed economic system than in a more market-based system.

> **TIP** Most economies are mixed. The extent of government involvement in the economy varies. This is a point to bear in mind when revising the topics in this section.

At a local level, the extent of decisions taken by government varies from country to country.

At national level, government has various functions including:

- ownership of key strategic industries, especially where there is a **natural monopoly** such as in railways, and water and electricity provision
- working in partnership with private sector firms
- as an employer in state-owned enterprises.

This involvement enables governments to carry out their macroeconomic aims, in particular that of economic growth.

At an international level, governments have an important influence on international trade, in particular the promotion of free trade. Some governments are members of trade blocs such as the European Union and ASEAN, the Association of Southeast Asian Nations, or the BRICS (Brazil, Russia, India, China and South Africa) organisation. Most are members of the World Trade Organization.

> **TERM**
>
> Natural monopoly: an industry where a single firm can produce at a lower average cost than two or more firms because of the existence of significant economies of scale.

Sample question

In Pakistan, the railways, and water and electricity supply, are government-owned natural monopolies. Give **three** reasons why government ownership is better than private ownership.

Sample answer:

In the case of natural monopolies, such as the railways, water and electricity, government ownership is likely to mean that the average cost of provision is less than if two or more firms were competing. It also would not make sense to duplicate rail, water and power networks, given that these are essential services. There are also economic and social welfare issues involved in their supply.

SKILLS FOCUS

Not all economists would agree. The wording of the sample question does not require any discussion as to why the private sector might be more efficient in some cases.

Progress check

Answer the following questions to check your understanding:

1. For a country you have studied, give examples of the role of the national government in the economy.
2. How can governments influence international trade?

Revision checklist

You should know:

- ☐ The role of government in the economy varies from one country to another.
- ☐ This role depends on the relative importance of the government and the free market.
- ☐ Most governments have an important role to play in promoting free international trade.

STRUCTURED SKILLS PRACTICE

1. Analyse the role of government locally, nationally and internationally in an economy that you have studied.

    TIP Much of the economic role of government is at national level. The question has three aspects, so remember to include something about the other two roles in your answer.

Exam-style multiple choice questions

1. Hong Kong is an example of a free enterprise economy. Why is this?

   A firms are extensively regulated

   B its government has no involvement in owning key industries

   C the government decides the wages for many employees

   D the government is the most important employer

2. A government decides to move from a planned to a more mixed economy. Which is the **most** likely result of this process?

   A commercial banks no longer want to give loans to small businesses

   B more subsidy is paid to the steel industry

   C the government has no plans to privatise the electricity supply industry

   D there is a reduction in the number of public sector workers

Chapter 25: The macroeconomic aims of government

Learning summary

By the end of this chapter, you should understand:

- the macroeconomic aims of government
- the reasons behind the choice of aims
- the criteria government set for each aim
- the possible conflicts between macroeconomic aims.

25.1 The macroeconomic aims of government

These are shown in Figure 25.1.

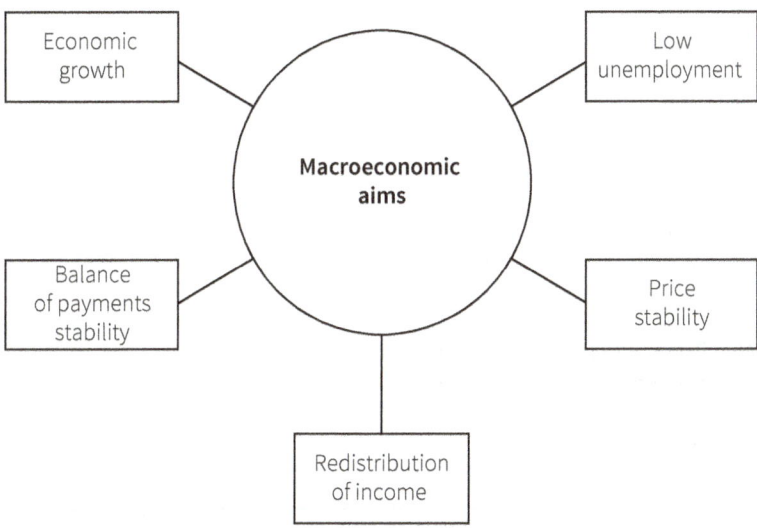

Figure 25.1 The macroeconomic aims of government

TERMS

Economic growth: an increase in the output of an economy and, in the long run, an increase in the economy's productive potential.

Total demand: the total demand for a country's product at a given price level – it consists of consumer expenditure, investment, government spending and net exports (exports minus imports).

Total supply: the total amount of goods and services that domestic firms are willing to supply at a given price level.

Economic growth

This objective is shown through an increase in output in the short run. In the long run, **economic growth** results in an increase in an economy's productive potential. This is illustrated in Figure 25.2 by means of a production possibility curve (PPC).

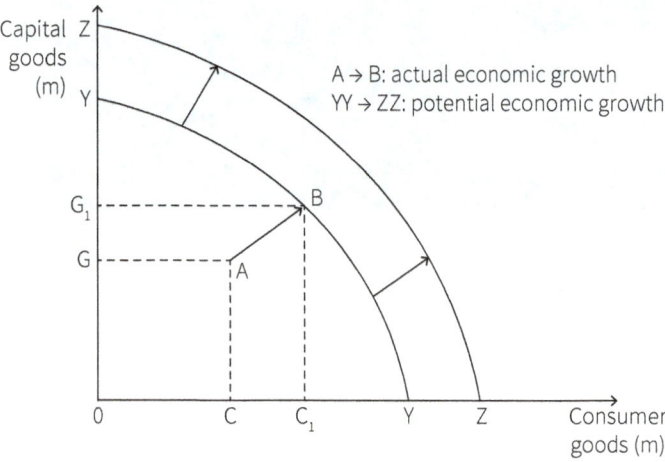

Figure 25.2 Economic growth

Economic growth can improve living standards through more goods and services being available. It increases life expectancy, and allows better health education and housing to be provided. Economic growth has a 'feel-good' impact, resulting in other macroeconomic aims being achieved.

Governments often set a target for economic growth. It is difficult to generalise but 2%–3% seems reasonable for most developed economies. For developing economies, the target is likely to be greater, although invariably more volatile.

Sample question

In 2017, the Asian Development Bank reported that Pakistan's economy grew at 4.7% in 2016 and was forecast to grow at 5.2% in 2017 and 5.5% in 2018. Explain how this growth is likely to benefit Pakistan's population.

Sample answer:

The most obvious benefit of this level of growth is through increased incomes. In turn, consumers will be able to purchase more goods and services, and experience a better lifestyle.

In turn, the government will receive increased revenue through a rise in the taxation it receives, especially from indirect taxes on goods purchased. This revenue can be spent on things that increase social well-being such as hospitals and schools. Some could be spent on new roads or modernising the railways, leading to further potential economic growth.

This growth can also aid Pakistan in achieving other macroeconomic objectives such as reducing unemployment or increasing exports. A warning is that an increase in the price level or import spending must be avoided to obtain the full benefits from growth.

> **SKILLS FOCUS**
>
> The sample answer is a very good one. It could be developed with a comment about growth being forecast to increase at an enhanced rate, so advancing the points already made in the answer.

Low unemployment

> **TERMS**
>
> Full employment: the lowest level of unemployment possible.
>
> Unemployment rate: the percentage of the labour force who are willing and able to work but are without jobs.

A low level of unemployment is usually interpreted as **full employment**. Just what this amounts to in terms of an **unemployment rate** varies from one country to another and over time – in the US in 2017, the unemployment rate was around 4.5% and seen as around full employment. In developing economies, the full employment level of unemployment will be greater, perhaps around 8%–10%.

> See Chapter 30.3 for the unemployment rate formula.

Price stability

> **TERM**
>
> Price stability: the price level in the economy not changing significantly over time.

Price stability is essential for international competitiveness. Firms can plan ahead by agreeing export prices, setting domestic prices and agreeing wage increases for workers. A target of a 2% inflation rate is set by many developed economies – it is higher for most developing economies. A slight rise in prices can actually be good for the economy – it encourages firms to become more efficient.

Balance of payments stability

This is where the revenue from selling exports is balanced from the money paid out for imports. Such a situation helps a country to avoid debt. Many economies are faced with having to borrow money because expenditure on imports is greater than receipts from exports. If this is short-term, then it is less of a problem than if the deficits are persistent.

Redistribution of income

Most governments have a policy of seeking to redistribute income from the rich to the poor. This is done by taxing high-earners more heavily than those on lower incomes, and by providing various types of subsidy and, in some cases, welfare and unemployment benefits.

> **TIP**
>
> It is useful to know some basic information on the macroeconomic position of any economy that you have studied in terms of its macroeconomic aims and whether the government has set any targets.

25.2 Possible conflicts between macroeconomic aims

Table 25.1 shows three of the most common conflicts between the macroeconomic aims of a government.

Table 25.1 Conflicting macroeconomic aims

Macroeconomic aim		Conflict
Full employment	versus	**Stable prices** An increase in total demand creates more jobs but increased costs of production lead to an increase in prices.
Economic growth	versus	**Balance of payments stability** An increase in productive potential is an increase in total supply – this can increase the need for more imported raw materials, creating instability in the balance of payments.
Full employment	versus	**Balance of payments stability** An increase in total demand leads to an increase in demand for imported consumer goods, leading to a deficit in the balance of payments.

Progress check

Answer the following questions to check your understanding:

1. What is the difference between actual and potential economic growth?
2. Define total demand and total supply.
3. What is a low level of unemployment?
4. Why is it difficult for an economy to have full employment and price stability at the same time?

Revision checklist

You should know:

- [ ] The macroeconomic aims of government are economic growth, low unemployment, stable inflation, balance of payments stability and the redistribution of income.

- [ ] For some aims such as economic growth and price stability, it is usual for governments to set an annual target.

- [ ] There are conflicts between macroeconomic aims, for example, between full employment and price stability, economic growth and balance of payments stability, and full employment and balance of payments stability.

STRUCTURED SKILLS PRACTICE

1. The table below compares four macroeconomic variables for Indonesia and Malaysia in 2016.

	Economic growth rate (%)	Unemployment rate (%)	Inflation (%)	Exports - imports ($bn)
Indonesia	5.0	5.6	3.0	+$9bn
Malaysia	4.2	3.5	1.8	+$21bn

    i Explain what evidence there is to support the view that in 2016 Malaysia had a stronger economy than Indonesia.

    ii Discuss whether or not the relationship between unemployment and inflation in each country indicates a possible conflict between macroeconomic objectives.

    > **TIP**
    > A good answer to part (ii) should include understanding of the theoretical relationship between unemployment and inflation. It should then consider whether the data matches this relationship.

Exam-style multiple choice questions

1. India's economy grew by 8% in 2015/16 and by 7.1% in 2016/17. What does this indicate?

   A people are better off in 2016/17 than in 2015/16

   B people are worse off in 2016/17 than in 2015/16

   C the balance of payments in 2016/17 was less stable than in 2015/16

   D the balance of payments in 2016/17 was more stable than in 2015/16

2. Which will lead to an increase in total supply?

   A an increase in imported consumer goods

   B an increase in the number of migrant workers

   C firms reducing their stocks of manufactured goods

   D more firms working overtime to meet orders

Fiscal policy

Chapter 26

Learning summary

By the end of this chapter, you should understand:

- what is meant by a budget
- the reasons for government spending
- the reasons for taxation
- how taxes are classified
- the principles of taxation
- the impact of taxation on consumers, producers, government and the economy
- what is meant by fiscal policy
- fiscal policy measures and how to calculate a budget deficit or surplus
- the effects of fiscal policy on government macroeconomic aims.

26.1 The budget

The budget is a statement where a government sets out its annual planned revenue and spending. There are three types of budget, as shown in Table 26.1.

Table 26.1 Types of government budget

Deficit budget	Surplus budget	Balanced budget
Government spending is greater than government revenue.	Government spending is less than government revenue.	Government spending is equal to government revenue.

26.2 The reasons for government spending

The amount spent by governments varies between countries. More is likely to be spent in countries with a large public sector relative to the private sector. The main reasons for government spending are to:

- influence economic activity in order to meet macroeconomic aims
- reduce market failure by spending on public goods and merit goods, and by regulating markets where there is a difference between social and private costs, and social and private benefits
- promote equity by providing benefits and services for the less-well-off and vulnerable groups
- pay interest on national debt.

Sample question

In 2015/16, the Pakistan government's budget deficit was expected to increase by 1350 billion rupees (Rs). Its spending was estimated to be Rs5800bn.

i   Calculate the government's expected revenue.

ii Give **two** likely reasons for the increased budget deficit.

Sample answer:

i   Revenue = spending − budget deficit

    = 5800 − 1350 (Rs bn)

    = 4450 (Rs bn)

ii Likely reasons for the increased budget deficit include additional spending on healthcare and social services, defence and debt servicing.

SKILLS FOCUS

An equally acceptable answer is that government revenue has fallen. It could also be explained by a combination of changes in both government spending and revenue.

26.3 Reasons for taxation

There are many reasons why governments levy taxes on people and businesses. These include:

- to fund government spending on things such as public services
- to reduce the income gap between the rich and poor
- to discourage consumption of demerit goods such as junk food
- to protect domestic industries from unfair competition from cheap imports
- to influence economic activity in order to meet macroeconomic aims.

TERMS

Direct taxes: taxes on income and wealth.

Indirect taxes: taxes on spending.

Progressive tax: one which takes a larger percentage of the income or wealth of the rich.

Regressive tax: one which takes a larger percentage of the income or wealth of the poor.

Proportional tax: one which takes the same percentage of the income or wealth of all taxpayers.

Virtually all types of economy have **direct** and **indirect taxes**. The balance between the two varies, although most economies have an increasing emphasis on indirect taxes such as the recently introduced goods and services tax in India.

Figure 26.1 shows some typical examples of taxes. In general, direct taxes aim to be **progressive** while indirect taxes are **regressive**.

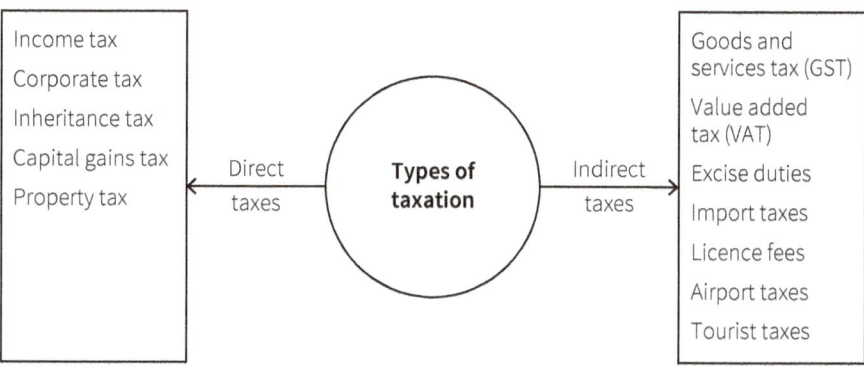

Figure 26.1 Types of taxation

26.4 The principles of taxation

There are various principles of taxation that governments should follow. The most important are:

- *Equity.* The tax burden should be fairly distributed. People with higher income or wealth should pay more tax than those with lower income or wealth.
- *Economy.* The cost of collecting the tax should be as low as possible.
- *Convenience.* A tax should be easy to pay and, for governments, easy to collect.
- *Certainty.* A tax should be clearly defined and, for taxpayers, it should be clear how much they should pay.

26.5 Impact of taxation

Taxation has an impact on consumers, producers, government and the economy as a whole. For consumers and producers, the impact can be shown by the incidence of taxation, the distribution of the burden of an indirect tax. This is shown in Figure 26.2.

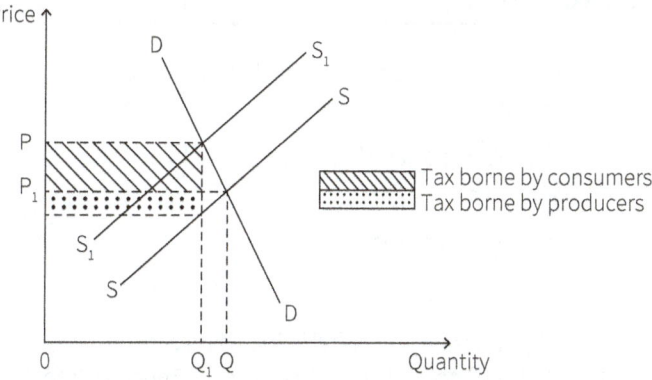

Figure 26.2 The impact of an indirect tax

Notice:

- An indirect tax is represented by a shift to the left of the supply curve.
- This increases the price to P_1 and reduces quantity to Q_1 from the equilibrium position of P and Q.

- Consumers are paying the largest proportion of the tax. This is because demand is inelastic.

Other points to make on the impact of taxation are:

- A high rate of income tax may discourage some workers from working harder.
- A high rate of corporation tax may discourage an entrepreneur from investing in new equipment.
- Increased indirect taxes are likely to lead to increased prices which in turn are inflationary.

26.6 Fiscal policy measures

> **TERM**
>
> Fiscal policy: decisions on government spending and taxation designed to influence total demand.

Sample question

The table shows estimated government revenue and spending in Mauritius in 2016/17 and 2017/18.

	2016/17 (Rs bn) (estimated)	2017/18 (Rs bn) (estimated)
Government revenue	94.7	112.2
Value added tax	30.2	32.8
Corporate tax and income tax	21.4	23.3
Customs and excise duties	18.3	21.5
Other revenues	11.1	20.0
Property and other taxes	13.7	14.7
Government spending	110.6	127.7
Wages and salaries	28.4	30.6

	2016/17 (Rs bn) (estimated)	2017/18 (Rs bn) (estimated)
Social benefits	27.4	29.6
Other expenses	22.6	25.9
Subsidies and grants	22.0	22.9
Capital expenditure	10.0	18.8

i Calculate the budget deficits in 2016/17 and 2017/18.

ii Calculate the change from 2016/17 to 2017/18 in:
- indirect taxes
- direct taxes.

iii The increase in capital expenditure from 2016/17 to 2017/18 accounts for much of the increased expenditure. Explain the likely reason for this change.

Sample answer:

i 2016/17 Expenditure Rs 110.6 bn
   Revenue Rs 94.7 bn
   Deficit = 110.6 bn − 94.7 bn
   = **Rs 15.9 bn**

   2017/18 Expenditure Rs 127.7 bn
   Revenue Rs 112.2 bn
   Deficit = 127.7 bn − 112.2 bn
   = **Rs 15.5 bn**

ii Indirect taxes are VAT and customs, and excise duty.

Total 2016/17 is Rs 30.2 bn + Rs 18.3 bn = Rs 48.5 bn

Total 2017/18 is Rs 32.8 bn + Rs 21.5 bn = Rs 54.3 bn

Change is Rs 54.3 bn − Rs 48.5 bn = + **Rs 5.8 bn**

Direct taxes are corporate tax and income tax.

Total 2016/17 is Rs 21.4 bn

Total 2017/18 is Rs 23.3 bn

Change is Rs 23.3 bn − Rs 21.4 bn = + **Rs 1.9 bn**

iii Given two deficit budgets, the increase in capital expenditure is designed to give a boost to the economy through increasing employment and growth.

26.7 Effects of fiscal policy on government macroeconomic aims

If a government wants to raise total demand in order to increase economic growth and employment, it will implement an **expansionary fiscal policy**. Alternatively, a government may implement a **contractionary fiscal policy** to reduce inflationary pressure.

TERMS

Expansionary fiscal policy: rises in government expenditure and/or cuts in taxation designed to increase total demand.

Contractionary fiscal policy: cuts in government expenditure and/or rises in taxation designed to reduce total demand.

Table 26.2 shows how fiscal policy can be used to achieve macroeconomic aims.

Table 26.2 Achieving macroeconomic aims with different fiscal policies

Macroeconomic aim	Fiscal policy	How it is achieved
Economic growth	Expansionary	Increasing government spending, especially on new roads, rail improvements, water and power supplies
Reduced unemployment	Expansionary	Reducing indirect and direct taxation, which increases demand from consumers
Reduced inflation	Contractionary	Cutting government spending or raising taxes
Reduced balance of payments deficit	Contractionary	Raising taxes to dampen demand

Progress check

Answer the following questions to check your understanding:

1. What is the difference between a budget deficit and a budget surplus? When might each be used?
2. Give examples of direct taxes and indirect taxes from a country that you have studied.
3. When is an indirect tax most effective in reducing the quantity demanded?
4. When might a government use a contractionary fiscal policy?

Revision checklist

You should know:

- There are three types of budget – deficit, surplus and balanced.
- Governments spend money for many reasons such as provision of public and merit goods, and to meet macroeconomic aims.
- Governments impose taxes to fund spending, to discourage consumption of demerit goods, to reduce income inequality and to meet macroeconomic aims.
- There are many types of taxation – direct and indirect, progressive and regressive.
- Fiscal policy refers to the use by government of measures relating to its own spending and taxation.
- Fiscal policies can be expansionary or contractionary depending on what macroeconomic aim is being pursued.

STRUCTURED SKILLS PRACTICE

A government wants to reduce the level of unemployment in its economy. Discuss whether or not this should be done through reducing taxation or increasing government spending.

TIP This is a typical question on fiscal policy. The 'discuss' command word is giving a strong hint that both policies can be used to reduce unemployment. You could mention that a combination of both is often used.

Exam-style multiple choice questions

1. Why is income tax referred to as a progressive tax?

    A high income earners pay a higher percentage than those on lower incomes

    B it generates increased revenue for governments, year by year

    C it is indicative of most modern economies

    D it is paid by many people in an economy

2. What is the likely effect of increasing an indirect tax on a demerit good?

	Price	Quantity demanded
A	increase	increase
B	increase	reduce
C	reduce	increase
D	reduce	reduce

3. How might fiscal policy be used to reduce the level of inflation in an economy?

	Government spending	Taxation
A	increase	increase
B	increase	reduce
C	reduce	increase
D	reduce	reduce

Chapter 27: Monetary policy

> **Learning summary**
>
> By the end of this chapter, you should understand:
>
> - what is meant by money supply
> - what is meant by monetary policy
> - the measures of monetary policy
> - the effects of monetary policy on government macroeconomic aims.

27.1 The money supply

The money supply consists of all the money in an economy at any one time. It can be measured in two main ways:

- *The narrow measure.* This includes notes, coins and what is held in current accounts at commercial banks – money used as the medium of exchange.
- *The broad measure.* This includes notes, coins, current accounts and deposit accounts – money used as the medium of exchange and the store of value.

27.2 Monetary policy

Monetary policy influences the supply and/or price of money.

> **TERM**
>
> Monetary policy: decisions on the money supply, the rate of interest and the exchange rate taken to influence total demand.

The money supply can be increased by:

- printing more notes and issuing more coins
- the government buying back government bonds
- an increase in lending by commercial banks.

Any of these will increase total demand.

Figure 27.1 shows how a change in the interest rate affects consumers and firms.

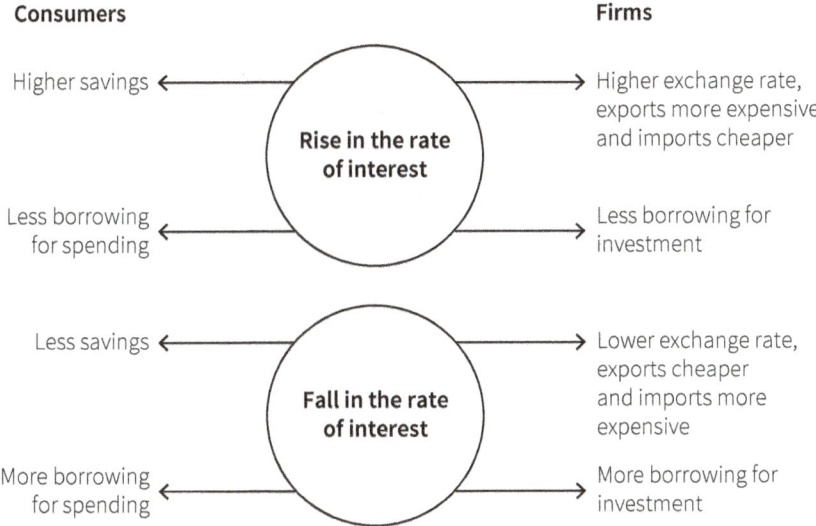

Figure 27.1 Effects of interest rate changes

27.3 Effects of monetary policy on government macroeconomic aims

If a government wants to increase the economic growth rate and reduce unemployment, it will use **expansionary monetary policy**, reducing the rate of interest or increasing the money supply. On the other hand, if it thinks that the price level is rising too quickly, it may increase the rate of interest or reduce the growth in the money supply, that is, use **contractionary monetary policy**, to reduce total demand and the upward pressure on prices.

> **TERMS**
>
> Expansionary monetary policy: increases in the money supply and/or a reduction in the rate of interest designed to increase total demand.
>
> Contractionary monetary policy: cuts in the money supply and/or an increase in the rate of interest designed to reduce total demand.

Table 27.1 shows how monetary policy can be used to achieve macroeconomic aims.

Table 27.1 Achieving macroeconomic aims with different monetary policies

Macroeconomic aim	Monetary policy	How it is achieved
Economic growth	Expansionary	Lowering interest rates and growing the money supply, leading to more investment
Reduced unemployment	Expansionary	Lowering interest rates and growing the money supply, leading to more output and employment
Reduced inflation	Contractionary	Raising interest rates and lowering the money supply to reduce total demand and prices
Reduced balance of payments deficit	Contractionary	Lowering interest rates which in turn lowers the exchange rate, making exports cheaper and imports dearer

Sample question

I   In August 2017, the Reserve Bank of India cut its lowest rate of interest from 6.75% to 6.5%. Give **two** possible reasons for this reduction.

II In 2017, the rate of interest in Japan was −0.1%. Explain what this means for consumers and firms and for the economy.

Sample answers:

I   The two obvious reasons are that inflation is not a problem, otherwise the rate of interest would not be cut, and it needs to stimulate India's growth rate by increasing consumer spending and private investment.

II The negative interest rate seeks to discourage consumers from saving and encourage them to spend. For firms, it makes the cost of borrowing cheap and should encourage new investment. For the economy, it is designed to boost total demand at a time of falling output and weak investor confidence.

SKILLS FOCUS

The case of Japan is unusual. Its experience over the past 20 years has defied almost all economic principles. Remember this when answering a question on Japan. The case of India is much more in line with economic theory.

Progress check

Answer the following questions to check your understanding:

1. What is the difference between monetary policy and fiscal policy?
2. What relationship is there between the rate of interest and the foreign exchange rate?
3. For what macroeconomic reasons might a government decide to increase the rate of interest?

Revision checklist

You should know:

- [ ] The money supply consists of narrow and broad money.
- [ ] Control of the money supply and control of the rate of interest are the main tools of monetary policy.
- [ ] Monetary policy is used to influence total demand.
- [ ] An increase in the money supply is likely to increase total demand.
- [ ] Monetary policies can be expansionary or contractionary depending on what macroeconomic aim is being pursued.
- [ ] In some economies, this includes managing the exchange rate.

TIP Be careful not to confuse monetary policy with fiscal policy – it is a common mistake.

STRUCTURED SKILLS PRACTICE

1 Discuss whether or not monetary policy is the best way for an economy to reduce a problem of inflation.

TIP The wording of this question makes clear that you need to consider other policies, as well as monetary policy. Then you can say which, if any, is best. A combination of policies is often widely applied.

Exam-style multiple choice questions

1 Which is **not** a monetary policy measure?

   A a decrease in the rate of interest
   B an increase in goods and services tax
   C an increase in the foreign exchange rate
   D an increase in the money supply

2 What would a decrease in the rate of interest normally lead to?

   A a fall in the money supply
   B a fall in the rate of inflation
   C an increase in investment by firms
   D an increase in unemployment

Chapter 28: Supply-side policies

Learning summary

By the end of this chapter, you should understand:

- what is meant by supply-side policy
- supply-side policy measures
- the effects of supply-side policy on government macroeconomic aims.

28.1 Supply-side policy measures

> **TERM**
>
> Supply-side policy: measures designed to increase total supply.

Supply-side policies are designed to help the economy to grow by increasing productive potential. They seek to increase the quantity and quality of resources, and improve efficiency in the economy. They can also help to lower unemployment and inflation.

Figure 28.1 shows some examples of supply-side policies and how they can improve efficiency and competitiveness in the economy.

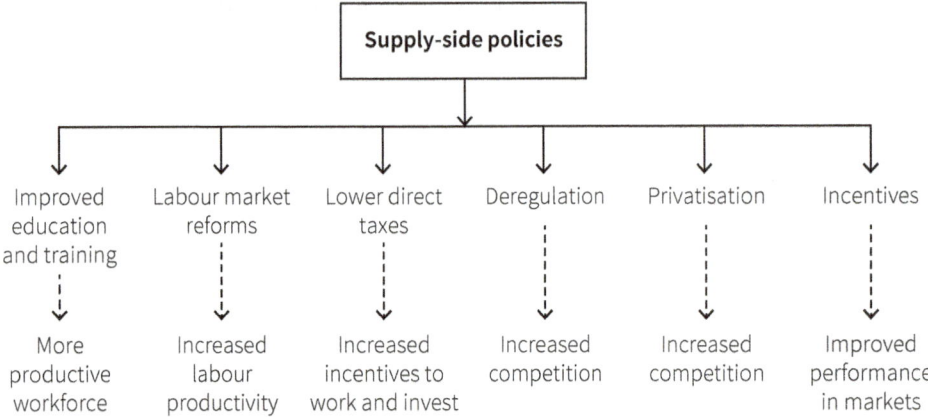

Figure 28.1 Examples of supply-side policies

> **TIP**
>
> The nature of supply-side policies is that they always aim to increase total supply, never reduce it.

Sample question

Explain how supply-side policy measures can be used to increase labour productivity.

Sample answer:

One possible supply-side policy to increase labour productivity would be to increase government investment in education and training. The funding might be used to keep more students in school longer and to promote vocational training.

Another supply-side policy would be to reduce direct taxes in order to stimulate entrepreneurial activity and to keep more people in employment. This would encourage more business investment.

Other policies might aim to reduce the power of the trade unions and to encourage more flexible working practices.

SKILLS FOCUS

All of these measures should improve competitiveness and will result in an increase in total supply. Do not confuse these policies with those designed to increase total demand.

28.2 Effects of supply-side measures on government macroeconomic aims

TIP: Supply-side policy measures take time to be effective. Fiscal and monetary measures take less time to work.

Supply-side policies aim to increase productive potential and efficiency, with total supply rising in line with total demand.

So, effective supply-side measures can:

- increase growth
- increase output and employment
- do so without increasing inflation
- improve the balance of payments position since exports increase and imports fall.

Progress check

Answer the following questions to check your understanding:

1. What is the purpose of supply-side policies?
2. Explain how deregulation and privatisation can increase the productive potential of an economy.
3. Why do supply-side policies take time to become effective?

Revision checklist

You should know:

- [ ] Supply-side policies are designed to increase total supply.
- [ ] They can be applied in the labour market and in product markets.
- [ ] They are particularly useful when there is a need for increased competition and efficiency.

STRUCTURED SKILLS PRACTICE

1. Explain **two** supply-side measures that might reduce the rate of inflation in an economy.

> **TIP**
> This is a simple, straightforward question. Make sure you say how each supply-side policy might reduce the rate of inflation.

Exam-style multiple choice questions

1. Which is a supply-side measure?
   A a decrease in government spending on armed forces
   B a decrease in interest rates
   C an increase in government spending on armed forces
   D an increase in taxation on corporate profits

2. In Country X, there is an increase in total supply but no change in total demand. Which is **most** likely?
   A the balance of payments deficit will fall
   B the productive potential of the economy has increased
   C the rate of inflation will increase
   D unemployment will increase

Economic growth

Chapter 29

Learning summary

By the end of this chapter, you should understand:

- what is meant by economic growth and how it is measured
- the causes and consequences of recession
- the causes and consequences of economic growth
- policies to promote economic growth.

29.1 Economic growth and how it is measured

Economic growth occurs when there is an increase in the real value of goods and services in an economy. This is measured through a rise in **real GDP**. Changes in the population can have a significant effect on real GDP. This is why changes in **real GDP per head** are usually used to measure a country's economic growth. This is an important statistic that is used when making international comparisons.

> **TERMS**
>
> **Real GDP:** GDP at constant prices and so adjusted for inflation.
>
> **Real GDP per head:** real GDP divided by size of population.

> **TIP**
>
> Real GDP per head (or per capita) is widely used to compare living standards. When making comparisons, ensure that you are using real and not nominal data, which measures GDP in money terms.

Sample question

The diagrams show the quarterly GDP growth rates of India and China from 2012 to 2016.

INDIA

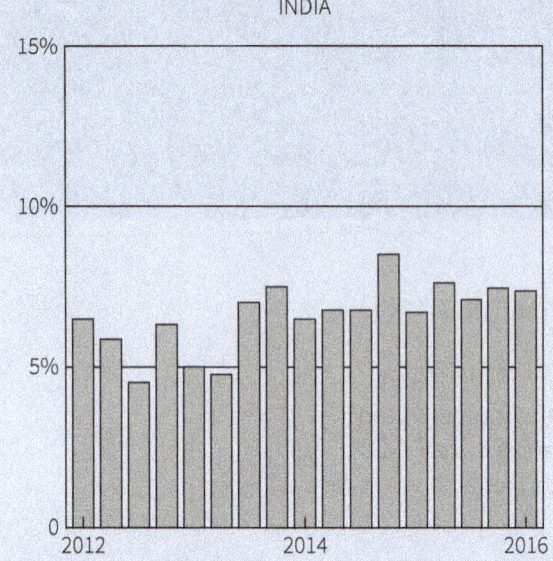

CHINA

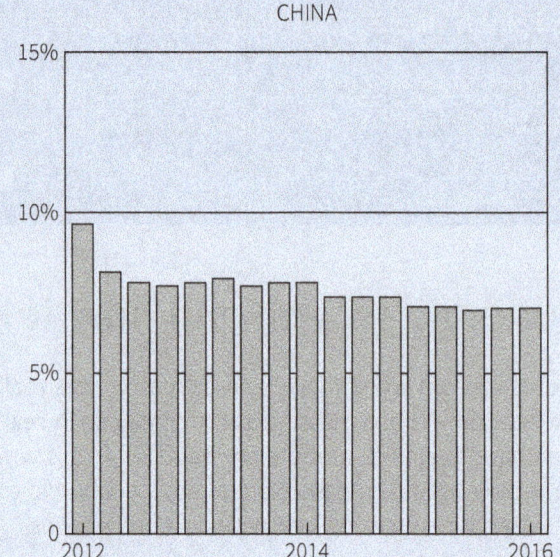

Quarterly GDP growth, 2012–2016

Source: Sections of a diagram from the Daily Telegraph, 9 February 2016, based on IMF statistics.

i   Describe the growth rates of India and China over this period.

ii Explain why the Indian government might feel positive about its economy being the 'fastest-growing major economy'.

Sample answer:

i   India's growth has fluctuated more than that of China, hitting a high towards the end of 2014. In contrast, China's growth has been steadily falling.

ii In the first quarter of 2016, India's growth for the first time was higher than that of China.

SKILLS FOCUS

There should be some caution with respect to (ii) – in all other quarters, China's growth exceeded that of India. It is also difficult to forecast future growth, which depends on many factors.

29.2 Causes and consequences of recession

> **TERM**
>
> **Recession:** a reduction in real GDP over a period of six months or more.

Figure 29.1 illustrates how an economy can move from a position of full employment to one of **recession** where fewer consumer goods and capital goods are produced.

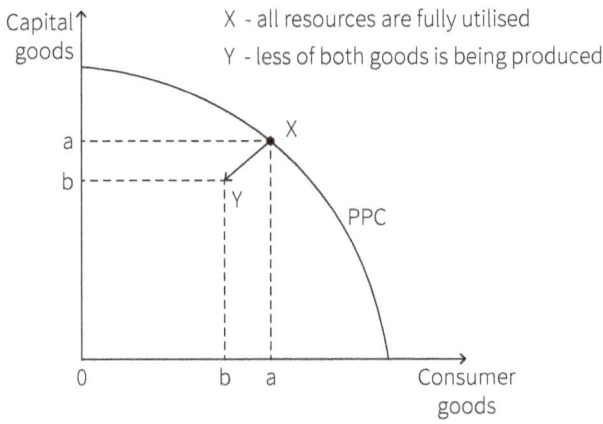

Figure 29.1 Recession and the PPC

The causes and consequences of recession are shown in Table 29.1.

Table 29.1 Causes and consequences of recession

Causes of recession	Consequences of recession
• A global economic shock – the financial crisis of 2008–2012 led to recession in many countries. Developing economies were particularly affected due to their dependency on trade with developed economies.	• Lower output, lower employment and lower living standards.
• An excessive decrease in total demand due to the need to combat rising inflation or rising debts.	• Multinational companies may be less inclined to risk foreign direct investment in an economy faced with recession.
• A decrease in total supply brought about by a rise in fuel prices affecting production and exports.	• A decline in tax revenue and the need to spend more on social benefits. This will increase a budget deficit.

29.3 Causes and consequences of economic growth

An economy experiences economic growth when there is:

- an increase in the quantity of productive resources
- an increase in the quality of productive resources.

Both can be shown on a PPC – see Figure 29.2. Short run growth, through an increase in total demand, is shown by a movement within the PPC from X to Y. Long run economic growth is shown by a shift outwards of the PPC from PPC to PPC_1, as a result of an increase in the total resources used.

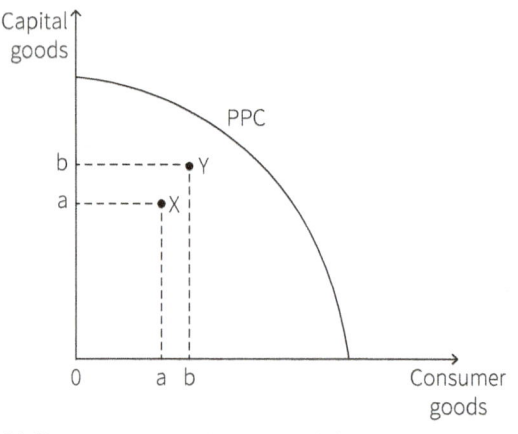
(a) Short run – unused resources being used

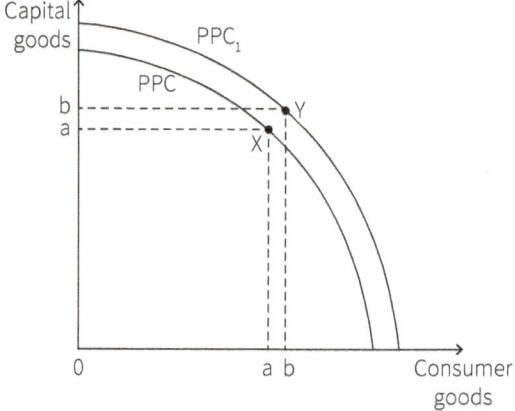
(b) Long run – an increase in the quantity of resources being used

Figure 29.2 Economic growth and the PPC

> **TIP**
> A good way to remember the causes and consequences of recession is to view them as the opposite of the causes and consequences of growth.

The main benefits and costs of economic growth are summarised in Table 29.2.

Table 29.2 Benefits and costs of economic growth

Benefits of economic growth	Costs of economic growth
• Improved living standards – this is the most obvious and it is why growth is pursued in most economies – people on average are better off, can afford more goods and services, and governments can fund more merit goods such as education and healthcare provision.	• Increased pollution, especially in big cities.
• Reduced poverty – governments should have more tax revenue to spend on those who are poor or not able to support themselves.	• Depletion of natural resources such as forests and fisheries and non-renewable resources.
• Increased life expectancy, especially in developing economies.	• Destruction of wildlife habitats.
	• Increased strain and stress, especially where people have to work long hours and in poor conditions.
	• A widening gap between the rich and the poor.

The benefits and costs of economic growth affect all economies. For many developing economies, rapid urbanisation may well have provided jobs and an increase in incomes but the costs in terms of pollution and quality of life are invariably considerable.

> **TIP**
> When discussing economic growth, remember that it comes with costs, as well as the obvious benefits.

29.4 Policies to promote economic growth

Government policies can promote the economic growth of a country in many ways. Some examples are given in Table 29.3.

Table 29.3 How government policies promote economic growth

Policy	Effect
Expansionary fiscal and monetary policies, e.g. reduction in tax on corporate profits, decrease in rate of interest.	Increased consumer expenditure and investment, leading to a rise in total demand to encourage firms to increase output.
Supply-side measures, e.g. improvements in education and training.	Raised labour productivity and increased productive capacity.
Foreign direct investment, incorporating new technologies.	Increased total demand with possible improvement to the balance of trade.
Any of the above.	A 'feel-good' factor promoting confidence in the economy.

Progress check

Answer the following questions to check your understanding:

1. How is economic growth measured?
2. What is a recession?
3. What are the main causes of economic growth?
4. Why is economic growth not always beneficial?

Revision checklist

You should know:

- [ ] Economic growth is the main macroeconomic objective of most economies.
- [ ] A PPC can be used to show short and long run economic growth.
- [ ] The largest rates of economic growth tend to be recorded by emerging and other developing economies.
- [ ] Government policies have an important influence on whether an economy grows.

STRUCTURED SKILLS PRACTICE

1. In 2017, it was reported that the Brazilian economy had moved out of recession for the first time since 2013. Explain the evidence on which this claim is likely to be based.

> **TIP** Start your answer with a definition of recession. From this, you can establish what data you need to say whether Brazil has moved out of recession.

Exam-style multiple choice questions

1. An economy experiences an increase in its real GDP but real GDP per head falls. Why is this?

   A a large informal economy is not counted in GDP

   B the economy has a high rate of inflation

   C the population has increased at a faster rate than real GDP

   D the top rate of income tax has increased for high income earners

2. Which is the **least** likely explanation of why the economic growth rate of China has been consistently high?

   A chinese families save a high percentage of their income

   B china has managed to control population growth

   C the Chinese economy has opened up to foreign investments

   D young people in China are very keen to increase their educational qualifications

Employment and unemployment

Learning summary

By the end of this chapter, you should understand:

- what is meant by employment, unemployment and full employment
- the nature and causes of changes in the pattern and level of employment
- how unemployment is measured
- the causes and types of unemployment
- the consequences of unemployment
- policies to reduce unemployment.

30.1 Employment, unemployment and full employment

> **TERMS**
>
> **Employment:** being involved in a productive activity for which a payment is received.
>
> **Unemployment:** being without a job while willing and able to work.

>  **TIP**
>
> Full employment is difficult to define numerically and varies from one country to another.

30.2 Changes in the pattern and level of employment

The pattern of **employment** in an economy changes over time. It is also a function of the type of economy and whether the economy is developed or developing.

Figure 30.1 shows some of most important reasons for changes in the pattern of employment.

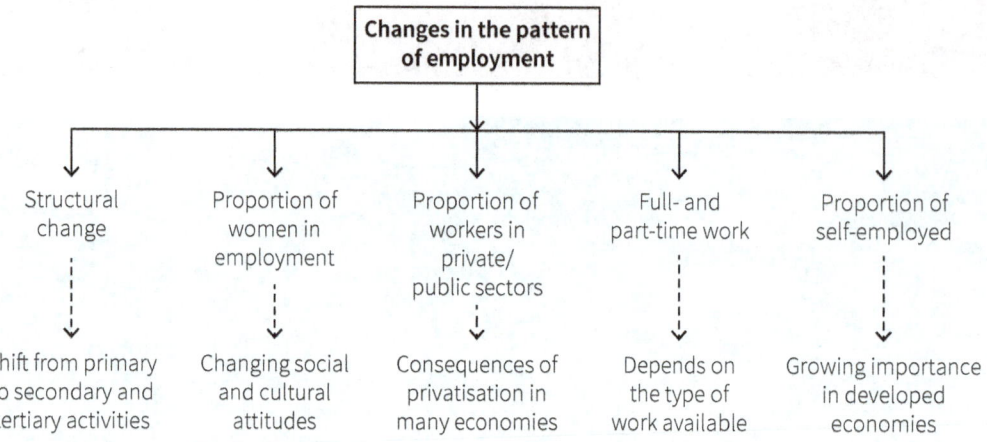

Figure 30.1 Reasons for changes in the pattern of employment

The level of employment refers to the total size of the labour force in an economy. This depends on:

- the size of the population and changes in its size
- the labour force participation rate, as measured by the proportion of the population of working age who are in the labour force.

The level of employment can also be affected by the flow of migrant workers in an economy. In economies such as Singapore, this figure is a significant proportion, although it is very dependent on the state of the economy.

30.3 How unemployment is measured

The **unemployment** rate is the proportion of unemployed people in the labour force.

$$\text{unemployment rate} = \frac{\text{unemployed population}}{\text{labour force}} \times 100\%$$

Unemployment is measured in two ways. These are:

- *Claimant count.* This is a tally of those unemployed in receipt of unemployment benefits.
- *Labour Force Survey Measure.* This counts people unemployed if they are without a job and have been actively looking for employment in the past month. This method is widely applied when making international comparisons.

There are practical problems in collecting the above information, particularly in many developing economies where there may be no formal benefits system or where people are not fully employed.

 **TIP** Underemployment is a particular issue in some economies – a worker may only work a few hours or work in a job involving low-level skills.

30.4 Causes and types of unemployment

Figure 30.2 shows the three main causes and types of unemployment.

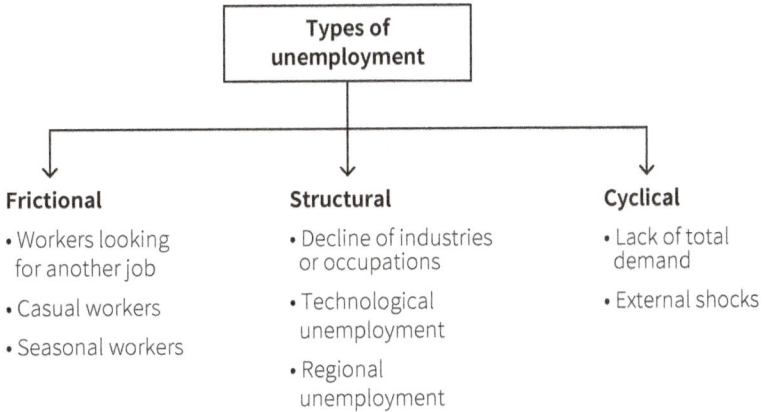

Figure 30.2 Types of unemployment

30.5 Consequences of unemployment

Unemployment means that potentially productive resources are not being utilised. Some short-term unemployment is inevitable in a market economy. It could also be the consequence of a macroeconomic policy to control inflation.

- For the individual, it usually means a loss of earnings. Psychological factors should also be considered.
- For firms, it could put downward pressure on wage rates and earnings – less total demand may reduce the demand for a firm's products.
- For the economy, there is an opportunity cost since not all resources are being used. It can mean lower tax revenue yet an increase in benefits paid to the unemployed.

30.6 Policies to reduce unemployment

Policies used to reduce unemployment are most likely to succeed if they are targeted at the cause of the unemployment, as shown in Table 30.1.

Table 30.1 Examples of unemployment reduction policies

Cause of unemployment	Policies to reduce unemployment
Frictional	• better information on job vacancies • reduction in unemployment benefits to encourage unemployed to rejoin the workforce • cut in income tax rate, or reduction in income tax threshold, both of which will increase the incentive to work
Structural	• supply-side policies to improve training • relocation allowances and grants • subsidies for firms willing to set up in areas of high unemployment
Cyclical	• expansionary fiscal policies • expansionary monetary policies

Sample questions

i   Analyse, using a production possibility curve diagram, how an economy moves from a position of unemployment to one of full employment.

ii In Country X, the unemployed have lost their jobs as a result of the closure of coal mines. Give examples of polices that might have been used to help them obtain new jobs.

Sample answer:

i   This PPC shows a move to full employment.

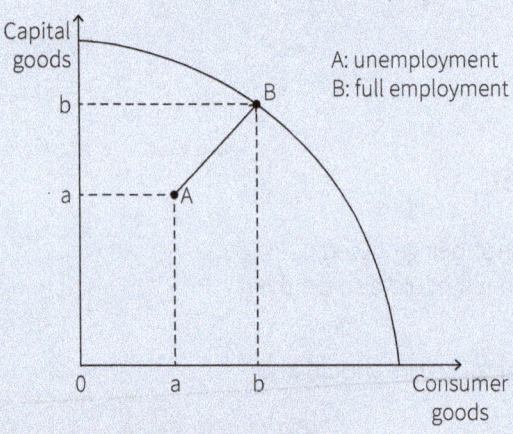

ii This is an example of structural unemployment. Supply-side policies are likely to be most effective and are likely to include government funding to re-train coal workers for the new jobs available, relocation incentives for unemployed workers to move to where new jobs are available and incentives for employers to take on unemployed coal miners.

SKILLS FOCUS

Fiscal and monetary policies lack the precision of most supply-side policies to deal with structural unemployment.

Progress check

Answer the following questions to check your understanding:

1 How is unemployment measured?
2 Give **two** reasons for recent changes in the pattern of unemployment in a country you have studied.
3 Give specific examples of frictional, structural and cyclical unemployment in a country you have studied.
4 Explain how supply-side policies can be used to reduce unemployment.

Revision checklist

You should know:

- [ ] Unemployment is a situation where someone who is able and willing to work does not have a job.
- [ ] Unemployment is usually measured by an unemployment rate.
- [ ] There are many reasons for the change in unemployment in an economy. These reasons tend to be a function of the type of economy and its stage of development.
- [ ] The causes of unemployment can be classified as frictional, structural or cyclical.
- [ ] Unemployment represents a serious waste of otherwise productive resources.
- [ ] Supply-side, fiscal and monetary policies can be used to reduce particular types of unemployment.

STRUCTURED SKILLS PRACTICE

1 Explain **two** policies that a government might use to reduce cyclical unemployment.

Be careful. Note that the question is about **one** of the types of unemployment. Think about which policies are most appropriate.

Exam-style multiple choice questions

1 The unemployment rate in an economy is 8%. There are 100 000 people in the labour force and 15 000 women who are seeking a return to work. What is the actual number of unemployed people?

   A 8 000
   B 23 000
   C 85 000
   D 100 000

2 A developing economy has seen many people leave farms in rural areas in search of work in cities. What type of unemployment is this?

   A frictional unemployment
   B structural unemployment
   C cyclical unemployment
   D a combination of frictional and cyclical unemployment

3 Supply-side policies can be used to reduce structural unemployment. Which supply-side policies is likely to be **least** effective in tackling structural unemployment?

   A an increase in the rate of income tax
   B a policy to re-train unemployed workers
   C a relocation allowance for workers to move to another job elsewhere
   D a subsidy for employers willing to employ someone who is unemployed

Chapter 31: Inflation and deflation

Learning summary

By the end of this chapter, you should understand:

- what is meant by inflation and deflation
- how to measure inflation and deflation
- the causes of inflation and deflation
- the consequences of inflation and deflation
- the policies available to control inflation and deflation and their effectiveness.

31.1 Meaning and measurement of inflation and deflation

> **TERMS**
>
> **Inflation:** a rise in the price level of goods and services over time.
>
> **Deflation:** a sustained fall in the prices of goods and services.

> **TIP**
>
> A fall in the inflation rate, say, from 6% to 4%, is known as disinflation. It is not **deflation**, as the general price level is still rising.

Inflation is usually measured by a consumer price index. This involves measuring the weighted average of a representative set (known as a 'basket') of goods and services. The index is constructed as follows:

- select a base year which is given an index of 100
- find out how households spend their money by allocating 'weights' to particular products
- find out price changes
- construct a weighted price index

Sample question

The data below shows the consumer price index for an economy over a five-year period. Explain what the data indicates.

	Year 1	Year 2	Year 3	Year 4	Year 5
Index	100	96	100	108	112

Sample answer:

The price level fell from Year 1 to Year 2 by 4%. This is consistent with deflation.

The price level increased from Year 2 to Year 3 by 4.2% returning to the same level as in Year 1. This is a period of inflation.

From Year 3 to Year 4, the price level rose by 8%. It rose again by 3.7% from Year 4 to Year 5 – the change from Year 4 to Year 5 is disinflation.

SKILLS FOCUS

Although the percentage increase in the price level has decreased from Year 4 to Year 5, average prices will have continued to increase. A common error is to say that prices have fallen.

31.2 The causes of inflation

Inflation is caused by **cost-push inflation** and **demand-pull inflation**.

TERMS

Cost-push inflation: rises in the price level caused by higher costs of production.

Demand-pull inflation: rises in the price level caused by excess demand.

Table 31.1 shows some of the main causes of each type of inflation.

Table 31.1 Causes of cost-push and demand-pull inflation

Cost-push inflation	Demand-pull inflation
• Increase in labour costs/wages.	• Increase in consumer spending.
• Increase in prices of raw materials.	• Increase in government spending.
• Increase in cost of imports.	• Increase in investment by firms.
• Increase in indirect taxes.	• Increase in demand for exports.

Each type of inflation can be represented by a demand and supply diagram, as shown in Figure 31.1.

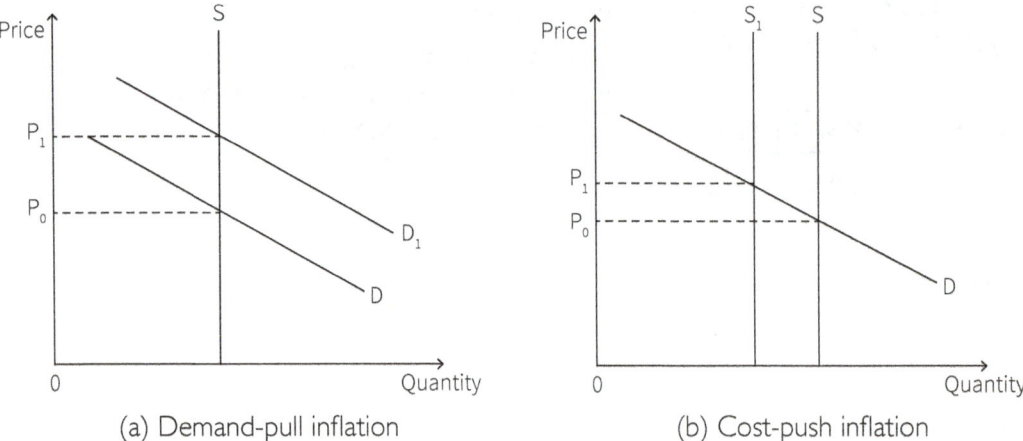

Figure 31.1 Demand-pull inflation and cost-push inflation

 A common error is to say that inflation is caused by rising prices. Rather, inflation is a rise in the price level and it occurs for many reasons.

31.3 The consequences of inflation

The consequences of inflation impact on consumers, workers, savers, lenders, firms and the economy as a whole. Some consequences are:

- Reduced purchasing power due to a fall in the value of money. As the price level rises, each dollar will buy fewer goods.
- Savers lose out relative to borrowers when the rate of interest is less than the inflation rate.
- Increased business costs. Firms have to change prices (menu costs) and, in some cases, seek out good financial returns as the money received loses value in the time period from billing to receipt (shoe leather costs).
- Depending on the level, inflation can create uncertain future economic prospects.
- There could be a negative effect on the balance of payments due to increasing export prices compared to trading competitors.
- The government may have to spend more on state benefits, pensions and wages.
- Mild inflation can make firms more competitive through the need to keep close control of costs.

31.4 Policies to control inflation

The most suitable policies to control inflation will depend on its cause, as shown in Table 31.2.

Table 31.2 Policies for controlling inflation

Cause of inflation	Policies to control inflation	Effectiveness of policies
Demand-pull	Contractionary fiscal policies: • reduce government spending • increase taxation Contractionary monetary policies: • increase rate of interest • reduce money supply	Could lead to: • increased unemployment • less economic growth
Cost-push	Supply-side policies: • improve education and training • privatise • deregulate • reform trade unions	Takes time to take effect Could increase costs in the short run

31.5 Deflation: causes, consequences and policies

The Japanese economy has suffered from deflation for the past 20 years or so. More recently, deflation has affected Greece, Portugal and Spain, albeit for much shorter periods.

Table 31.3 summarises the causes and consequences of deflation and what can be done to combat it.

Table 31.3 Deflation: causes, consequences and policies

Causes of deflation	Consequences of deflation	Policies to combat deflation
• Falling total demand.	• Unemployment increases.	• Low or negative interest rates.
• External shock.	• Weak business confidence.	• Increased government spending.
• Consumers postponing purchases.	• Firms may be reluctant to invest or increase investment.	• 'Helicopter money'.

> **TIP** Deflation occurs when the general price level is falling even though some prices might be increasing.

Progress check

Answer the following questions to check your understanding:

1. How is inflation measured?
2. What is the difference between cost-push inflation and demand-pull inflation?
3. Why do savers lose out relative to borrowers at a time of rapid inflation?
4. How might inflation affect the balance of payments of an economy?
5. Why are consumers reluctant to spend at a time of deflation?

Revision checklist

You should know:

- Inflation is when there is a rise in the general price level in an economy.
- Cost-push and demand-pull are two main causes of inflation.
- A period of rapid inflation affects various groups in the economy, some negatively, others positively.
- Fiscal, monetary and supply-side policies can all be used to reduce the rate of inflation.
- Deflation is when there is a fall in the general price level over two consecutive quarters.

STRUCTURED SKILLS PRACTICE

1. Discuss whether or not an increase in the rate of inflation might lead to conflict between workers and their employers.

   TIP
   When answering this question, it is a good idea to make an assumption about the rate of inflation. Is it 2%, 20% or 200%? The degree of conflict will depend on this.

Exam-style multiple choice questions

1. Which is a possible cause of cost-push inflation?

   A a fall in the rate of income tax

   B an increase in government spending

   C a reduction in spending by employees on new apprenticeships

   D a rise in wages not matched by a rise in productivity

2 Who, is **most** likely to lose out during a period of rapid inflation?

   A a firm with an extensive holding of stock

   B fixed income earners such as retired persons

   C property owners

   D those who borrow money from the bank

3 Which is a supply-side policy for reducing inflation?

   A an increase in the scope of regulations relating to a firm's production

   B a relaxation in the laws governing strikes

   C a subsidy for firms investing in new technology

   D a tax on labour training schemes

Exam-style structured questions for Section 4

Data response question

Read the source material carefully before answering the question.

Source material: Economic growth in Pakistan since 2012

Pakistan's economic growth since 2012 has been very encouraging. It has increased from 3.8% in 2012 to 4.7% in 2016 and is forecast to grow to over 5% in 2017 and 2018.

This change has been put down to economic reforms. These have involved cutting inefficient subsidies and privatising some loss-making state-owned companies. A recent International Monetary Fund (IMF) report has stressed that, in order to maintain its recent growth, there is an urgent need to strengthen Pakistan's manufacturing industries by making them more competitive. This will not be easy and the IMF failed to say how it should be done. Such a move should increase exports and cut down on goods which are currently imported but which could be produced in Pakistan. This has the added benefit of reducing a balance of trade deficit.

Much of Pakistan's growth since 2012 has been due to a deliberate policy of infrastructure improvement. This has included much needed investment in electricity supply and roads. There has also been a $57bn investment in projects connected to the Beijing-funded China–Pakistan–Economic Corridor. The consequences of change, which include falling unemployment, are now reaping rewards for Pakistan's economic prospects. Whether this will lead to improved living standards for all is by no means certain.

Source: Rewritten from an article in the Indian Express, 6 April 2017.

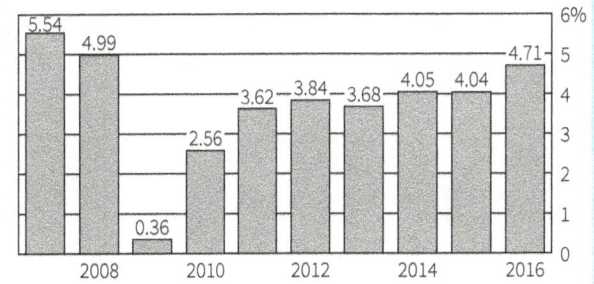

Figure S4.1 GDP growth rate, 2007–2016, Pakistan

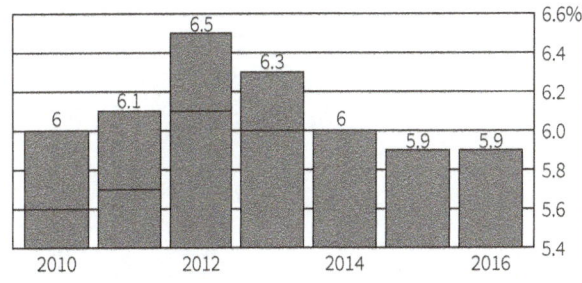

Figure S4.2 Unemployment rate, 2010–2016, Pakistan

Answer all parts of the question. Refer to the source material in your answers.

a. Define 'economic growth'. [1]
b. Describe how Pakistan's growth rate has changed from 2010 to 2016. [2]
c. Identify the relationship between the unemployment rate and economic growth in Pakistan from 2010 to 2016. [2]
d. Analyse, using a production possibility curve diagram, how Pakistan's economy is expected to grow from 2016 to 2019. [4]
e. Explain why a subsidy might be inefficient. [4]
f. Analyse how an improvement in the quantity and quality of resources has boosted economic growth in Pakistan. [5]
g. Discuss whether or not further supply-side policies might help Pakistan's manufacturing industries to become more competitive. [6]
h. Discuss whether or not the costs of increased economic growth might outweigh the benefits for the people of Pakistan. [6]

Four-part question

This question is introduced by stimulus material. In your answer, you may refer to this material and/or to other examples that you have studied.

In 2017, the average rate of unemployment in Malaysia was 3.5%. It was reported that industrial output was increasing but there had been a drop in palm oil production and some service sector activities such as tourism. An even bigger concern was the rate of graduate unemployment, estimated to be as high as 18% among young graduates.

a. Define 'unemployment rate'. [2]
b. Explain **two** types of unemployment in Malaysia. [4]
c. Analyse how fiscal policy might be used to reduce the unemployment rate in Malaysia. [6]
d. Discuss whether or not supply-side policies are the best way of reducing graduate unemployment in Malaysia. [8]

Section 5:
ECONOMIC DEVELOPMENT

Chapter 32: Living standards

Learning summary

By the end of this chapter you should understand:

- how living standards can be measured
- the advantages and disadvantages of real GDP per head and HDI as indicators of living standards
- how income and wealth inequality can be measured
- the reasons for differences in living standards and income distribution within and between countries.

32.1 Real GDP per head

Real GDP per head is the most widely used measure of living standards in an economy. (The 'real' bit is important since it is adjusted for inflation.)

An increase in real GDP per head is indicative of a rise in living standards. A word of caution, though ...

- Data only involves estimates and is subject to accuracy issues.
- The measure is an average and is not necessarily representative of the entire population, some of whom may have experienced a fall in living standards.
- An increase in production of some goods, for example armaments, will not improve living standards.
- Non-marketed output, for example subsistence farming, is not included in the data.
- The quality of life could fall even though GDP per head is increasing.

> **TIP**
> Purchasing power parity (PPP), which takes into account the buying power of a domestic currency, is an alternative measure to the use of a given currency, usually US dollars.

Sample question

The table opposite shows real GDP per head and GDP per head (PPP) for selected economies in 2017.

i Explain the difference between the two measures of GDP per head for New Zealand and Malaysia.

ii Explain why real GDP per head might be a poor measure of living standards for developing economies?

	Real GDP per head ($) (estimated)	GDP per head (PPP) ($) (estimated)
Australia	55215	50817
China	8481	16676
Indonesia	3895	12432
New Zealand	41100	38707
Pakistan	1468	5375
Malaysia	9623	28636

Source: Knoema.

152

Sample answers:

i In terms of real GDP per head, living standards in New Zealand are on average over four times greater than those in Malaysia. The difference is much closer when measured in PPP terms – this mainly reflects a much lower cost of living.

ii Real GDP per head may be a poor measure as income from the subsistence sector is not included. There will be a large informal economy that is not included in GDP. In addition, the distribution of income is not taken into account.

> **SKILLS FOCUS**
>
> It should be clear from the sample answer that you need to be aware of the weaknesses when using GDP per head data. It is best to see this data as a rough guide rather than precise economic data.

32.2 The Human Development Index (HDI)

Developed by the United Nations, this is a wider measure of living standards than GDP per head. It includes, as well as GDP per head, life expectancy at birth, and the mean and expected years of schooling to produce an index.

In 2016, Norway and Australia were the highest ranked at 0.95 and 0.94. The lowest ranked were countries in Africa – Central African Republic and Chad. Their indexes were typically 0.36 and indicative of 'low human development'.

The HDI can be criticised for not including other items and, in many poorer countries, there is a gender gap between men and women, and between rural and city dwellers.

32.3 Income distribution

The distribution of income is uneven in all economies. It is usually measured in terms of the percentage of the population relative to their share of income. For example, the poorest 10% of the population may earn 4% of income or the richest 10% of the population may earn 65% of income.

Differences in income are to be found within and between economies. In developing economies:

- employed city workers are likely to earn more than rural workers
- professional and skilled workers with more qualifications will earn more than unskilled workers
- male workers may earn more than female workers.

Progress check

Answer the following questions to check your understanding:

1. Why is real GDP per head widely used as a measure of living standards?
2. Country A has a GDP per head of $6 000 and Country B has a GDP per head of $12 000. Does this mean that the living standards in Country B are twice those in Country A?
3. What is meant by the distribution of income?

Revision checklist

You should know:

- GDP per head is a widely used measure of living standards.
- The HDI takes a wider perspective than just national output.
- Some households are rich because they earn high incomes. This can often lead to an unequal distribution of income.

STRUCTURED SKILLS PRACTICE

1. Discuss whether or not the distribution of income in a developing economy is likely to be more uneven than that in a developed economy.

TIP You could enhance your answer by referring to an economy or economies you have studied. With a question like this, there is no correct conclusion. Make this clear in your final sentences.

Exam-style multiple choice questions

1. What does real GDP per head measure?

    A average output per person

    B average output per person, taking account of inflation

    C the average earnings of each employed person

    D the total output of an economy

2. Which is **not** included in the Human Development Index (HDI)?

    A income per head

    B life expectancy at birth

    C mean years of schooling

    D number of doctors per 10 000 population

Poverty

Chapter 33

Learning summary

By the end of this chapter, you should understand:

- ☐ the difference between absolute poverty and relative poverty
- ☐ the causes of poverty
- ☐ the policies to alleviate poverty and redistribute income.

33.1 Absolute and relative poverty

TERMS

Absolute poverty: where people's income is too low to enable them to meet their basic needs.

Relative poverty: where people are poor in comparison to others in their country; their income is too low to enable them to enjoy the average standard of living in their country.

People who live in **absolute poverty** do not have enough income to pay for basic needs such as adequate food, clothing, housing, sanitation and healthcare.

By contrast, people who live in **relative poverty** are poor compared to the norm or average living standard in that country.

TIP An income level consistent with absolute poverty may be the same as one that represents relative poverty in a less developed economy.

33.2 The causes of poverty

There are various causes of poverty including:

- being in low-paid work – earnings are insufficient to meet basic needs
- being unemployed – any benefits are likely to be less than when in employment
- poor health
- growing old
- many dependants in the family
- poor education.

33.3 Policies to alleviate poverty and redistribute income

There are many policies a government may employ to reduce poverty. Some of these also have the effect of redistributing income.

Typical policies include:

- a progressive direct taxation system with a threshold that means low-income earners do not pay income tax
- a national minimum wage
- an equitable state benefits system that helps those not able to work or who are too old to work
- an education policy that enhances the earnings of the poorest groups
- an increase in the economic growth rate that leads to better distribution of improved living standards
- foreign aid from national governments and international organisations.

Sample question

The diagram shows how absolute poverty and relative poverty in the UK have changed over 20 years from 1995/96.

i   Describe how absolute poverty and relative poverty have changed over the period 1995/96 to 2015/16.

ii Explain **two** policies a government might use to reduce poverty and make the distribution of income more equal.

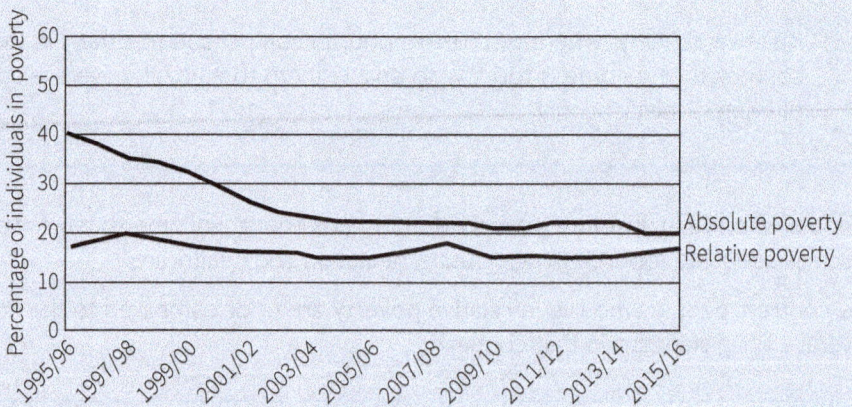

Poverty in the UK, 1995/96–2015/16

Source: Department for Work and Pensions, adapted from the original to show only 'after housing costs'.

Sample answer:

i   Absolute poverty has fallen over the period. There was some modest increase from 2010 to 2013 (presumably as a result of recession) but with a further decrease in 2015.

Relative poverty has hardly changed over the period.

ii A change to the progressive tax system is an obvious method to reduce poverty and improve the distribution of income. This approach is one that is widely used in economies where incomes are directly taxed.

A second method could be to introduce a minimum wage, which is designed to raise the standard of living of the lowest earners.

SKILLS FOCUS

Many governments have a policy of seeking to make the distribution of income more equal. See what examples you can find for a country you have studied.

Progress check

Answer the following questions to check your understanding:

1. What is the difference between absolute poverty and relative poverty?
2. Why might a poor education be a cause of poverty?
3. Why will imposing a new indirect tax be likely to increase poverty and make the distribution of income less equal?

Revision checklist

You should know:

- Poverty can be measured in two ways – absolute poverty and relative poverty.
- The causes of poverty are many and it happens for economic and non-economic reasons.
- Most governments seek to reduce poverty and make the distribution of income more equal.

STRUCTURED SKILLS PRACTICE

1. In 2012, in the USA, an income of around $11 000 was seen as necessary for a one-person household to just avoid absolute poverty. Explain why this level of income might not be entirely representative as applying to all one-person households.

    TIP Averages like this can be misleading. The wording of the question hints at this.

Exam-style multiple choice questions

1. Abdul has recently lost his job as an IT manager. Although his family can still afford to buy food and pay the bills, they cannot now match the lifestyle of others in the area where they live. What is this an example of?

   A absolute poverty

   B a family in need of state benefits

   C relative poverty

   D the opportunity cost of employment

2. Which government policy is **least** likely to improve the distribution of income?

   A a reduction in secondary school fees

   B an increase in the tax on cooking oil

   C an increase in the top rate of income tax

   D free healthcare for young children

Population

Learning summary

By the end of this chapter, you should understand:

- ■ the factors that affect population growth
- ■ the reasons for different rates of population growth in different countries
- ■ the effects of changes in the size and structure of population in different countries.

34.1 Factors that affect population growth

Birth rate and **death rate** affect population growth. So do **emigration** and **net migration** figures.

> **TERMS**
>
> **Birth rate:** the number of births in a year per 1000 population.
>
> **Death rate:** the number of deaths in a year per 1000 population.
>
> **Emigration:** the act of leaving a country to live in another country.
>
> **Net migration:** the difference between immigration and emigration.

Figure 34.1 shows some of the factors that affect population growth in a country.

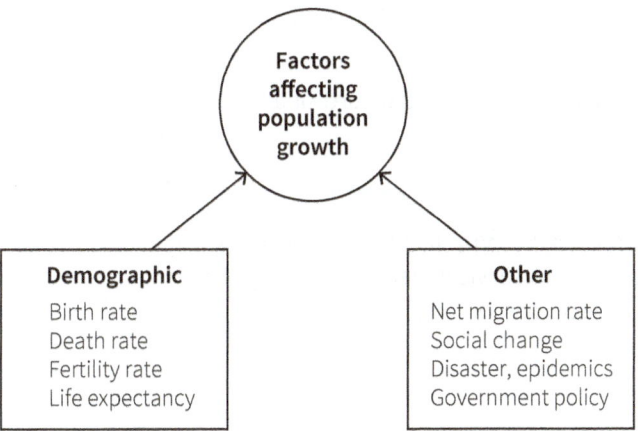

Figure 34.1 Factors affecting population growth

34.2 The reasons for different rates of population growth in different countries

This is a complex topic and the reasons differ from one country to another.

> **TIP**
>
> A good way to determine what is affecting the rates of population growth in a country is to consider how the factors given in Figure 34.1 can be applied.

Here are a few basic reasons:

- A population grows when its birth rate is greater than its death rate.
- Birth rates and death rates tend to be higher in developing economies compared with developed economies.
- Net migration is an important consideration in some Middle East countries, Germany and Singapore.
- Infant mortality rates are falling but remain high in some developing countries with poor healthcare facilities.
- In some developed economies, such as Italy and Russia, the population is falling due to social factors such as more women in work.

34.3 The effects of changes in the size and structure of populations

> **TERMS**
>
> Optimum population: the size of population which maximises the country's output per head.
>
> Population pyramid: a diagram showing the age and gender structure of a country's population.

The concept of an **optimum population** is shown in Figure 34.2. It is reached when, given all resources, there is the maximum output of goods and services per head of population. If there are more people, given the same level of resources, output per head will decline.

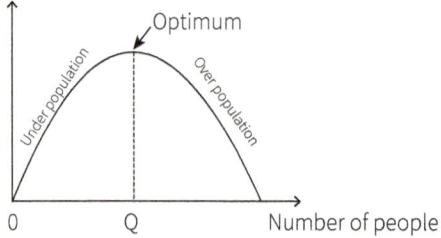

Figure 34.2 The concept of optimum population

Sample question

These diagrams show two **population pyramids**.

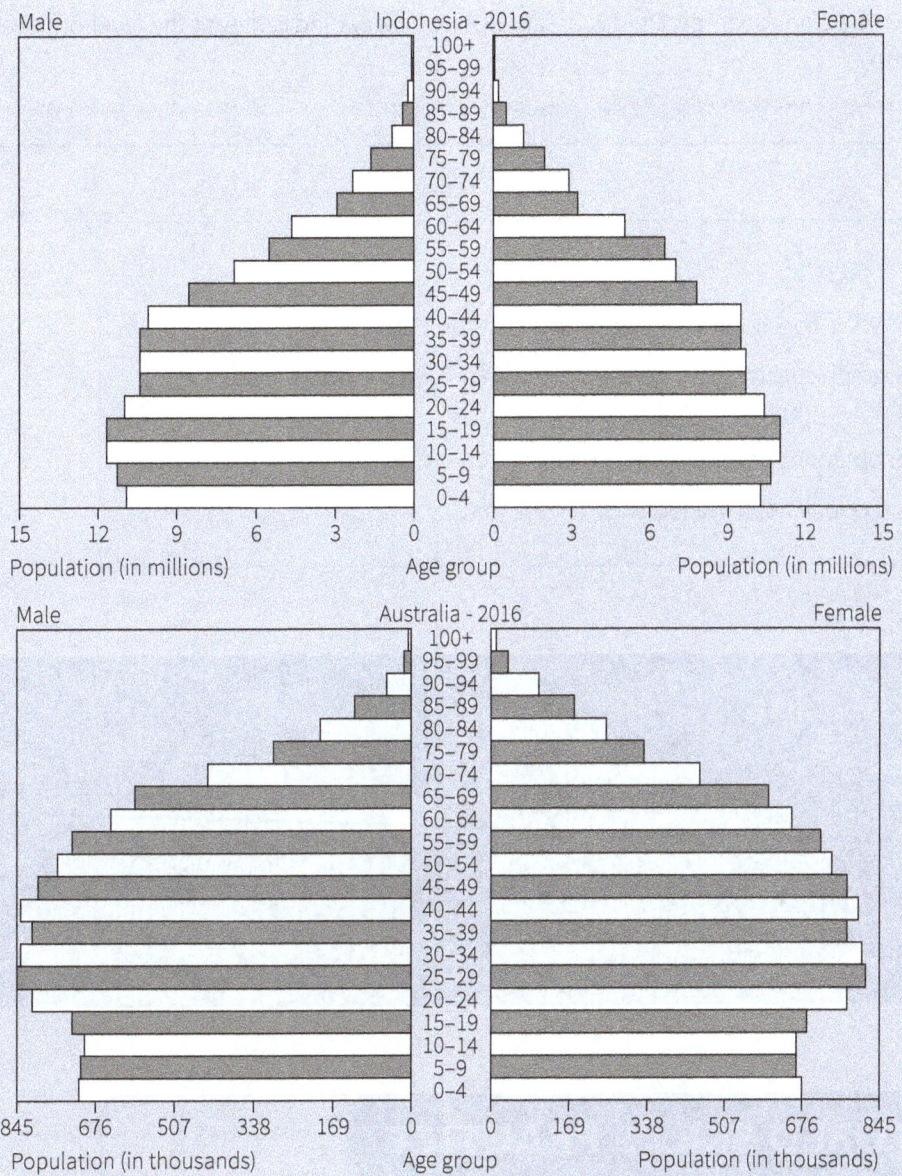

Population pyramids of Indonesia and Australia, 2016
Source: CIA World Factbook.

i Describe the age and gender structure of the populations of Indonesia and Australia in 2016.

ii Explain two differences between the population pyramids.

Sample answer:

i The population pyramid for Indonesia has a pyramid shape, whereas the one for Australia does not. Indonesia has a relatively fewer percentage of its population aged 70 and over compared to Australia. Indonesia has similar numbers of males and females, while Australia has more males.

ii Some of the differences can be explained by variations in birth rates and death rates. These are likely to be higher in Indonesia than in Australia. The relatively higher number of males compared to females in Australia is more difficult to explain – it could be accounted for by the large number of male migrant workers in Australia.

SKILLS FOCUS

The shape of a population pyramid is usually, but not always, indicative of the level of development of an economy.

Progress check

Answer the following questions to check your understanding:

1. What demographic factors can be used to explain how the population of a country grows?
2. What is the optimum population of a country?
3. What does a population pyramid show?

Revision checklist

You should know:

- ☐ Population growth in an economy is dependent upon demographic and other factors.
- ☐ An optimum population is achieved when output per head is maximised.
- ☐ A population pyramid is a useful way of representing the age and sex structure of a country's population.

STRUCTURED SKILLS PRACTICE

1. The population of Italy continues to fall. Explain **two** demographic reasons for this.

    TIP The obvious ones are birth rate and death rate. Make sure you use them in your answer to explain a falling and not a rising population.

Exam-style multiple choice questions

1. The table below shows some population statistics for a country in 2016.

Population	1.5 million
Residents moving to live elsewhere	100 000
New migrant workers	30 000
Migrant workers returning home	10 000

   Calculate the total population at the end of 2016.

   A 1 370 000

   B 1 380 000

   C 1 420 000

   D 1 640 000

2. Which is a consequence of over-population?

   A output per head is constant

   B output per head is declining

   C output per head is fluctuating

   D output per head is increasing

3. A country has a large proportion of young people. What would be the shape of its population pyramid?

   A relatively narrower at its base

   B relatively narrow at its top

   C relatively wider at its base

   D relatively wide at its top

Chapter 35: Differences in economic development between countries

Learning summary

By the end of this chapter you should understand:

- the nature of economic development
- the causes of differences in economic development between countries
- the impacts of differences in economic development between countries.

35.1 Economic development

> **TERM**
>
> Economic development: an improvement in economic welfare.

Economic development, like economic growth, is seen in improved living standards for a country's population. It also involves reducing poverty, expanding choices of employment and social change, coupled with increasing freedom and self-esteem. As an economy develops, the economic welfare of its people increases.

> Economic development is much wider than economic growth.

35.2 Causes of differences in economic development between countries

The main reasons why countries have different levels of economic development are shown in Figure 35.1.

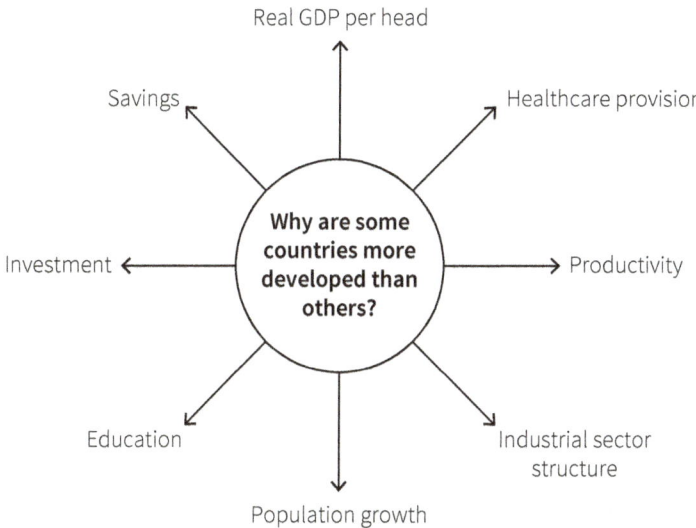

Figure 35.1 Reasons for differences in economic development between countries

Sample question

The table shows some data for Tanzania and Zambia in 2016.

	Real GDP per head ($)	Life expectancy (years)	Percentage of workforce in agriculture	Mobile phones per 1000 population
Tanzania	880	65.5	32.0	750
Zambia	1299	53.6	9.2	740

i Identify the evidence that you would use to conclude that 'Zambia is more developed than Tanzania'?

ii State what additional information you might use to confirm this assertion.

Sample answer:

i In terms of living standards and employment structure, it appears that Zambia is more developed than Tanzania. There is, however, a significant difference in life expectancy, implying that living conditions in Tanzania may be better than in Zambia.

ii Data on education and health would be particularly useful in providing a more complete snapshot.

SKILLS FOCUS

When looking at differences in levels of economic development, real GDP per head is very important but does not necessarily give a full picture.

35.3 Impacts of differences in economic development between countries

For economic development to occur there needs to be an improvement in the quantity and quality of resources. More investment, better education, training and healthcare are required so as to increase real GDP and the quality of people's lives.

The development process can be held back for many reasons, as shown in Table 35.1. Differences in any, or all, of the factors can result in varying levels of economic development among countries.

Table 35.1 Factors affecting economic development

Factors affecting the development process	Impact
High rate of population growth	Uses up resources that could otherwise increase productive potential
High level of international debt	Repayments can severely affect government spending.
Heavy reliance on primary exports	Many primary products have experienced a fall in real prices, meaning more have to be exported for the same revenue
Lack of investment	Holds back increases in productivity and improvements in social capital

Progress check

Answer the following questions to check your understanding:

1. How does economic development differ from economic growth?
2. Two countries have the same real GDP per head. Give **two** reasons why their economic development may be different.
3. Explain **two** reasons why a developing economy may not experience an improvement in its level of economic development.

Revision checklist

You should know:

- ■ Economic development is concerned with improvements in economic welfare.
- ■ Economic development can be measured in terms of higher real GDP per head and other economic and social indicators.
- ■ Countries with low economic development face various internal and external pressures.

STRUCTURED SKILLS PRACTICE

1 Analyse **two** ways in which the government of a country can improve its economic development.

TIP: Think about the quality and quantity of resources. Supply-side policies involving labour and capital are the obvious ones. The 'analysis' command word should indicate that you need to focus your answer in terms of the relationship between labour and capital and economic development.

Exam-style multiple choice questions

1 Which is **not** a measure of a country that is experiencing an improvement in its economic development?

A a decline in productivity

B an increase in savings rates

C a rise in GDP per head

D more spending on state education

2 A country is experiencing deterioration in its level of economic development. What might be the reason for this?

A a fall in the birth rate

B a reduction in foreign direct investment

C a rise in life expectancy

D less employment in agriculture, more in vehicle assembly

Exam-style structured questions for Section 5

Data response question

Read the source material carefully before answering the question.

Source material: Differences in the economic development of China and India in 2016

In 2016, in terms of economic development, China and India appeared to be worlds apart. This can be seen from the indicators of living standards shown in the table. But what about the future? Much has been made of how, in 2016, India's growth rate exceeded that of China, making India the fastest growing major economy in the world. Moreover, this trend is expected to persist, with India quietly closing the gap in its living standards compared to China.

Table S5.1 Selected indicators of economic development in China and India

	China	India
GDP per head ($)/Purchasing Power Parity (PPP)	15 400	6 600
Growth rate (% real GDP)	6.7	7.1
Birth rate (per 1000 population)	12.3	19.0
Life expectancy (years)	75.5	68.5
	China	India
Adult literacy rate	96.4	71.2
Health expenditure (% GDP)	5.5	4.7
Population below poverty line (%)	3.3	21.9
Savings ratio (% GDP)	45.8	30.5
% employment in agriculture	28.3	47.0

Source: CIA Word Factbook.

China has one potentially crucial weakness – its ageing population. In October 2015, the Chinese government announced that it would change its one-child policy to allow all couples to have two children in order to address its rapidly ageing population. Although China has managed to curb population growth, it has meant that the birth rate has remained below that required to replace the population. In contrast, India's population is growing at a rate of around two children per female. Figure S5.1 shows the population pyramids for China and India.

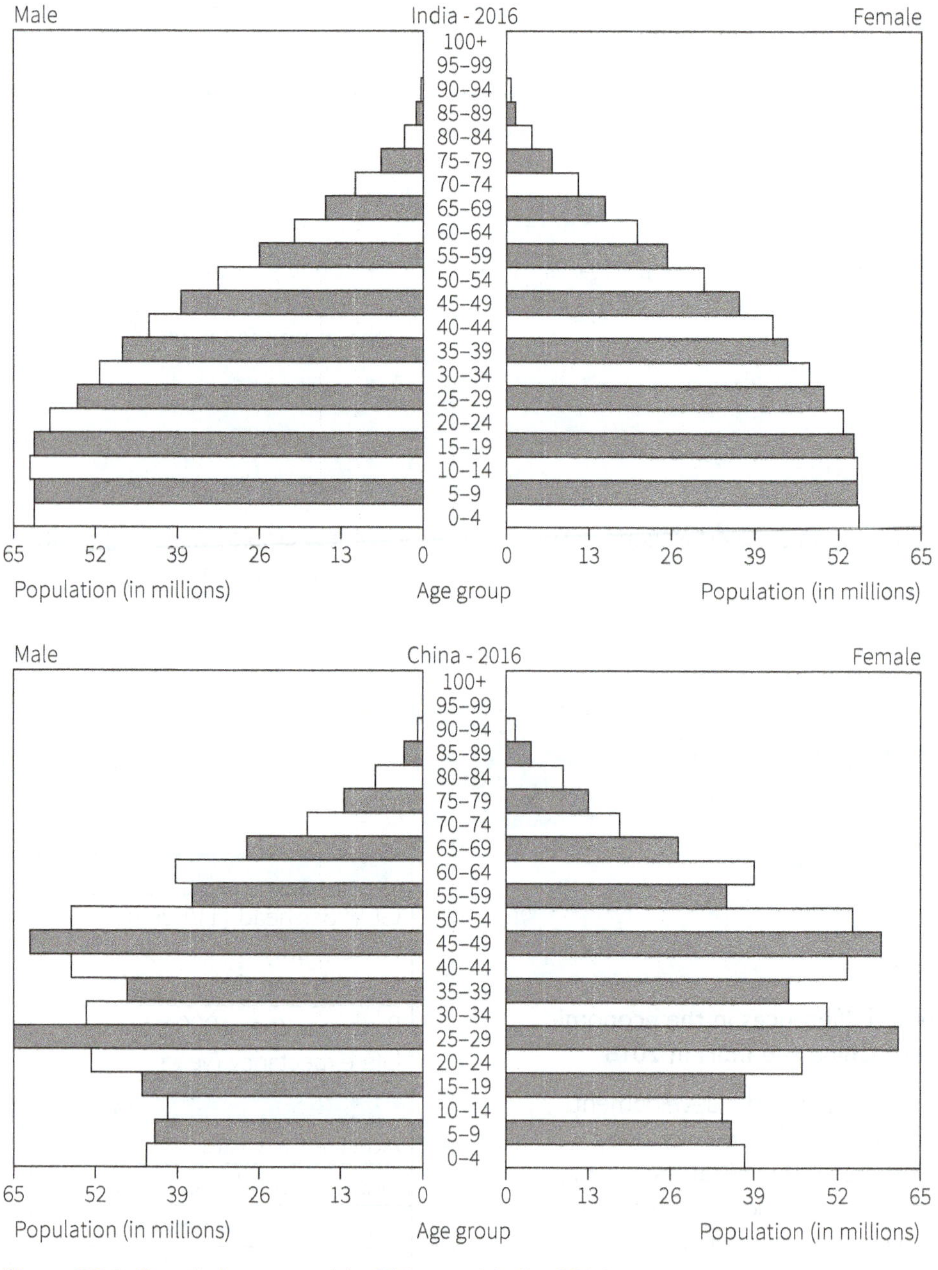

Figure S5.1 Population pyramids, China and India, 2016

Source: CIA World Factbook.

The economic implications of an ageing population for China are clear – rising pension and healthcare costs, a declining workforce and lower tax receipts. In contrast, in India, more young people will be joining the workforce, providing hope of an expanding production base. The challenge for India will be to generate economic opportunities on a sustained basis through an improvement in the quantity and quality of resources for its economic development.

Answer all parts of the question. Refer to the source material in your answers.

a Define 'purchasing power parity'. [1]

b State what is meant by 'population below poverty line'. [2]

c Identify **two** possible reasons for the higher life expectancy in China. [2]

d Explain **two** indicators that will have to be improved if India is to increase its economic development. [4]

e Analyse the population pyramids for China and India. [5]

f Explain whether evidence from the population pyramid supports the forecast that the population of China will fall after 2025. [4]

g Discuss whether or not China's ageing population is likely to have an adverse effect on its future economic development. [6]

h Discuss whether or not there is one particular policy that the Indian government could use to close the gap in its economic development compared to China. [6]

Four-part question

This question is introduced by stimulus material. In your answer, you may refer to this material and/or to other examples that you have studied.

Tanzania is one of the poorest countries in the world. Despite being rich in natural resources, as many as 80% of the population in rural areas experience absolute poverty. Most depend on livestock and subsistence agriculture for their livelihoods. In recent years, the government has provided small cash transfers for the poorest families in an attempt to release them from the underlying problems of subsistence farming.

a Define 'absolute poverty'. [2]

b Explain **two** possible causes of absolute poverty. [4]

c Analyse possible policies that could be used by the Tanzanian government to reduce poverty. [6]

d Discuss whether or not policies to alleviate poverty can lead to a redistribution of income. [8]

Section 6:
INTERNATIONAL TRADE AND GLOBALISATION

Chapter 36: International specialisation

> **Learning summary**
>
> By the end of this chapter, you should understand:
> - what is meant by specialisation at a national level
> - the advantages and disadvantages of specialisation at a national level.

36.1 Specialisation at a national level

Specialisation at a national level depends on the quantity and quality of resources that are available in an economy. In broad terms, this explains why some countries produce agricultural products, others manufactured goods and, in some cases, a range of services.

> **TIP**
> Think about a country you have studied. What is it good at producing and why is this so?

In the global economy, trade takes place as a result of specialisation. Countries specialise in those goods and services where they have a relative cost advantage over another country.

36.2 Advantages and disadvantages of specialisation at a national level

Countries usually concentrate on producing what they are best at making, taking into account global demand for the products and the resources they have most abundantly available. But there are benefits and challenges associated with trading with other countries, as shown in Table 36.1.

Table 36.1 Advantages and disadvantages of specialisation at a national level

For whom	Advantages	Disadvantages
Consumers	• More and wider range of goods and services. • Higher living standards. • Lower prices. • Better quality. • Develop particular skills.	• Over-dependency on a narrow range of goods and services. • Disruption to supplies.

For whom	Advantages	Disadvantages
Firms	• Lower average costs due to benefits from economies of scale. • New ideas and technology.	• Dependent on supplies from elsewhere. • Vulnerable to changes in demand.
Economy	• Increased efficiency and welfare. • Improved living standards. • Economic growth generated.	• Over-reliance on some goods and services.

Sample question

Explain why a country such as the UK manufactures cotton shirts but also imports these products from other countries such as China and Bangladesh.

Sample answer:

The basis of these specialisms is the quality and quantity of resources. The UK has a long history of manufacturing cotton shirts – there is a skilled workforce producing a high-quality but relatively expensive products. China and Bangladesh also have skilled workforces but the emphasis is on large-scale production, leading to cost advantages per shirt. They also grow and produce cotton which can be made into material for the manufacture of shirts.

SKILLS FOCUS

This answer focuses on the resources available in the three countries. The reality is much more complex. For example, some consumers may prefer to buy locally produced shirts. Another reason is that shirts produced in China and Bangladesh will have a lower price in the UK market.

Progress check

Answer the following questions to check your understanding:

1. What is meant by 'specialisation at a national level'?
2. Why does it occur?
3. Explain **one** advantage and **one** disadvantage for the economy of specialisation at a national level.

Revision checklist

You should know:

- ■ Specialisation for a country can increase output, reduce costs and spread new ideas and technology.
- ■ There are risks of specialisation and these can impact on consumers, firms and the economy.

STRUCTURED SKILLS PRACTICE

1 Apple iPhones are designed in the USA and manufactured in various different countries. Explain **two** reasons for this specialisation.

TIP: This question is all about specialisation. Think about factors of production and why Apple would want to manufacture its iPhones in other countries, yet retain their design in the USA. Make sure your answer covers both.

Exam-style multiple choice questions

1 A country chooses to specialise in producing coffee. What is the **most** likely reason for this?

   A its climate is suitable for coffee production

   B it is expensive to export coffee beans

   C other countries produce coffee beans

   D the global demand for tea is increasing

2 A manufacturer of trainers in a developed economy decides to close its production plant, opting to source its market from a lower-cost country such as the Philippines. Which is **not** likely to be a disadvantage?

   A imported trainers will be 20% cheaper in retail shops

   B imported trainers will be subject to an annual quota

   C it will have no control over changes in demand

   D supplies could be disrupted

Free trade and protection

Chapter 37

Learning summary

By the end of this chapter, you should understand:

- what is meant by globalisation
- the role of multinational companies
- the benefits of free trade
- the methods of protection
- the reasons for and consequences of protection.

37.1 Globalisation

> **TERM**
>
> Globalisation: the process by which the world is becoming increasingly interconnected through trade and other links.

Markets across the world have become more integrated through developments in transport, communications and trade. As well as through trade, **globalisation** can be evidenced through global brands (such as Microsoft, Toyota, Nestlé, Coca-Cola) and, increasingly, through the global sourcing of products in international trade.

37.2 Role of multinational companies

A multinational company (MNC) is one that has business interests in more than one country. There are many examples, particularly in food and drink provision, vehicle manufacturing and financial services.

> Think what MNCs there are in a country you have studied and where their host countries are.

The role of MNCs, especially in developing economies, is a controversial one. Table 37.1 summarises some of the benefits and costs.

Table 37.1 Benefits and costs of MNCs

	Benefits	Costs
Host country	• Creates employment • Adds to GDP • Transfer of knowledge and technology • Reduced import bill • Taxes paid	• MNC not always well liked • Can displace local firms in the market • Can pull out of the host country quickly • Profits are repatriated to the home country
Home country	• Cheaper products • Profits are returned to the home country • Growth of business	• Less employment • Fewer exports

37.3 The benefits of free trade

Free trade occurs when there are no restrictions on trade between two or more countries. This produces various benefits including:

- a more efficient allocation of scarce resources – countries can specialise in those products which they can produce more cheaply than their competitors and import products which they are not able to produce efficiently
- world output, employment and living standards are higher than if there are trade restrictions
- consumers have a wider variety of goods at lower prices.

37.4 Methods of protection

The benefits of free trade are extensively promoted by the World Trade Organization – and restrictions on free trade have been gradually reduced. More recently, though, protection has increased, particularly from developed countries. There are various forms of restrictions applied by developing, as well as developed, economies. The methods of protection are shown in Figure 37.1.

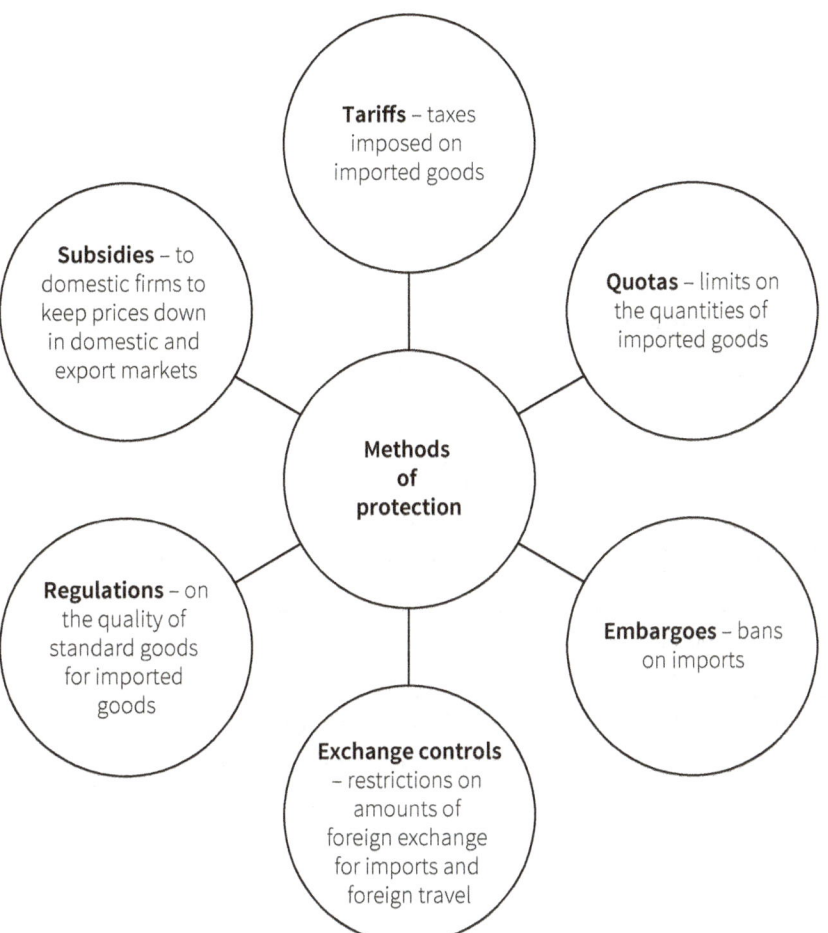

Figure 37.1 Methods of protection

Sample question

Analyse why the USA, the world's richest country, wishes to increase the tariff on imported tyres from China.

Sample answer:

The purpose of the tariff is to increase the price at which Chinese tyres are sold in the US market. This is to protect US producers as they are not able to compete with such imports in terms of price. There is also a need to protect employment, particularly in states where manufacturing employment has been falling. There are also balance of payments benefits if the value of imports is reduced.

The increased tariff discriminates against Chinese producers compared, for example, to tyre manufacturers elsewhere in Asia who supply the US market. It can be argued that US consumers are not benefiting from lower prices and that the tariff could actually encourage Chinese manufacturers to set up manufacturing capacity in the US.

SKILLS FOCUS

The answer considers both sides of a controversial topic. Although concerned with tyres, some of the arguments can be more widely applied.

37.5 Reasons for and consequences of protection

This is a controversial issue, with arguments being made for and against protection by developed and developing economies.

Table 37.2 summarises these arguments.

Table 37.2 Reasons for and consequences of protection

Method of protection	Why protect?	Consequences
Protect infant (sunrise) industries	Allows them to grow and benefit from economies of scale	Can become too dependent on protection
Protect declining (sunset) industries	Retains employment	Not easy to remove protection
Protect strategic industries	Is essential for development and security of supply	Less dependent on imports
Protect from dumping	Could drive domestic firms out of production as price is less than cost	Safeguards production and employment
Protect from unfair subsidies	Could drive domestic firms out of production as price is less than cost	Safeguards production and employment

Progress check

Answer the following questions to check your understanding:

1. Define globalisation.
2. Explain the benefits for a developing economy when a German motor manufacturer sets up a new vehicle assembly plant in the country.
3. What is the difference between a tariff and a quota?
4. Why are some forms of protection desirable for a developing economy?

Revision checklist

You should know:

- Globalisation can be seen through the increasing trade flows between countries.
- Reduced transport costs and developments in IT and communications have helped to promote the global economy.
- Multinational companies generate benefits and costs to the host country where they are located and also to their home country.
- Free trade in the global economy leads to the best allocation of resources.
- Developed, and developing, economies find it necessary to use methods of protection, for various reasons and with various consequences.

STRUCTURED SKILLS PRACTICE

1 Discuss whether or not the European Union (EU) is justified in subsidising food production, as well as imposing tariffs on the same types of food from the rest of the world.

TIP

The key point here is to answer in terms of the 'same types of food'. You need to look at the case for subsidy, the case for a tariff and then say which is in the best interests of the EU. Include consumers, as well as producers, in your answer.

Exam-style multiple choice questions

1 Which is a feature promoting globalisation?

A higher shipping costs from Asia to Europe

B increased use of the internet for international transactions

C more protective measures being imposed by the USA

D restrictions on the movement of business capital

2 Which is a reason why a multinational company may not always be welcomed in a developing economy?

A the company provides jobs for local people

B the company's products widen consumer choice

C the company sends its profits back home to its shareholders

D there is less of a deficit on the balance of payments

3 The European Union (EU) imposes a 10% tariff on vehicles imported from non-EU countries. What is the **most** likely reason for this?

A EU producers are not as efficient in producing vehicles

B it is a way of protecting employment

C there is less of a deficit on the balance of payments

D vehicle production in some Asian countries is subsidised

Chapter 38

Foreign exchange rates

Learning summary

By the end of this chapter, you should understand:

- what a foreign exchange rate is
- the nature of floating and fixed exchange rate systems
- how foreign exchange rates are determined
- the causes of foreign exchange rate fluctuations
- the consequences of foreign exchange rate fluctuations
- the advantages and disadvantages of floating, and fixed, foreign exchange rates.

38.1 Floating and fixed foreign exchange rate systems

TERMS

Foreign exchange rate: the price of one currency in terms of another currency or currencies.

Floating exchange rate: an exchange rate which can change frequently as it is determined by market forces.

Depreciation: a fall in the value of a floating exchange rate.

Appreciation: a rise in the value of a floating exchange rate.

TIP

A **foreign exchange rate** is a price and is determined by demand and supply in the foreign exchange market. Most foreign exchange rates compare a local currency with the US dollar.

A **floating exchange** rate is determined by market forces.

- A fall in demand, or a rise in supply, for a currency causes the price to fall. This is called a **depreciation**.
- A rise in demand, or a decrease in supply, for a currency will lead to a rise in the price of a currency. This is known as an **appreciation**.

Figure 38.1 shows a depreciation and an appreciation of the Malaysian ringgit against the US$.

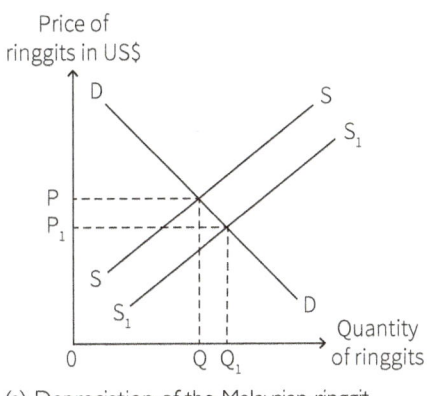
(a) Depreciation of the Malaysian ringgit

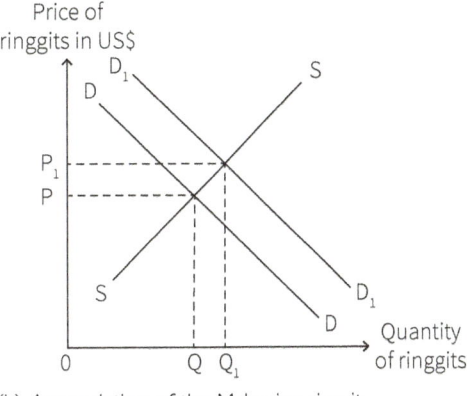
(b) Appreciation of the Malaysian ringgit

Figure 38.1 Depreciation and appreciation of the Malaysian Ringgit

> **TIP**
> When drawing diagrams, remember that the vertical axis should always be labelled 'Price of a currency in terms of another, normally US dollars ($)'.

A **fixed exchange rate** is different as it is set at a particular value in terms of another currency, usually the US$. This value is maintained by the government through the buying and selling of the currency.

- If the value of the currency is falling, the central bank will buy more of its currency to increase the exchange rate back to its agreed level. The currency has been **devalued**.
- If the value of the currency is rising, the central bank will sell some of its currency to reduce the exchange rate to its agreed level. The currency has been **revalued**.

> **TERMS**
>
> Fixed exchange rate: an exchange rate whose value is set at a particular level in terms of another currency or currencies.
>
> Devaluation: a fall in the value of a fixed exchange rate.
>
> Revaluation: a rise in the value of a fixed exchange rate.

> **TIP**
> When using the terms **depreciation**, **appreciation**, **devaluation** or **revaluation**, be clear whether you are referring to a floating or fixed exchange rate system.

38.2 Determination of foreign exchange rates and causes of fluctuations in the foreign exchange rate market

Like any price, a foreign exchange rate is determined by market forces, namely the demand and supply of a particular currency.

Table 38.1 shows some of the factors affecting the demand and supply of a foreign currency (e.g. the Malaysian ringgit).

Table 38.1 Factors affecting demand and supply of a foreign currency

Demand for a currency	Supply of a currency
• Demand for exports – those wishing to buy goods from Malaysia must pay in ringgits.	• Demand for imports – importers have to pay in foreign currency, bought with ringgits.
• Foreign direct investment (FDI) – a foreign firm setting up business in Malaysia will have to pay in ringgits for locally produced goods.	• FDI – Malaysian firms investing abroad require a supply of ringgits to buy foreign exchange.
• Interest rates – higher interest rates attract more money to Malaysia, hence more demand for ringgits.	• If interest rates away from Malaysia are higher, savers will need to buy foreign currency with ringgits.
• Speculation – demand for ringgits will increase if speculators see a good return.	• Speculation – supply of ringgits will increase if speculators decide to sell.

> **TIP** It is easy to confuse the demand and supply sides of the foreign exchange market. Firms buying a country's exports pay in that country's currency, increasing its demand. Firms importing goods into a country require foreign currency, increasing its supply.

38.3 Consequences of a change in the exchange rate

There are two main consequences of a change in the exchange rate. These are:

- *Export and import prices.* A depreciation of a foreign exchange rate will make exports relatively less expensive and imports relatively more expensive. The final effect on export and import revenue will depend on the price elasticity of demand. If import demand is inelastic, then the total value of imports will increase. An elastic demand for exports will increase export revenue.

- *Macroeconomic considerations.* A fall in the exchange rate which leads to increasing import prices could generate cost-push inflation. An increase in exports due to lower prices could increase output and employment if the economy has spare capacity. If not, it could lead to demand-pull inflation.

Sample question

The diagram shows how the foreign exchange rate of the Malaysian ringgit changed against the US$ between July 2014 and October 2017.

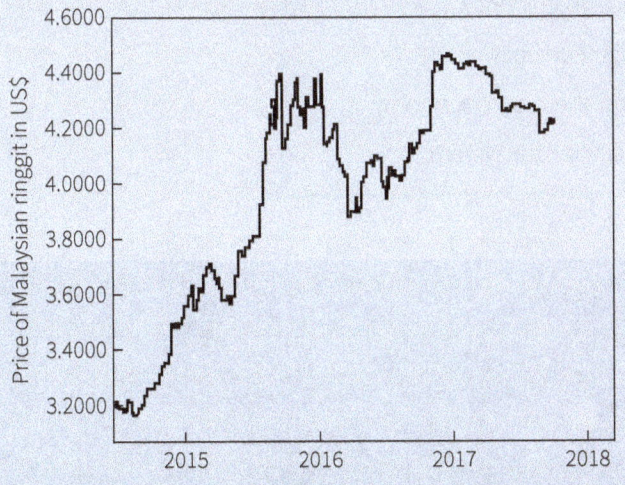

US dollar–Malaysian ringgit foreign exchange rate

Source: TradingView.

i   Describe the changes shown in the diagram.

ii Analyse the likely consequences of the changes for trade between Malaysia and the USA.

Sample answers:

i   The ringgit appreciated against the US$ from the middle of 2014 until the start of 2016. It then experienced a depreciation of around 10%. For the rest of 2016, it appreciated back to its peak at the end of 2016. A slight depreciation has occurred up to October 2017.

ii The appreciation of the ringgit US$ exchange rate means that Malaysian exports to the US will become more expensive, yet imports from the US will be relatively cheaper. The opposite applies when it comes to the periods of depreciation.

The scale of the appreciation from mid 2014 to the beginning of 2016 is significant and will have had a disturbing impact on trade due to the uncertainty of exchange rates facing exporters and importers.

SKILLS FOCUS

The first part of the answer consists of basic principles, while the second part looks at these and makes a relevant point for discussion.

38.4 Advantages and disadvantages of floating and fixed foreign exchange rates

Table 38.2 summarises some of the main points about these exchange rate systems.

Table 38.2 Floating and fixed exchange rate systems: advantages and disadvantages

Exchange rate system	Advantages	Disadvantages
Floating	• Automatic correction of balance of payments deficit or surplus. • Less chance of a financial crisis. • Protects from inflationary pressures elsewhere. • Fewer foreign exchange reserves required.	• Uncertainty for day-to-day trade. • May discourage foreign direct investment. • Hot money flows.
Fixed	• Creates certainty for business. • Inflation can be better managed.	• Reducing a balance of payments deficit is deflationary. • A crisis or external shock can lead to a devaluation. • More foreign exchange reserves needed.

Progress check

Answer the following questions to check your understanding:

1. What is the difference between a floating and a fixed exchange rate system?
2. Give **two** reasons for an increase in demand for a foreign currency.
3. Give **two** reasons for a reduction in supply of a foreign currency.
4. Explain how a currency depreciation affects prices and the macroeconomy.
5. Discuss the advantages of a floating and a fixed exchange rate system.

Revision checklist

You should know:

- An exchange rate is the price of a currency in terms of another currency, usually US dollars ($).
- There are many reasons for the demand and supply of a currency – payment for exports and imports is particularly important.
- A fall in the exchange rate is likely to increase export revenue and reduce import expenditure, depending on the price elasticities of demand.
- A deficit in the balance of payments can be automatically adjusted in a floating exchange rate system. In a fixed exchange rate system, a transfer of currency reserves is required.

STRUCTURED SKILLS PRACTICE

1. For some time, the US government has believed that the Chinese renminbi is over-valued relative to its dollar. Analyse what this means for the US economy and for the Chinese economy.

   TIP Make sure your answer is a balanced analysis of the effects on each country of an over-valued renminbi. Be careful not to write about a depreciated renminbi.

Exam-style multiple choice questions

1. What is meant by a depreciation of a currency?

   A a fall in value caused by market forces

   B a fall in value due to government intervention

   C a rise in value caused by market forces

   D a rise in value due to government intervention

2. How would Indonesia's currency be affected if there was a big increase in foreign direct investment (FDI) in the country?

   A there would be a decrease in demand for Indonesian bahts

   B there would be a decrease in supply for Indonesian bahts

   C there would be an increase in demand for Indonesian bahts

   D there would be an increase in supply for Indonesian bahts

3. What would happen as a result of the Indian rupee falling in value against the US dollar?

   A it would be cheaper for Indian tourists to visit the USA

   B the price of India's exports to the USA would fall

   C the price of India's imports from the USA would fall

   D there would be an increase in the number of US tourists visiting India

Chapter 39: Current account of balance of payments

Learning summary

By the end of this chapter, you should understand:

- the structure of the current account of the balance of payments
- the causes of a current account deficit and surplus
- the consequences of a current account deficit and surplus
- the policies to achieve balance of payments stability.

39.1 Structure of the current account

Remember that the balance of payments is a record of international business transactions between residents of one country and the rest of the world, usually over a year.

The current account of the balance of payments shows the value of all exports and imports. These consist of primary income, that is, trade in goods and services, investment income and current transfers.

Investment income and current transfers are now referred to as primary income and secondary income. The terminology can be confusing.

The current account consists of:

- *Trade in goods.* Often called visible exports and imports, and includes food, vehicles, machinery and so on.
- *Trade in services.* Often called invisible exports and imports, and includes travel, financial services and tourism.

Together, these give a balance of trade in goods and services.

Two further parts are:

- *Primary income.* This includes earnings by employees working abroad, profits from multinational companies and investment income generated from assets held abroad.
- *Secondary income.* This covers transfers of money by migrant workers and aid that is paid to governments.

> **TERM**
>
> Current account balance: a record of the income received and expenditure made by a country in its dealings with other countries.

Sample question

The table below shows the balance of payments for Mauritius in the first quarter of 2017.

	Rupees (millions)
Exports of goods	19 687
Imports of goods	39 188
Exports of services	26 233
Imports of services	19 001
Primary income (net)	8 869
Secondary income	−1 584

i   Calculate the balance of trade in goods and services.

ii Calculate the current account balance.

Sample answer:

i   Balance of trade in goods = 19 687 − 39 188
$$= -19\,501$$
Balance of trade in services = 26 233 − 19 001
$$= 7232$$
Therefore, balance of trade in goods and services
$$= -19\,501 + 7232$$
$$= -12\,269 \text{ Rs(m) (deficit)}$$

ii Current account balance
$$= -12\,269 + 8869 - 1584$$
$$= -4984 \text{ Rs(m) (deficit)}$$

SKILLS FOCUS

Tourists visiting Mauritius, or any other country, are an export and are recorded as a positive item in the current account of the balance of payments.

39.2 Causes and consequences of a current account deficit

There are many causes and consequences of a current account deficit. The main ones are summarised in Figure 39.1.

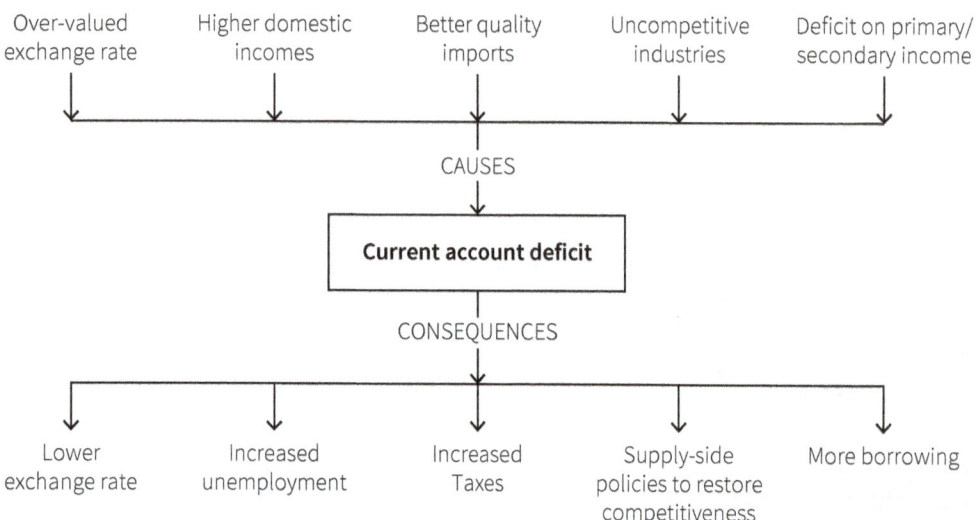

Figure 39.1 Causes and consequences of a current account deficit

39.3 Causes and consequences of a current account surplus

There are many causes and consequences of a current account surplus. The main ones are shown in Figure 39.2.

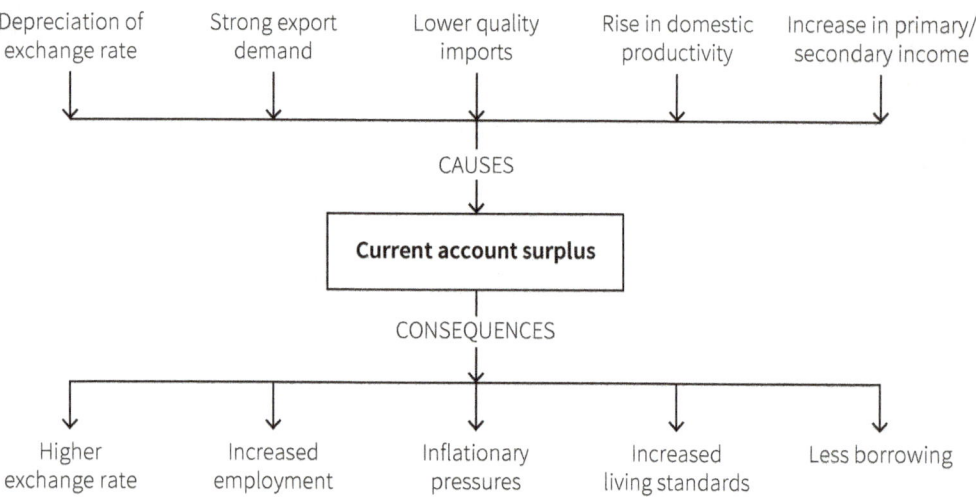

Figure 39.2 Causes and consequences of a current account deficit

> **TIP** The consequences of a current account deficit or surplus will depend on the size, duration and causes of the deficit or surplus.

39.4 Policies to achieve balance of payments stability

In principle, governments will want to achieve stability in their balance of payments – they will not want to see persistent current account deficits or surpluses. In reality, this objective may be far from being achieved.

Reducing a current account surplus is less common. Relevant policies tend to be the opposite of those to reduce a deficit. Revaluation of a currency is likely to be most effective, though controversial.

Progress check

Answer the following questions to check your understanding:

1. How are the balance of trade and the current account balance calculated?
2. How are receipts from international tourism recorded in the balance of payments?
3. Explain **two** causes and **two** consequences of a deficit in the current account.
4. Explain **two** causes and **two** consequences of a surplus in the current account.
5. Analyse how a depreciation of a currency is likely to affect a country's current balance.

Revision checklist

You should know:

- The balance of payments is a record of international business transactions of one country with the rest of the world.
- The current account consists of trade in goods, trade in services, primary income and secondary income.
- A current account deficit or surplus may be caused by a range of factors at home or abroad. Changes to the exchange rate are particularly important for many countries.

STRUCTURED SKILLS PRACTICE

1. Analyse how a government can improve a deficit on the current account of its balance of payments.

> **TIP**
>
> Note that the question is about the current account only. Be clear what this includes and does not include. It will enhance your answer if you include some reference to invisible earnings such as tourism.

Exam-style multiple choice questions

1. When migrant workers from Pakistan send money home to relatives, where is this transaction recorded in the current account of the balance of payments?

   A primary income

   B secondary income

   C trade in goods

   D trade in services

2. In 2017, international visitors to Mauritius spent US$20m, of which US$8m was spent on imported food and drink. How will these changes affect the current account of the balance of payments?

	Trade in goods	Trade in services
A	improve it	worsen it
B	worsen it	improve it
C	improve it	improve it
D	worsen it	worsen it

3. Which is **most** likely to reduce a surplus on the current account of the balance of payments?

   A a fall in income tax

   B a fall in the value of the currency

   C a fall in unemployment

   D a rise in the value of the currency

Exam-style structured questions for Section 6

Data response question

Read the source material carefully before answering the question.

Source material: Malaysia and Pakistan – contrasts in the balance of payments

Malaysia and Pakistan are emerging economies yet their current accounts of the balance of payments are in marked contrast (see Figure S6.1 and Table S6.1).

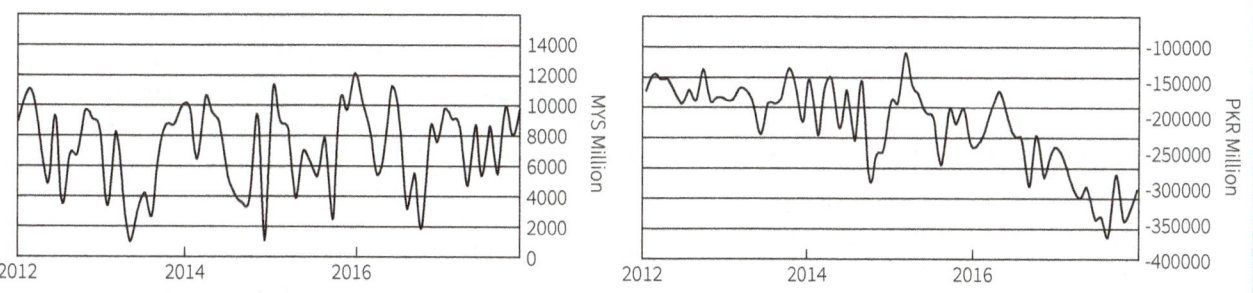

Figure S6.1 Malaysia and Pakistan, Balance of Trade, 2012–2016

Trading Economics.

Table S6.1 Balance of payments current account summaries, Malaysia and Pakistan, 2016

	Malaysia (MYRm)	Pakistan ('000 Rsm)
Exports of goods and services	82 200	176 400
Imports of goods and services	72 400	471 100
Balance of trade	9 800	−294 700
Current account balance	9 642	−4 419

Trading Economics.

Malaysia has had a surplus balance of trade for many years. This has been achieved through its strong exports of oil, gas, rubber and timber products. Its imports are mainly food and supplies for its growing manufacturing industries. The current account balance has benefited by a consistent flow of FDI from multinationals in the oil and gas industries, and a growing number of international tourists.

A disappointment has been Malaysia's failure to become Southeast Asia's regional automotive hub, now firmly established in Thailand. Foreign car makers have been put off by the high taxes imposed by the Malaysian government in order to protect its own producers. In a shock move, in 2016, import tariffs on cars from Japan and Australia were slashed to 15% and 13.6%. Further reductions or even a removal of these tariffs has been supported.

In sharp contrast to Malaysia, Pakistan's trade deficit has widened for most of 2017. Imports remain at a high level. A strong rupee, especially against the US dollar and the Chinese renminbi, has resulted in a flood of cheap imports, hurting domestic producers. In contrast, the export of goods has fallen, widening the deficit and increasing the burden of external debt. The one positive aspect of this situation remains the growth in remittances made back home by overseas Pakistani workers employed in the Middle East and elsewhere.

It is against this background that in July 2017, on a single day, the Bank of Pakistan did not intervene in the market when the rupee fell by over 3% to 108.1 against the US dollar. This was its biggest fall in nine years. A Karachi-based economist commented that the drop was 'long overdue'. The International Monetary Fund had in 2016 stated that the rupee was over-valued at a time when China, India, Thailand and Turkey, all trading competitors, had devalued their currencies.

a Define 'balance of trade'. [1]

b Describe **two** ways in which Pakistan's balance of trade differs from that of Malaysia over the period from 2012 to late 2017. [2]

c Identify, with a reason, whether Pakistan has a fixed or floating exchange rate. [2]

d Explain **two** reasons for the difference in the current account balance and the balance of trade for Malaysia and Pakistan in 2016. [4]

e Analyse the effects if Malaysia were to remove tariffs on imported vehicles from Australia and Japan. [4]

f Explain why the removal of the tariffs may not increase demand for Australian and Japanese vehicles in Malaysia. [5]

g Discuss whether or not a depreciation of Pakistan's currency is likely to affect consumers in Pakistan and in its trading partners. [6]

h Discuss whether or not Malaysia or Pakistan should be more concerned about its current account position. [6]

Four-part question

This question is introduced by stimulus material. In your answer, you may refer to this material and/or to other examples that you have studied.

In 2016, the World Trade Organization (WTO) reported that world trade growth had fallen to below world GDP growth for the first time since 2001. Prospects for reducing protection received a further setback in March 2017 when the USA opposed plans from the WTO to renew their longstanding pledge to bolster free trade.

a Define 'free trade'. [2]

b Explain **one** advantage and **one** disadvantage of free trade. [4]

c Analyse how multinational companies impact on the current account of the balance of payments of a developing economy [6]

d Discuss whether or not a developing economy should protect an infant manufacturing industry. [8]

Suggested answers

Except for the multiple choice questions, all answers are suggested only. Other answers may be acceptable.

Answers to Progress Check Questions are brief. If you are unsure about any answer, you will find it useful it to read the appropriate chapter in the Coursebook.

The suggested answers to structured skills practice questions outline the main points. As part of your exam preparation, you may wish to write out the answers in more detail.

For exam-style structured questions at the ends of Sections 1–6, the suggested answers are accompanied by comments to help you develop your skills and improve the quality of your responses. All exam-style questions and sample answers in this title were written by the author. In examinations, the way marks are awarded may be different.

Section 1 The basic economic problem

Chapter 1

Progress check questions

1 Wants are unlimited; needs are limited yet necessary and include food, clothing and housing.

2 The economic problem is the term used to denote a situation where consumers, firms and governments have unlimited wants in relation to the resources available to them. This means choices have to be made.

3 Free good – clean air, sunshine, wild fruit (limited examples).

   Economic good – many examples such as cars, chocolate bars, bottled water.

Structured skills practice

1
- The small clothing manufacturer has limited resources for the business in relation to wants.
- Decisions have to be taken on, say, whether to purchase new sewing machines or cutting equipment, or whether resources would be best invested in new premises.
- The manufacturer could decide to do nothing and save any profits for the future.

2
- The free power is an economic good because resources are required to produce this power.
- The fact that there is no charge to farmers is irrelevant.

Exam-style multiple choice questions

1 B

2 D

Chapter 2

Progress check questions

1 Land – the physical area on which the food stall is built.

   Labour – staff employed at the food stall.

   Capital – cooking equipment.

   Enterprise – the owner of the stall who is responsible for organising the business.

2 Occupationally immobile – due to limited skills which could seriously restrict other possible employment.

   Geographically immobile – reluctant to move for family reasons or for cultural attachment to the home region.

3 Through use of mechanisation/robots, improved education and training for workers.

Structured skills practice

1
- All factors of production – land, labour, capital and enterprise – are required for the production and assembly of motor vehicles.
- Japan has limited land and expensive labour.
- Other Asian countries have room for new developments, skilled and cheaper labour, and possibly capital incentives for new factories.
- Enterprise can be applied through the possible risk involved in moving production outside Japan.

Exam-style multiple choice questions

1 A

2 C

3 B

Chapter 3

Progress check questions

1. Opportunity cost is the cost of the best alternative that has been forgone.

2. The business has various alternatives including to:
   - spend the $10 000 on new equipment for the business
   - hire consultants to identify new markets to sustain the development of the business
   - put the money in a bank for future use.

Structured skills practice

1.
   - Opportunity cost is the best alternative that is forgone.
   - Choices have to be made, for example, should the farmer produce both fruit and vegetables or more fruit than vegetables?
   - If so, what type of fruit should be produced and what are the alternatives that have to be forgone?

Exam-style multiple choice questions

1. B
2. C

Chapter 4

Progress check questions

1. Reproduce Figure 4.2.

2. Movement along the PPC – show two separate points on the PPC. This represents a change in the allocation of resources.

   Outward shift of the PPC – show the entire PPC shifting outwards, indicating that more of each good will be produced. This can be achieved through an increase in the labour force or technological advance increasing the output of both products.

Structured skills practice

1. (a) Oil sector / Non-oil sector showing PPC 2015 and PPC 2016.

(b)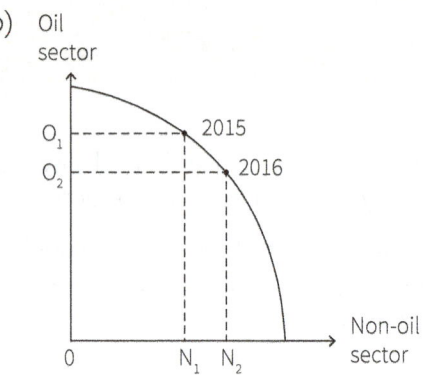

- The negative economic growth is shown by a shift to the left of the entire PPC. There will be less production in both sectors.
- The reallocation of resources is shown by a movement along the PPC from O_1N_1 to O_2N_2.

Exam-style multiple choice questions

1. B
2. B

Exam-style structured questions for Section 1

Data response question

a. The answer is 27%.

   An approximate answer could be 25%–28%.

b. The total amount of money has increased. There was a steady increase from 2011 to 2014. There was a slight drop in funding from 2015 to 2016.

   Note that the answer must cover the entire time period, unlike part (a). Any two of the three points above for 1 mark each.

c. The data for spending is in local currency. It does not take into account inflation. So-called real data is best when looking at this type of change over time.

   When you see this type of data, check to see if the data is absolute or real.

d. Two factors of production are labour and land. Labour includes doctors, nurses and a range of other staff that are required to provide healthcare services. Land includes the site and buildings for hospitals and clinics.

   Capital is an alternative factor of production. This is a common type of question where 1 mark is for recognition and 1 further mark is for elaboration of each factor. There is no need to write a long answer.

e   A free good is one that does not require any resources to make it. This is not the case with healthcare, which is provided by factors of production that have to be paid for. This therefore means that healthcare is an economic good.

Whether or not a charge is made is irrelevant.

f   Healthcare is important for the well-being of the economy. A fall in expenditure on healthcare could mean that more people suffer illnesses with the result that output decreases. In principle, this will shift the PPC of an economy downwards, resulting in less output of both types of good.

Although not stated in the question, a PPC diagram would enhance the quality of this answer. The 'analyse' command word hints at this. Make sure that you refer to the diagram in your answer.

g   Opportunity cost is the best alternative that is forgone. It could be applied in this case although it would only be a crude way of ranking the various areas of government spending covered by the budget. The concept can also be applied to identify priorities in the healthcare budget. Other methods will have to be used, such as looking at costs and benefits and how value for money can be achieved.

The key point is that opportunity cost can be used but it does have limitations.

h   The source material indicates that this is a controversial topic, particularly in a developing economy like Zambia. For healthcare users, there is an opportunity cost. Additional charges for healthcare are likely to mean that something else has to be forgone. It could also mean that the cost of treatment becomes so expensive that treatment has to be forgone.

Additional income from higher charges would provide the government with more resources, ideally for the health service. It also seems right that those who can afford to pay for healthcare should do so. Both would help to overcome the problem of a reduction in expenditure from the budget.

The answer looks at both sides. It could be improved with an additional paragraph that has a clear conclusion on whether out-of-pocket charges should be increased.

Four-part question

a   Enterprise is a factor of production concerned with risk taking and making decisions in business.

This is a standard term but note the two aspects to the definition.

b   Of the four factors of production, three are mobile. Labour is most mobile for the typical situation mentioned in the stimulus material. Enterprise through the involvement of an entrepreneur is geographically mobile and there can also be circumstances where a firm's owner can decide to take a risk and move into a new area of business. Capital is also mobile, as clearly shown through the globalisation of business, although this is likely to take time. Land, by definition, is immobile.

This is a good answer. Note how it concentrates on the mobility of factors of production with valid reference to examples including the stimulus material. The wording of the question does not require definitions of the factors of production.

c   An obvious reason why workers wish to migrate to countries such as Singapore is to earn higher wages than they might earn in their own country. They then hope to remit most of their earnings back home for their family. The stimulus material makes clear that migrant workers are from lower income countries compared to Singapore.

This answer is too brief for the 6 marks available. There is only one reason, but a very good one, given for why labour migrates. Other reasons are required to give a bit more depth to the answer. These could include high unemployment in the migrant's home country, no jobs available relative to a migrant's skills and political considerations.

d   Singapore needs migrant workers as the data in the stimulus material indicates. Restricting numbers is a way of ensuring that local workers remain employed. When economic prospects are weak, there will be a cutback by firms in the number of migrant workers and a tightening of restrictions on those already working in Singapore.

The regulation of migrant workers seems to be controversial. There will inevitably be situations where migrants are paid less than Singapore workers doing the same job. Migrants will often do the jobs locals would not do. They are unlikely to have the same access to healthcare and social care facilities.

The benefits and costs to Singapore's economy should be considered in order to arrive at a conclusion as to whether numbers should be regulated.

This answer is good but could be improved by expanding the third paragraph to include a more explicit list of benefits and costs to an economy, not necessarily Singapore. The 'such as' wording provides an opportunity to write about an economy you have studied.

Section 2 The allocation of resources

Chapter 5

Progress check questions

1. For example:

    Microeconomic issue – an increase in goods and services tax on chicken meat has increased the cost of the weekly shopping.

    Macroeconomic issue – recession has reduced the number of job opportunities for school leavers.

2. Typical examples are:
    - the market for mobile phones
    - the labour market
    - the foreign exchange market
    - the market for coffee beans.

Structured skills practice

1. i There are various possibilities including:
    - whether to reduce indirect taxes to boost total demand
    - whether to impose a tariff on some imported goods to reduce a balance of payments deficit.

   ii The opportunity costs are:
    - reducing direct taxes to increase total demand – the best alternative forgone
    - imposing a quota on certain imports as the best alternative forgone for reducing a balance of payments deficit.

Exam-style multiple choice questions

1. C
2. B

Chapter 6

Progress check questions

1. What to produce?

    How to produce?

    Who are the products to be produced for?

2. The role and importance of government – and the role and importance of the price mechanism.

3. A market is in equilibrium when demand and supply are equal at the current price.

4. i Demand falls → Falling prices → Farmers grow less maize → Producers refine less cooking oil → Prices increase → Market equilibrium is restored.

   ii Demand increases → Prices increase → Farmers grow more maize → Producers refine more cooking oil → Prices fall → Market equilibrium is restored.

Structured skills practice

1. - It has come about as a result of less government involvement in the economy.
    - Possible means include privatisation of state-run industries and opening up markets through deregulation to increase competition.

Exam-style multiple choice questions

1. D

Chapter 7

Progress check questions

1. An inverse one, whereby a decrease in price leads to an increase in quantity demanded and an increase in price leads to a decrease in quantity demanded.

2. i A contraction in demand is shown by a movement up the demand curve. This is a consequence of a rise in the price of the product.

   ii A decrease in demand is shown by a shift to the left of the demand curve. This means that there is a fall in demand at any given price.

3. Reasons:
    - an increase in the price of chocolate
    - a growing awareness of the health risks of consuming too much sugar
    - greater availability of healthier alternatives

Structured skills practice

1.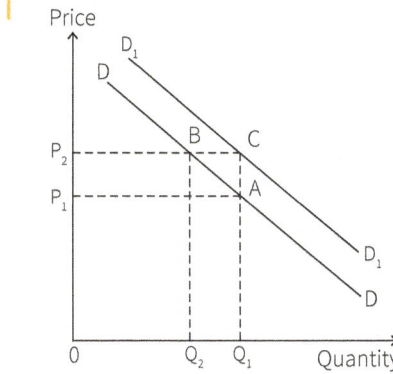

    i   The original position is at A where price is P_1 and the quantity demanded is Q_1. An increase in the price of this brand of cola is shown by a movement up the demand curve to point B, where price is now P_2 and the quantity demanded is reduced to Q_2.

    ii An increase in the price of a substitute brand of cola is represented by a shift outwards of the demand curve to D_1D_1. At any price, such as P_2, more will be demanded.

2. The increase in demand can be explained by:
    - an increase in the price of petrol vehicles (substitutes)
    - a positive shift in favour of electric vehicles for environmental reasons
    - an advertising campaign by electric vehicle manufacturers
    - an increase in disposable incomes.

Exam-style multiple choice questions

1. C
2. C
3. A
4. B

Chapter 8

Progress check questions

1. A positive one whereby an increase in price leads to an increase in the quantity supplied and a decrease in price leads to a decrease in the quantity supplied.

2. Reproduce Figure 8.1.

    i   An extension in supply is shown by a movement up the supply curve. This is a consequence of a rise in the price of the product.

    ii An increase in supply is shown by a shift to the right of the supply curve. This means that there is an increase in supply at any given price.

3. Reasons:
    - less disruption of supplies due to adverse weather conditions
    - an increase in subsidies from governments to coffee farmers
    - a large increase in the price of tea
    - a fall in the cost of cultivating coffee beans.

Structured skills practice

1.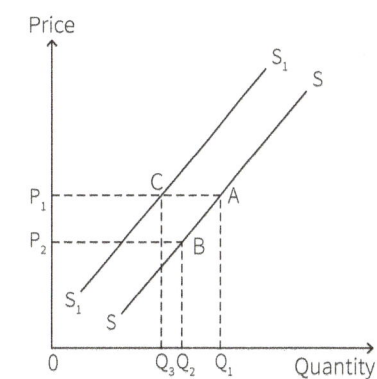

    i   This is represented by a movement down the supply curve SS from A to B. If US wholesalers reduce the price they are willing to pay from P_1 to P_2, the Bangladeshi garment manufacturer will only be willing to supply Q_2 and not Q_1.

    ii The effect of a subsidy by the Chinese government for its manufacturers leads to a shift to the left of the supply curve since Bangladeshi garments are relatively more expensive. So, at any one price, fewer garments will be supplied.

2.
    - Changes in supply come about through the actions of suppliers (such as OPEC and US shale oil producers). An increase in supply can be shown by a shift to the right of the supply curve for oil. This would cause the price of oil to fall.
    - A change in demand could also have occurred. The reduction in the price of oil by 2017 could indicate a decrease in demand from 2014. This is less likely to have occurred.

197

- It is not easy to say which has had the most influence on price – more than likely, it is due to supply factors. Additional data is required to be more certain.
- The diagram below could be used to explain the change in price.

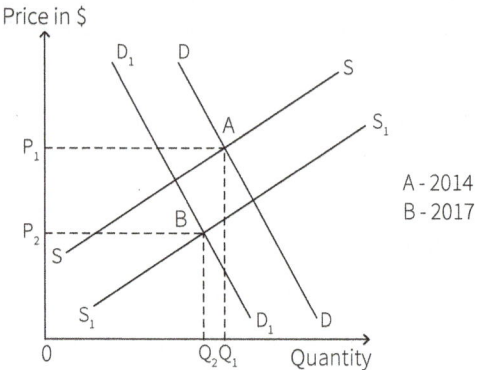

Exam-style multiple choice questions

1. B
2. C
3. C

Chapter 9

Progress check questions

1. A market is in equilibrium when demand and supply are equal.
2. When in equilibrium, a market clears since there is no reason for the price or quantity to change.
3. Excess demand – when the quantity demanded outstrips the quantity supplied.

    Excess supply – when the quantity supplied is greater than the quantity demanded.

    Both of these situations lead to disequilibrium in the market since demand and supply are not equal.

Structured skills practice

i
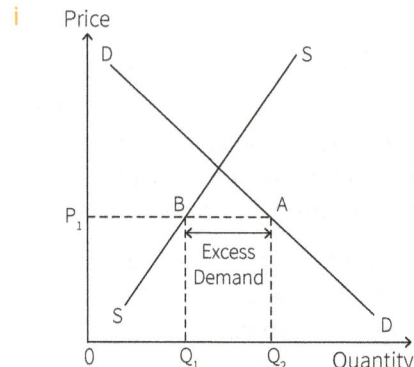

The market is in disequilibrium because the quantity demanded is not equal to the quantity supplied. OQ_2 is demanded but only OQ_1 is supplied at price P_1.

ii The excess demand is shown by the distance BA on the diagram. The excess demand will be eliminated if supply increases – this can be shown by a shift to the right to point A, resulting in the market now being in equilibrium.

iii When there is excess demand, producers benefit since they can increase supply. If they continue to restrict supply, price is likely to increase. Consumers will only benefit if, with the increase in supply, price remains at P_1. When the market is in disequilibrium, they are not able to buy all of the chicken they would like to purchase.

Exam-style multiple choice questions

1. D
2. A

Chapter 10

Progress check questions

1. Prices change due to changing market conditions. For example, there may be an increase or decrease in demand, or an increase or decrease in supply in a market; any of these will lead to price changing.

2. Reproduce Figure 9.1.

    i A decrease in demand is shown by a shift to the left of the demand curve DD. As a result, the equilibrium price falls and the equilibrium quantity also falls.

    ii A decrease in supply is shown by a shift to the left of the supply curve SS. As a result, the equilibrium price rises and the equilibrium quantity falls.

Structured skills practice

1. i More efficient production methods are shown by a shift to the right of the supply curve for mobile phones. The increase in demand is shown by a shift to the right of the demand curve. When combined, given a larger shift of the supply curve, prices of mobile phones have fallen from P to P1.

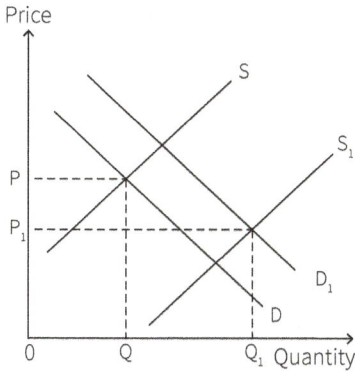

ii The diagram shows a shift to the right in the demand curve and the supply curve. The outcome is that the equilibrium price remains at P with an increase in the quantity traded to Q_1. As a result, sales have increased.

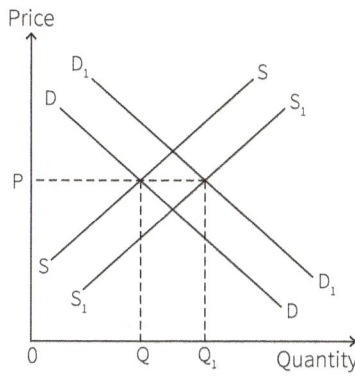

Exam-style multiple choice questions

1 A
2 C
3 B

Chapter 11

Progress check questions

1 The left-hand diagram shows an elastic demand curve. The relative change in quantity demanded is greater than the relative change in price.

The right-hand diagram shows an inelastic demand curve. The relative change in quantity demanded is less than the relative change in price.

2 30%.

3 A producer should not increase the price of a product when its PED is elastic as this will decrease the revenue received.

Structured skills practice

1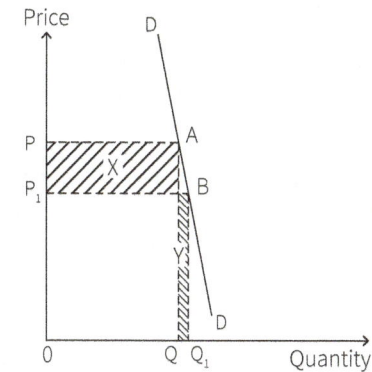

When the price falls from P to P_1, the quantity demanded increases from Q to Q_1. At price P, the revenue from sales is OPAQ. At price P_1, the revenue from sales is OP_1BQ_1 which is less than when price was at P. The loss of revenue, area X, is greater than the gain, area Y.

2 The values for PED change from elastic to inelastic with a movement down the demand curve. (The values for each change in price are 4, 4.7, 2.4, 0.72, 0.5 and 0.18.)

3 Both estimates are inelastic, the short run figure being more inelastic than that for the long run. This indicates that in the short run, if, say, price increases, people in Mauritius will buy less gasoline but have little opportunity to switch to other forms of fuel. There is more opportunity for them to do this in the long run when the alternatives become known to them.

4 • If PED is elastic, a fall in price will increase revenue. An increase in price reduces revenue.

• If PED is inelastic, an increase in price will increase revenue. A reduction in price will lead to a fall in revenue.

• The assumption is that price is the only factor that influences the quantity demanded. This is invariably not the case, as other factors have to be considered.

Exam-style multiple choice questions

1 C
2 B
3 A

Chapter 12

Progress check questions

1. The left-hand diagram shows an elastic supply curve. The relative change in quantity supplied is greater than the relative change in price.

   The right-hand diagram shows an inelastic supply curve. The relative change in quantity supplied is less than the relative change in price.

2. 3%.

Structured skills practice

1.
   - Agricultural goods are usually inelastic in their supply. This is due to the time it takes to increase or decrease production, limitations of what can be grown and where particular crops can be grown, and problems of supply due to weather conditions.
   - Most manufactured goods are price elastic in supply. They can be stored and released, or withdrawn from the market depending on price fluctuations.

2.
   - If PES is elastic, then it makes sense for a producer to expand production if there is a large increase in the market price. This could be done through releasing stocks or expanding production using existing resources.
   - If PES is inelastic, the response is less clear. The increase in supply will take time, during which other suppliers may have increased supply causing the market price to fall.
   - PES is just one factor that the producer should consider. Others include whether the large increase in price can be sustained and the opportunity cost of increasing production.

3.
   - The fall in supply of OPEC's crude oil would be expected to result in an increase in price as shown by a shift to the left of the supply curve.
   - This has not happened largely on account of other sources increasing supply, more than offsetting OPEC's cut in supply.
   - It is difficult to tell if PES is elastic or inelastic as the fall in price is not given. The limited evidence suggests it is elastic due to increased supply from other producers.

Exam-style multiple choice questions

1. B
2. C
3. B

Chapter 13

Progress check questions

1. Typical examples are:
   i. McDonald's
   ii. railways
   iii. steel production.

2.
   i. Private firms do not have to pay directly for the environmental problems they cause. Also, there may be no regulations restricting such problems. It is therefore easiest and cheapest for firms to discharge waste into rivers, the atmosphere or landfill.
   ii. It is the government's responsibility to reduce inequality. In a market system, there are no such policies due to a lack of government intervention.

Structured skills practice

1.
   - An emerging market economy is not only a developing one but also one where the private sector and the free market have an increasingly important role to play.
   - Pakistan has gone through, and continues to go through, a process of privatisation, especially of former state-owned manufacturing and utility services providers.
   - The market has also been through a process of deregulation in order to encourage more competition.

2.
   - Advantages are efficient resource allocation, increased competition, innovation and the market being more responsive to customer needs.
   - Disadvantages are market failure due to lack of regulations, widening inequality of income and wealth, and less government provision of social welfare services.
   - Any economy has to weigh up the respective importance of the advantages and disadvantages.

Exam-style multiple choice questions

1 D
2 D

Chapter 14

Progress check questions

1 i Private costs: costs of producing tuna.

Private benefits: wages paid to workers, profits for factory owners.

External costs: noise and smells from the factory, depletion of tuna stocks for others.

External benefits: wider benefits to the local economy.

ii Private costs: costs to government of funding more university places.

Private benefits: a better education and job prospects for students receiving this funding.

External costs: additional cost to taxpayers.

External benefits: an enhanced rate of economic growth resulting from a better-educated population.

2 i Free dental care is a merit good since it generates a positive externality in the form of a healthier population that is more productive. Due to information failure, many people in the population do not appreciate the problems that can be caused through consuming excessive amounts of sugar and the damage this can cause to teeth.

ii Junk food such as burgers, fried chicken and soda are demerit goods when their excessive consumption leads to additional costs on the community for waste disposal and combatting obesity amongst young people.

3 i A local fire protection service is an essential service that is usually provided by the government. It is impractical to charge an annual fee or call-out charge when it is used. No one can be excluded from the benefits it provides; it is also non-rival when provided in sufficient quantity.

ii Anyone purchasing a new moped has to pay for it. It is excludable since no one else can use it without the owner's permission. The owner is the only person who receives the benefits of ownership.

Structured skills practice

1 i
- Car users can travel more quickly and at reduced cost since the car is being used more efficiently.
- There is better air quality for pedestrians and city residents.
- Fewer accidents happen to pedestrians and cyclists.

ii
- Car users are likely to under-estimate the full social costs of using their vehicles in crowded cities.
- Car users may not be aware of the personal and wider advantages of using mass transit due to information failure.

Exam-style multiple choice questions

1 B
2 A
3 A
4 A

Chapter 15

Progress check questions

1 It is best to impose an indirect tax on a product that has an inelastic demand curve. The change in quantity demanded will be relatively less than the increase in price and there will be an increase in tax revenue. With an elastic demand, there will be a greater decrease in demand compared to the increase in price and a decrease in tax revenue.

2
- This could be achieved through an increase in taxation to fund an expansion of health provision. It is best funded through increased income taxes on higher-income earners. No charge at the point of use is likely to be the most effective way.

- As above for taxation but with a small charge to be made at the point of use for some treatments. This is also effective and provides a way of charging for those who can afford to pay for health provision.

- Additional tax revenue could be generated by increasing indirect taxes on some demerit goods. This has some value since those who consume demerit goods such as tobacco and alcohol are most likely to require health provision at some stage of their lives.

- Increasing the quality of provision is likely to be difficult for a developing economy. A feasible option could be for the government to form a partnership with a private sector provider.

Structured skills practice

1 i

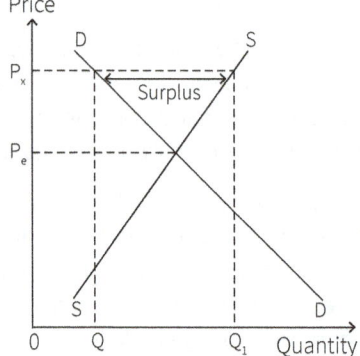

- The maximum price P_x, to be effective, has to be below the market equilibrium price. As the diagram shows, at this price, the quantity demanded exceeds that which suppliers are willing to provide.

ii
- A shortage may not develop if some form of rationing is used, for example food coupons.
- The risk is that supplies could be sold on the illegal market, bypassing the official market.

2 i Price

(diagram showing surplus between P_x and P_e, with quantities Q and Q_1)

- The minimum price has to be above the market equilibrium price to be effective. A surplus results, since suppliers are willing to supply more than is demanded by consumers.

ii The government is forced into buying surplus stocks in order to avoid a fall in the price.

Exam-style multiple choice questions

1 D

2 B

3 B

Exam-style structured questions for Section 2

Data response question

a Market failure is when the market mechanism results in a misallocation of resources.

This is the basic definition of the term.

b Car sales have increased continuously from 2008 to 2017. The rate of increase has been variable, particularly from 2010 to 2012 when there was only modest growth in sales. This contrasts with 2008 to 2009, when sales grew by over 50%.

'Level and trend' is a good way of tackling this type of question when the data is a time series.

c Two possible reasons are:
- an increase in disposable income
- the convenience of owning a car.

The command word 'state' means that only a brief answer is needed. Note that the question says 'increase in demand' and not 'increase in quantity demanded'.

d Price

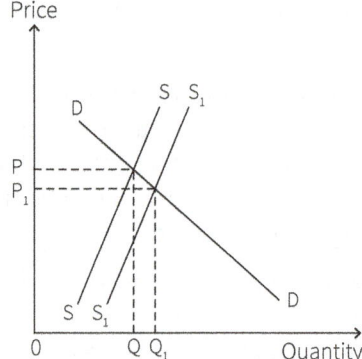

The reduction in the rate of taxation will result in a shift to the right of the supply curve for small-engine cars. This will cause a fall in price and an increase in the quantity traded. The extent of the increase in demand for small-engine cars will depend on the price elasticity of demand.

The price elasticity point is required for a higher level answer.

e Two external costs are:

- the additional costs to the medical services of treating young people who have respiratory problems
- the strain and stress experienced by inhabitants as a result of continuous traffic noise.

The question clearly requires information from the last paragraph. Remember that it is third parties who face these external costs. A third external cost is the cost of traffic accidents involving cyclists and motor cyclists.

f A consequence of external costs in the market is that private costs are not equal to social costs. This is why there is a misallocation of resources. The market price is lower than it should be and the quantity produced and consumed is more than it should be.

The answer could be improved by using one of the examples identified in the previous part to explain why there is a misallocation of resources.

g External benefits include:

- lower incidence of respiratory diseases in young people
- less noise from traffic.

Both will result in benefits to third parties not directly involved in using NEVs and so represent a better allocation of resources. It is, though, doubtful whether there will be fewer accidents involving cycles and motorcycles since NEVs are quieter than conventional vehicles. It will also take time for the benefits to accrue since petrol and diesel vehicles will continue to be used for many years. It is really difficult to make a conclusion even though China has a large number of these vehicles. The early evidence would seem to point to their being external benefits. These will fall if there is no Chinese supplier.

The last two sentences provide a relevant discussion. Based on the evidence, the conclusion appears to come out in favour of NEVs. Referring back to what you have written is a good way of presenting a conclusion to this type of question.

h Subsidies were cut because many producers who had received subsidies had not actually produced any NEVs. This is a waste of scarce resources that could be put to better use. In the absence of Chinese-produced NEVs, there is a danger that the import of electric vehicles will continue to increase. Whether or not this drastic policy is the best one is not clear – an alternative policy would be to concentrate on giving subsidies to larger manufacturers who are in a much stronger position to supply NEVs to the China market.

Again, two points of discussion are in this answer. The second one in the last sentence is offering an alternative policy. Rather more could be said about the loss of jobs and technical knowledge for China in what is clearly a growing means of sustainable transport.

Four-part question

a Price elasticity of supply is a measure of the responsiveness of the quantity supplied to a change in price.

This is a basic definition. Make sure you get it the right way round.

b The price elasticity of supply is likely to be inelastic because:

- it takes time for cashew nut farmers to plant more crops in response to an increase in the market price, meaning that supply cannot be quickly increased
- they may not have spare stocks to release onto the market when price rises and they cannot hold back stocks if price falls.

Both these factors mean that supply is insensitive to a change in price.

Two relevant reasons are provided with some elaboration.

c The stimulus material refers to:

- an 11% fall in the supply of cashew nuts
- rising demand for cashew nuts.

This situation can be represented on a diagram.

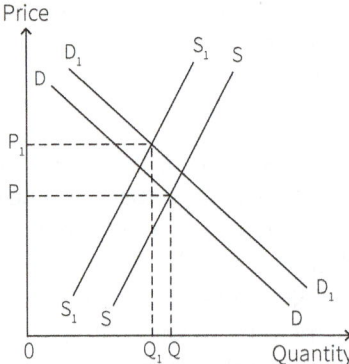

The diagram shows that if the fall in supply and increase in demand are combined, there will be a fall in quantity traded from Q to Q_1 and a large increase in the price from P to P_1. The extent of change in the market depends on the respective shifts of the market supply and demand curves.

A diagram is a good way of addressing this question. Note how the suggested answer makes clear use of the diagram. This is good practice. The first part of the answer makes clear what the changes are in the market.

d   The response of producers is varied. In Vietnam, producers of cashew nuts may try to compensate for drought by investing in irrigation systems or water storage facilities in order to safeguard supply. If practical, another approach would be to diversify into other types of crop production, ideally not requiring heavy supplies of water. Away from Vietnam, other producers may increase their land devoted to cashew nuts – this would be a desire to take advantage of rising prices in a market where demand continues to increase.

For consumers, the response will depend on whether or not they see other types of nut as a substitute for cashew nuts or whether their demand is price inelastic, meaning that they are prepared to pay higher prices.

The market response will take both of these into account. It is, though, very difficult to say what the outcome will be as there are many factors involved.

A diagram might also be used to enhance this answer. The paragraph on consumers' response could be extended. The third paragraph has only limited discussion – another one or two sentences would improve this answer.

Section 3 Microeconomic decision makers

Chapter 16

Progress check questions

1   As a medium of exchange. The remaining functions depend on money being acceptable to buyers and sellers.

2   In the past, salt has served as money in some economies. It was scarce, acceptable as a medium of exchange, could be stored and, by weight, acted as a unit of account.

3   Consumers and producers rely on commercial banks for day-to-day banking transactions. Commercial banks also lend money, provide advice and assist producers when exporting and importing goods.

4   The central bank in most economies controls the supply of notes and coins. This is essential in order to maintain the integrity of the currency. It also holds gold and foreign exchange reserves and manages loans that an economy may have with third party governments and multinational organisations such as the World Bank. In some economies, the central bank has an important role to play in determining interest rates and foreign exchange rates.

Structured skills practice

1   i
    - Commercial banks provide a safe place for consumers' money. They also lend to consumers and provide a range of banking services.
    - Producers are able to borrow money from commercial banks to fund expansion or new investment in a business. They can also provide support for overseas transactions.

    ii
    - A central bank can have considerable influence over economic policy, for example in the determination of interest rates.
    - A central bank manages the national debt, and holds reserves of gold and foreign exchange.

Exam-style multiple choice questions

1   B

2   D

3   A

Chapter 17

Progress check questions

1. Disposable income is income after tax has been deducted and state benefits have been added. It is the most important determinant of household spending since any change in disposable income causes a change in household spending. The relationship is positive.

2. Particularly in Asian countries, the reason is largely cultural. Households have a higher savings ratio in order to put money aside for the future, especially old age. People are concerned about the costs of healthcare and whether state benefits will change over time. There are also concerns about future economic prospects and, in some economies, a reluctance to borrow money.

3. Savings are the amount of disposable income which is not spent on consumption. Borrowing, in contrast, is where more money is needed; it enables people to spend more than their current disposable income.

Structured skills practice

1. There are various reasons including:
   - to save for future needs such as welfare provision
   - it has been the Asian custom for savings to be a high percentage of disposable income
   - to provide support for the education of selected family members
   - a possible lack of confidence in China's economic prospects
   - household consumption has lagged behind growth in earnings
   - to support government investment.

Exam-style multiple choice questions

1. D
2. D
3. A

Chapter 18

Progress check questions

1. The wage rate is the basic pay a person receives, usually per hour. Earnings are the total pay a worker receives, including overtime pay and bonuses, as well as the payment for how many hours a person has worked.

2. In general, the most likely reason is non-wage factors. For example, a worker experiencing little or no job satisfaction may decide to move to a lower paid post with, say, a charitable organisation. The fringe benefits and holiday entitlement of a job may also result in a person changing jobs for less pay. Some work is physically demanding and conditions are dirty – a person may decide to take a less onerous job offering less pay.

3. The demand and supply of hotel managers are inelastic. In other words, supply is limited and demand is strong. This means that the wage rate is high. For cleaning staff, in contrast, demand and supply are elastic. There is a good supply of workers willing to work at the equilibrium wage rate; firms know that they can get all the workers they need at this rate.

4. i An increase in the use of robots in the assembly process and a fall in demand for motor vehicles.

   ii An increase in the number of call centres and improved communications technology.

Structured skills practice

1.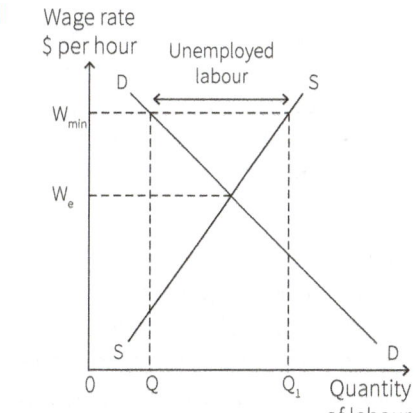

   - To be effective, the new minimum wage must be above the market equilibrium.
   - At this wage, Q_1 workers are willing to be employed. Employers demand fewer workers at Q.
   - The obvious conclusion is that some unemployment is likely when a new minimum wage is introduced.
   - With the minimum wage, employers may require existing workers to work harder – an informal labour market could develop.

2

Graph: Wage rate ($ per hour) on y-axis, Quantity of nurses on x-axis. Original demand curve D and supply curve S intersect at wage W, quantity Q. New curves D₁ (shifted right) and S₁ (shifted right) intersect at the same wage W but at a higher quantity.

- The simultaneous increase in demand and supply of nurses would leave the wage rate at W but with an increased number of nurses employed.

Exam-style multiple choice questions

1 C
2 D
3 C

Chapter 19

Progress check questions

1 The role of the trade union is to represent the interests of its members when negotiating with an employer. Such negotiations cover issues such as wage rates, working conditions, workplace pensions and other issues relating to the employment of such workers.

2 Some trade unions have weak bargaining power due to there being an elastic supply of workers in the market. Such workers will be unlikely to have specialist skills and could be easily replaced in the firm. A trade union is likely to have weak bargaining power where it has a low percentage of workers in full-time employment. Weak bargaining power is also a reality in most sunset industries – an unwarranted pay rise could push the firm into liquidation.

Structured skills practice

1
- A trade union, in principle, can restrict the supply of labour in order to increase wages.
- This can be very effective where labour has special skills or is in short supply. This will protect those employed by a firm.
- This can be effective where a trade union has a high percentage of members in a firm and where the firm has a strong order book and economic prospects look good.
- A trade union's actions are for the benefit of its members, not for the benefit of the total labour force.
- A conclusion might suggest that it is unlikely for a trade union to be able to increase the wages of its members while protecting the total number in employment. (Note how this last sentence uses the wording of the question. This is often good practice.)

Exam-style multiple choice questions

1 C
2 B

Chapter 20

Progress check questions

1 Size – value of output, value of sales and value of capital employed in the business.

Ownership – private sector, public sector, mixture of each.

Other – stage of production.

2 Firms grow either from within or through a merger or takeover. Internal growth is usually a slow process as firms increase their output and market share. External growth is quicker and occurs when one firm takes over another firm or where two firms agree to a merger.

3 i Internal economies of scale, as the name suggests, are benefits that accrue to a firm from within its own business. In contrast, external economies of scale can benefit all firms in a particular location.

ii Economies of scale are the benefits to be gained by firms producing on a larger scale. They can be shown by falling long run average costs. Diseconomies of scale occur when long run average costs increase as the scale of output increases.

Structured skills practice

1 There are high costs of operating a steel-making plant.
- The market is dominated by large firms. Steel manufacture is a very competitive industry, with cutbacks in supply in many countries.

2 - Possible economies of scale are lower long run average costs due to lower fuel costs per passenger, discounts on bulk-buying supplies for passengers and lower average administrative costs.

- Possible diseconomies of scale are the difficulty of managing a larger number of passengers at airports, problems of communication and staff possibly feeling that they are providing a less than personal service.

Exam-style multiple choice questions

1. D
2. C
3. A

Chapter 21

Progress check questions

1. Production is the total output of a firm. Productivity is the output of a factor of production, for example the output of a person employed per hour or per day.
2. The reason is that it takes time to change factors of production. In the short run, a firm can change the number of workers it employs quite easily to increase or reduce production. Installing new capital equipment or building a new factory takes much more time. Such fixed factors can only change in the long run.
3. Capital-intensive: steel production, vehicle assembly, food production.

   Labour-intensive: agriculture, restaurants, retailing.

Structured skills practice

1.
   - An increase in the number of workers employed will increase total output.
   - Investment in new, more efficient machines will increase output per machine.
   - There are other possibilities such as an increase in the hours worked (production) and making bonus payments when production targets are exceeded (productivity).

Exam-style multiple choice questions

1. D
2. A

Chapter 22

Progress check questions

1. Average total cost = total cost / output
2. The average cost curve is best described as 'U-shaped'. This indicates that as output increases, average cost falls up to a point where it is at a minimum. Beyond this point, average cost begins to increase.
3. Profit is the difference between total revenue and total cost. This difference must be positive for a firm to earn profit.
4. An important concept when studying firms is that, in theory, firms aim to maximise their profits. This underpins how they respond to market conditions and is irrespective of whether they are small or large firms. Profit maximisation is pursued by many private sector firms and occurs when the positive gap between revenue and cost is greatest.

Structured skills practice

1.
   - Profit maximisation is the objective used in economic theory. It is difficult for firms to know how much they need to produce and at what price to sell their products to achieve this ideal.
   - There are more realistic objectives such as survival, social welfare and increasing sales. These objectives are more recognisable for all firms, irrespective of size.
   - The most likely conclusion is that there is a difference between economic theory and what actually happens in businesses. The content of the answer could be improved with references to types of firm such as a market stall, a small manufacturer or a publicly owned company, noting the problem of how to recognise where profits are maximised and why each has an alternative objective.

Exam-style multiple choice questions

1. B
2. A
3. C

Chapter 23

Progress check questions

1. A competitive market is one where there are a number of firms competing with each other. A more competitive market is one that has a large number of sellers and buyers, neither of whom can influence price. For this to occur, there has to be relatively free entry into and exit from the market.
2. Normal profit is when a firm earns just enough profit to keep producing in the short run. If it is

not earning this, then it is likely that the firm should leave this market. Abnormal (or supernormal) profit is when a firm earns profits higher than normal profit. In a competitive market, these profits will act as a clear signal for new firms to enter a market. As supply increases, the price of the product falls and profit returns to its normal level.

3 In India, for example, Indian Railways and Coal India are monopolies. Their monopoly power goes back many years through legislation that prohibits any other business from operating railways or mining coal. (Coal India's monopoly is under threat due to not meeting production targets.)

Structured skills practice

1
- A monopoly is defined as a single supplier in a market.
- A monopolist is often criticised for charging high prices due to a lack of competition. Other costs are that monopolists can be inefficient compared to a more competitive market, can sell products of poor quality and can be slow to respond to change.
- A monopolist with large-scale production can be more efficient than a smaller firm and benefit from economies of scale. A natural monopoly is desirable in certain situations – for example, high profits can fund research and development.
- So, in some, but not all, cases a monopoly can act in the best interests of consumers. The early part of the answer could be enhanced by including an inelastic demand curve that explains how the monopolist can fix a price but cannot control the quantity demanded.

Exam-style multiple choice questions

1 C

2 D

Exam-style structured questions for Section 3

Data response question

a A market with a single seller.

This is a basic definition.

b A public sector firm is government-owned. Its business is managed, overseen and regulated by the government.

This is mentioned in the first sentence. With 2 marks available, an elaboration is needed.

c
- Total production has increased.
- There was no particular growth in 2016.

The 2 marks indicate that two points are required.

d This means that fixed costs constitute a high proportion of total costs. Variable costs are therefore a smaller proportion. Typical examples of fixed costs are the capital costs of the steel making plant. The high percentage of fixed costs means that it is very important that the firm is using as much of its capacity as possible.

The identification of some fixed costs is fine, though explaining their significance is rather more difficult. The last sentence could be supplemented with something about the implication of high fixed costs for prices.

e
- There is a guaranteed market for steel rails (which means there is no threat from competitors).
- Monopoly can provide a cover-up for inefficiency (production targets have not been achieved).

There are 2 marks available for each advantage, 1 mark for identification and a further mark for the elaboration in brackets. The above suggested answers are drawn from the source material – others are possible as profits are likely to be high and there is little incentive for change.

f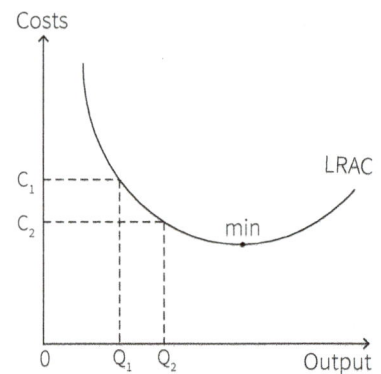

The above figure shows that long run average costs for SAIL fall as the scale of output increases. The LRAC curve falls steeply due to the high percentage of fixed costs in relation to total costs. At Q_1 the LRAC is C_1, then at a higher output, Q_2, it falls to C_2. SAIL is not operating at the minimum average cost although it is benefiting from economies of scale, as the LRAC clearly shows.

A very good answer that includes a reference to SAIL. The command word 'analyse' is used here as a prompt for a diagram to be used. This is not essential as the question does not require it – the diagram, though, makes the analysis clearer.

g As things stand, SAIL is operating in a protected market and it continues to let down Indian Railways through its inability to supply what is required annually. A more competitive market should result in lower prices for steel rails purchased by Indian Railways and may also improve the reliability of supply. It is also likely to make SAIL more efficient due to the threat of other producers moving in to supply this market.

This answer could be improved as it is short and only covers two possible benefits for Indian Railways. No potential costs are mentioned. These could include the fragmentation and possible uncertainty of supplies from private firms or the danger that, in the future, steel rails could end up being provided by a private monopoly. This is necessary given the 'discuss' command word of the question.

h The current level of subsidy received by Indian Railways is substantial. It is paid by the government to support its day-to-day passenger and freight services, and its investment in modernising the network. It is clear from the material provided that Indian Railways provides a vital, essential service in transporting people to work in cities, linking remote rural communities, contributing to tourism and moving freight in this huge country.

Whether or not more subsidy should be provided is a fair point. Some economists would argue that subsidy can lead to inefficiency, especially in a big organisation like Indian Railways. There are also opportunity cost considerations given that government funds are limited.

So, to conclude, given the scale and importance of railways to India, on balance there does seem a strong case for more subsidy, provided this is properly controlled.

The answer looks at both sides and finishes with a clear final sentence that answers the point of the question.

Four-part question

a A trade union is an organisation that represents its members and seeks to protect their interests in the workplace.

Two points are made.

b In a competitive market, wages are determined by the forces of demand and supply. A wage rate is a type of price and is therefore affected by any changes in the conditions of demand and supply. For example, if a firm demands more labour, and there are no other changes in the market, the wage rate will increase.

The answer could also mention the effect of increased supply on the wage rate. A diagram could also be used but is not essential.

c An important reason for the difference in earnings between skilled and unskilled workers is due to their supply. In general, there is a huge supply of unskilled workers and a much lower supply of skilled workers. This means that the supply of skilled labour is relatively inelastic – it is not very responsive to an increase in wage rates. Unskilled labour is price elastic with many workers willing to work for low wages. A related reason is that skilled workers, by definition, will have acquired more skills and educational qualifications. They are also likely to have more bargaining power with employers.

This is a good answer with relevant analysis. It would additionally benefit from some specific examples and a diagram.

d One thing the government could do is introduce a minimum wage. This should improve the earnings of the lowest paid unskilled workers. The government could also revise the benefits system and provide more help for those most in need.

Trade unions are likely to face more obstacles, not least because of their weak bargaining power when dealing with the concerns of unskilled workers. It is likely that some form of industrial action may have to take place and, even then, there is no certainty that the earnings of unskilled workers would increase.

So, to conclude, it would seem that the government rather than trade unions has more opportunity to increase the earnings of unskilled workers.

This is a well-structured answer, with a relevant conclusion. Reference could also have been made to how the government could fund training schemes to improve the skills of unskilled workers.

Section 4 Government and the macroeconomy

Chapter 24

Progress check questions

1. In Pakistan, for example:
   - Pakistan Railways and WAPDA (the Water and Power Development Agency) are state-owned and the responsibility of the national government.
   - The government is partway through an extensive privatisation programme which it believes will increase the country's economic growth.
   - The ministry of finance has a central role in determining government economic policy. The State Bank of Pakistan determines interest rates.

2. Governments can influence international trade through:
   - imposing tariffs and quotas on imports, and subsidies on exports
   - participation in the World Trade Organization and membership of trading groups such as ASEAN and MERCOSUR.

Structured skills practice

1. A typical answer could cover the role of government:
   - in setting local rates of taxation
   - in deciding how to allocate funds to different areas of public expenditure
   - in deciding whether to impose protective tariffs on certain imported goods.

   This is a very general question with many possible answers. Do make reference to an economy that you have studied as directed by the question.

Exam-style multiple choice questions

1. B
2. D

Chapter 25

Progress check questions

1. Actual economic growth occurs in the short run. It can be represented by a movement from within to the boundary of the PPC. Potential economic growth is shown by a shift outwards of the PPC, indicating that the economy is capable of producing more of each good.

2. Total demand: the total demand for a country's product at a given price level.

   Total supply: the total amount of goods and services that domestic firms are able to supply at a given price level.

3. This is a situation where those willing and able to work at the going wage rate can find employment. It is very difficult to put a percentage unemployment rate on this as it varies from one economy to the next.

4. The difficulty arises because the aims are conflicting. An economy at full employment is very likely to experience inflationary pressures due to the increase in total demand and increased costs of production. Prices will be increasing, which is not consistent with price stability.

Structured skills practice

1. i   Malaysia has a stronger performance in three of the four macroeconomic variables in 2016. Indonesia, though, has a higher rate of economic growth.

   ii
   - Comparatively, the higher rate of inflation in Indonesia is matched by a higher rate of unemployment. For Malaysia, inflation and unemployment rates are lower than in Indonesia.
   - This relationship does not match what might be expected in theory – a low rate of unemployment usually coincides with a high rate of inflation. (Information over a longer time period would allow a better conclusion to be made.)

Exam-style multiple choice questions

1. A
2. B

Chapter 26

Progress check questions

1. Budget deficit: government spending is greater than government revenue. It is used when there is a need to increase total demand to stimulate employment.

Budget surplus: government spending is less than government revenue. It is used when there is a need to reduce total demand to curb inflationary pressures.

2   Examples of taxes in Indonesia:

Direct taxes: income tax – regionally variable rates up to 40%

corporation tax – 25%

Indirect taxes: GST (goods and services tax) –10%

land tax – annual charge on buildings

vehicle taxes – various charges

petroleum tax – approx 25%

3   When the price elasticity of demand is elastic.

4   A government would use a contractionary fiscal policy when there is a need to reduce total demand. This is where the aim is to reduce inflation or to reduce expenditure on imports when there is a balance of payments deficit.

Structured skills practice

1
- Reducing taxation or increasing government spending will increase total demand.

- Reducing taxation, especially indirect taxation, will have a more immediate impact than increasing government spending.

- Reducing direct taxation is good because it puts additional disposable income directly into the pockets of consumers.

- It is likely that there will be inflationary pressure if taxes are reduced. This will depend on how close the economy is to full employment. This point is very relevant when writing a conclusion to this answer.

Exam-style multiple choice questions

1 A
2 B
3 C

Chapter 27

Progress check questions

1   Monetary policy controls total demand through changes in the money supply and the rate of interest. Fiscal policy controls total demand through changes in taxation and government spending.

2   An increase in the rate of interest will reduce consumer expenditure. This will reduce total demand by encouraging a rise in the foreign exchange rate. The price of exports will rise; the price of imports will fall resulting in lower net exports.

3   A government might decide to increase the rate of interest to encourage consumers to save more and spend less of their incomes. It is the usual policy response when the rate of inflation is increasing or there is a growing deficit of imports over exports.

Structured skills practice

1
- To reduce a problem of inflation, monetary policy can be used to increase the rate of interest, to cut back on the supply of money or to achieve a combination of both.

- The above policies will reduce total demand and inflationary pressure.

- Fiscal policy through reducing government spending or raising direct taxes on consumers will also reduce total demand.

- The underlying cause of the inflation may have to be tackled through supply-side policies, which can take time.

- Another issue is the particular rate of inflation that has to be reduced – if this is high, then other measures, as well as monetary policy, will need to be implemented.

Exam-style multiple choice questions

1 B
2 C

Chapter 28

Progress check questions

1   Supply-side polices are designed to increase total supply in the economy with the purpose of facilitating economic growth.

2   Deregulation and privatisation are supply-side polices which aim to improve the efficiency of an economy. They are based on the premise that competitive markets and private sector ownership are appropriate ways of improving competitiveness and, hence, the productive potential of an economy.

3   A typical example of a supply-side policy is where a government invests in education and training by encouraging more students to train for jobs or

more students to go to university. These are not short-term policies – it can take a few years for young people to be trained and for more university graduates to be educated.

A second supply-side policy is when a government reduces corporate taxes in order to encourage new investment. It takes time for firms to decide whether or not to invest and, if they do, it takes time for new capital items to be ready for production.

Structured skills practice

1.
   - Supply-side measures increase total supply.
   - Legislation to curb the power of trade unions could result in a reduced increase in wage rates and an increase in labour productivity.
   - Deregulation in markets will increase competition and drive down costs and prices.
   - Other measures include privatisation or increasing the numbers of migrant workers.

Exam-style multiple choice questions

1. B
2. B

Chapter 29

Progress check questions

1. By a change in real GDP, usually on an annual basis.
2. A recession is when there is a fall in real GDP over two quarters (six months) or more.
3. The main causes of economic growth are increases in the quantity and quality of productive resources available in an economy. Typical examples are through an increase in net investment or the size of the labour force (quantity of resources), and technological change and improved education (quality of resources).
4. Economic growth may not always be beneficial. Increased environmental pollution of the land, sea and air is a consequence of economic growth in virtually all economies. There are many recent examples such as the problems associated with the disposal of waste plastics, the poor air quality in many cities and discarding used batteries in the street. Natural resources and fisheries are being exploited to the point of near exhaustion as nearly all countries strive to increase their growth rates.

Structured skills practice

1.
   - A recession is when there have been two successive quarterly periods of a reduction in real GDP.
   - To move out of recession, the change in real GDP should be positive for at least two quarterly periods.
   - This is likely to be accompanied by a fall in the unemployment rate.

Exam-style multiple choice questions

1. C
2. B

Chapter 30

Progress check questions

1. Unemployment is usually measured by counting the total number of people who are without a job and who have been actively looking for employment in the past month.
2. Possible reasons are:
   - an increase in the number of unemployed school leavers or university graduates for demographic reasons
   - an increase in unemployment among factory workers due to new capital-intensive production methods.
3. Typically for India:

   Frictional unemployment: hotel workers in Goa who are casual labourers.

   Structural unemployment: garment workers replaced by machinery.

   Cyclical unemployment: financial services workers who become unemployed due to global recession.
4. See Chapter 28, answer to Q3. Each of these polices can be used to reduce unemployment. Retraining workers, young and old, provides new skills which aim to enhance employability. A fall in the rate of corporate taxation increases total demand, resulting in firms employing additional workers.

Structured skills practice

1.
   - Cyclical unemployment occurs when there is a lack of total demand or when the economy has experienced an external shock which has had a negative impact.

- Expansionary fiscal and monetary policies can reduce cyclical unemployment by increasing total demand.
- A reduction in taxation, an increase in government spending, a fall in the rate of interest and an increase in the money supply will boost total demand and reduce cyclical unemployment.

Exam-style multiple choice questions

1. B
2. B
3. A

Chapter 31

Progress check questions

1. Inflation occurs when there is a rise in the general price level in an economy. An index, often the consumer price index, is used to measure the change in prices from one year to another.

2. Cost-push inflation is caused by supply-side factors such as higher costs of production due to workers receiving large wage increases. Demand-pull inflation is caused by too much demand in the economy as a result of excessive tax reductions or increases in government spending.

3. At a time of rapid inflation, interest rates will be at a high level, usually below the prevailing rate of inflation. Savers receive the interest on their savings but lose out to borrowers who end up paying back less in real terms than what they borrowed.

4. Inflation can make the price of domestic exports uncompetitive relative to similar products made in a competitor economy with a lower inflation rate. The price of domestically produced goods may become uncompetitive compared to imported goods. Each will have an adverse effect on a country's balance of payments.

5. Consumers are reluctant to spend at a time of deflation in case prices fall even lower. This especially applies to 'big ticket' products such as cars and electronic goods.

Structured skills practice

1. - An increase in the rate of inflation means that the value of money has fallen – fewer goods can be bought for each unit of currency.

- Workers will clearly seek to maintain or even increase their wage rates in these circumstances, bringing them into conflict with employers.
- Employers will be mindful that an increase in the rate of inflation will also increase other costs as well as labour costs.
- The employer's reaction will depend on the extent to which any increased costs can be passed on to customers.
- It is also relevant to note that the degree of conflict is likely to depend on the financial position and stability of the firm, and the strength of the trade union. Both of these points will enhance the conclusion.

Exam-style multiple choice questions

1. D
2. B
3. C

Exam-style structured questions for Section 4

Data response question

a. Economic growth is when there is a rise in real GDP in an economy.

This is not a complete definition but it's adequate. An alternative definition could be in terms of the quantity and quality of resources in the economy (see part (f)).

b. Pakistan's growth rate increased over the period 2010 to 2016, with a slight upward trend. The year 2013 was a minor exception.

Two points are made, given 2 marks are available.

c. In theory, a fall in the unemployment rate will lead to an increase in economic growth. This is because more resources are being employed and adding to real GDP.

There is some evidence of this relationship from 2012 to 2016 when the increase in the growth rate coincided with a steady fall in the unemployment rate.

A very good answer could suggest a time lag before the fall in unemployment is reflected in an increased growth rate. Note how the two sets of data have different start points.

d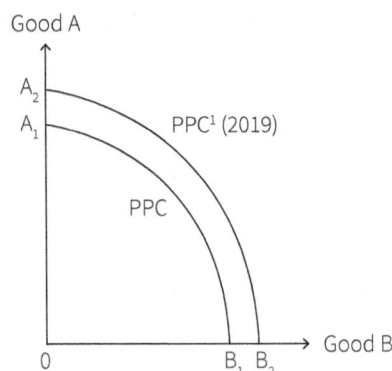

The diagram shows that, as a result of growth, the PPC has shifted outwards, indicating that more of each of the goods will be produced in 2019.

Be careful to label the axes correctly.

e A subsidy can be inefficient since there may be little or no incentive for firms to want to reduce the payments they receive from the government. This means that their costs are higher than they should be. Also, a producer may not pass on the full benefit of the subsidy to consumers in the form of lower prices.

The usual assumption is that subsidies are paid to producers and not consumers.

f The last paragraph of the source material refers to an increase in the quantity and quality of resources for promoting growth. The US$57bn Chinese investment in the China–Pakistan–Economic Corridor and the investment by the Pakistan government are examples of an increased quantity of resource for growth. The 'improvement' for electricity supply and roads is a means of increasing the quality of resources.

The point is clearly understood although the answer could be improved with reference to the possible quality gains through cutting inefficient subsidies and privatisation of loss-making public sector businesses.

g Supply-side policies are those that are designed to increase total supply. The infrastructure schemes referred to in the data are typical examples. The issue is really whether further supply-side policies could improve the competitiveness of Pakistan's manufacturing industry.

One obvious way would be to invest more in education and training, especially the latter, in order to upgrade the skills level of the working population. Another supply-side policy would be to reduce corporate taxes to allow firms to invest in more modern equipment and technology.

Whether or not the above policies would improve Pakistan's manufacturing competitiveness is by no means certain. It would also take time – the IMF stresses urgency. There is also much to be done to convince consumers in Pakistan that home-produced goods are more than a match for similar imports.

This is a very good answer. Supply-side policy is defined, two possible examples are provided and the third paragraph contains a clear discussion of the point of the question.

h The benefits and costs of growth are a controversial topic, especially for developing economies like Pakistan that are hoping to repeat the experience of other economies that are now developed.

A clear benefit of growth is that of improved living standards – people are better off and can afford more goods and services. Many may move out of absolute poverty. The government may also be able to help by providing more merit goods from its increased taxation.

There are costs of growth, too. These are clear to see in the world around us. Climate change and its devastating effects, the depletion of natural resources and the destruction of wildlife are making the world in which we live a less prosperous place.

This is a sound answer that could be improved by including a little more on the costs of growth and how growth might have affected the people of Pakistan. It could be further improved by a clear evaluation as to whether the benefits of growth outweigh the costs as far as the people are concerned.

Four-part question

a The unemployment rate is a percentage of the total unemployed divided by the total number in the labour force.

Note that the question asks for 'unemployment rate'.

b The introduction refers to:

  i graduate unemployment, which is a type of frictional unemployment

  ii unemployment in tourism, which is likely to be cyclical unemployment.

The drop in palm oil production (structural unemployment) could also be used.

c   Fiscal policy is used by governments to influence total demand through taxation and government spending. When there is a need to reduce the unemployment rate, as in Malaysia, there is a need to increase total demand. This can be done through an increase in government spending or a reduction in taxation or maybe a combination of both.

d   A supply-side policy is one that increases total supply. Graduate unemployment in Malaysia could be reduced if more job opportunities were available for these graduates.

One way that this could happen would be for the Malaysian government to provide tax incentives for companies to take on unemployed graduates. The government could pay a graduate's salary for, say, the first year of employment.

A second supply-side policy would be for graduates lacking in employability skills to be re-trained for work. The government could provide incentives for this to come about.

The problem with supply-side policies is that they take time to have any effect. There is also some uncertainty as to whether firms and unemployed graduates will respond to what might be offered.

This is a good answer. It could be improved by making more use of the introduction, in particular whether more graduates could work in the expanding industrial sector. The lack of jobs in the service sector is also bad news for many graduates.

Section 5 Economic development

Chapter 32

Progress check questions

1   Real GDP per head measures the goods and services that are typically available on average for people living in an economy. The measure is widely used since it takes into account differences in population size and is adjusted for inflation.

2   The simple answer is 'No'. A better measure for comparative purposes would be for GDP per head to be in terms of purchasing power parity as this takes into account the actual buying power of domestic currency when converted from US dollars. Many other factors need to be considered when making comparisons.

3   The distribution of income refers to the way in which income is shared among different groups in the economy. These groups are usually deciles (tenths) or quintiles (fifths). The distribution of income can be expressed in terms of the share of income, say 4%, earned by the poorest 20% of the population.

Structured skills practice

1
- The distribution of income is uneven in all economies. It is measured in terms of the percentage of the population relative to their share of income.
- The employment structure, especially the high percentage employed in agriculture, means that a large percentage of the population in developing economies earn very low incomes.
- There is also likely to be a lower percentage of the population in developing economies with professional or higher educational qualifications which invariably lead to higher incomes.
- Despite there being a greater proportion of higher earners in developed economies, they have less overall effect on the distribution of income.
- This is a very general question. It is worth noting in the conclusion that there may be exceptions in economies that have less emphasis on a market system.

Exam-style multiple choice questions

1   B

2   D

Chapter 33

Progress check questions

1   Absolute poverty is when people's income is below the poverty line, in other words, too low to enable them to meet their basic needs. Relative poverty is when people are poor relative to others and therefore cannot claim to enjoy the average standard of living.

2   A poor education is likely to mean that someone is only capable of doing low-paid work at best. This invariably means that they will earn a low income.

3   A new indirect tax will be regressive. The tax will affect poor people relatively more than

richer people, assuming both groups consume the product. The new tax will take up a higher proportion of the income of poorer people.

Structured skills practice

1.
   - Absolute poverty is where people's income is too low to enable them to meet their basic needs.
   - The USA is a large diverse economy – the cost of living varies enormously between cities such as New York and poor rural areas such as New Mexico.
   - The minimum level of income applies to an employed person in a low-paid job and to someone who is retired and much more able to exist on $11 000 per year.

Exam-style multiple choice questions

1. C
2. A

Chapter 34

Progress check questions

1. The main factors are birth rate, death rate and net migration.
2. The optimum population is the size of population which maximises a country's output per head.
3. A population pyramid is a diagram that shows the structure of a country's population in terms of gender and age (usually in five-year bands).

Structured skills practice

1.
   - The population of Italy is falling because the death rate is higher than the birth rate.
   - An obvious demographic factor is a falling birth rate.
   - A third possible reason is that net migration may be positive. This means that more Italians are leaving the country to live and work elsewhere than there are people from elsewhere obtaining permanent residence in Italy.

Exam-style multiple choice questions

1. C
2. B
3. C

Chapter 35

Progress check questions

1. Economic development and economic growth measure living standards in an economy and are therefore very close. Economic development, though, is wider and covers improvements in the economic welfare of a country's population.
2. Their economic development may be different due to variations in economic welfare. For example, there may be differences in education and health – free education and free healthcare in one country but not in the other. The nature of work and working conditions may be harder in one country compared to the other. People in one country may be happier than those in the other country and experience much greater freedom in their daily lives.
3. Two reasons are:
   - a high rate of population growth – this means that resources have to be used to feed and educate the increased population
   - external debt – most developing economies have had to borrow from developed economies and the World Bank. Interest charges and the repayment of loans can seriously affect the ability of a developing economy to spend on services such as improving education and healthcare.

Structured skills practice

1.
   - Economic development occurs when a country is able to improve the economic welfare of its people.
   - Two ways in which this could happen are through more investment into education and healthcare, both merit goods.
   - These two merit goods are important for improving the quality of people's lives from an economic and social perspective.
   - There are other ways to improve economic development including increasing investment by the private and public sectors, and increasing exports.

Exam-style multiple choice questions

1. A
2. B

Exam-style structured questions for Section 5

Data response question

a   Purchasing power parity is a way of taking into account what a currency is able to buy in a particular country.

This is a reasonable definition. Be careful not to confuse PPP and the 'real' in real GDP per head.

b   This refers to those whose income is below the level necessary to enable them to meet their basic essential needs.

Very similar to 'absolute poverty'.

c   A greater percentage of expenditure on healthcare. Lower percentage of population below poverty line.

The question implies that you need to use the information in Table S5.1. Other reasons not in the table could be better sanitation and control of infectious diseases, cultural factors and better working conditions.

d   India's economic development could be improved if the adult literacy rate increased. This would mean that more people could be trained and assisted to get jobs in the emerging manufacturing and service sectors.

Economic development could also occur if there was a switch of resources from agriculture to more productive sectors.

Be careful to only use information from the table as directed by the question.

e   India's population pyramid is more even than that of China. There is also a higher proportion of its population under 20 years of age. India has more males than females in almost all age groups. China has a larger proportion of its population in the 80+ age group.

Four valid points. The question is only asking for a comparison of the two shapes. Note how the answer is written in a comparative way.

f   The short answer is 'Yes'. Future population can be determined by taking the last two bands (5–9 and 0–4 age groups) and moving them upwards. Given the life expectancy information, if the 65–69 and 70–74 age groups were removed, then more people would be dying off relative to those in the younger age groups.

This is not an easy question. Reference to the birth rate is outside the scope of the question.

g   There are two aspects to be considered. First, the ageing population will mean a fall in the quantity of workers that are in the productive labour force. Potentially, this will have an adverse effect on future economic development. The ageing population will be an increasing burden for the government and families. More resources will have to be allocated for healthcare and there is also the opportunity cost involved when members of a family have to look after ageing relatives. The opportunity cost is that these resources could be used more productively to increase economic development.

These are valid points but it lacks an overall conclusion. The answer could be improved by noting that the evidence provided seems to indicate that China's ageing population is a real constraint on future economic development.

h   Referring to the table of data, an increase in the savings ratio would lead to an increase in investment. In particular, this could be used to improve India's infrastructure, transport, energy and sanitation especially. This would lead to an increase in the growth rate and help to close the substantial gap in GDP per head compared with China.

This is just one of a range of policies that could be used. Others include various supply-side policies such as improving literacy rates, training workers from poor households and making it easier for foreign businesses to set up in India. These are all policies that China has used to enhance its economic development.

It is difficult, if not impossible, to identify one particular policy since what is needed is a combination of the above and other policies that have the common objective of closing the gap in economic development compared to China.

This is a very good answer that is focused on the point of the question throughout. It has a highly appropriate last sentence.

Four-part question

a   Absolute poverty occurs when a household's income is too low to enable basic needs of food and housing to be met.

This is a basic definition, not to be confused with relative poverty.

b Two causes of absolute poverty are:
   i   earnings are insufficient to meet basic needs
   ii the family has many dependants who are unable to earn wages.

   Although in employment, the wages that are paid to household members are low and insufficient to meet basic needs.

   In many developing economies, there are large families with few earners. Family members who earn a wage are required to support old relatives and young children.

   The answer could be better set out on the same basis as other examples of this type, namely identification followed by explanation.

c Given the nature of the absolute poverty, one way of trying to reduce it is to provide more support for subsistence agriculture. This could involve giving advice on how to improve crop yields, how to develop marketable crops and, possibly, measures designed to increase the size of agricultural holding in order to increase efficiency.

   Such measures would require additional government funds. There may also be limited opportunities for subsistence farmers to take on part-time work, say, in tourism.

   To comply with the 'analysis' command word, the answer could be improved by a brief analysis of how the support for agriculture and part-time job opportunities for farmers affect their disposable incomes.'

d There are a range of policies that can be used to alleviate poverty. These include

   a progressive tax system, a minimum wage, a state benefits system to support the less-well-off and foreign aid.

   The first three, if effectively applied, could lead to a redistribution of income. For example, a progressive tax system charges higher rates of income tax on high earners compared to those on lower earnings. Receipts from this tax could be used to assist families on low incomes. An equitable benefits system can also assist those households on low levels of income and who are in need.

   Whether any of these policies is effective in redistributing income is difficult to say. From past experience, any noticeable change takes time and is likely to be very minor.

A very good concluding paragraph. Possibly a sentence could be added to describe the two policies that are mentioned but that have not been explained.

Section 6 International trade and globalisation

Chapter 36

Progress check questions

1 Specialisation is the process by which an economy concentrates on producing those goods and services where they have an advantage over others.

2 Specialisation occurs for many reasons mainly related to the quantity and quality of resources available. For example, Brazil, Vietnam and Indonesia specialise in growing coffee due to having fertile land and the type of climate that produces a good supply. Mauritius has good beaches, a pleasant climate and a good supply of labour to specialise in international tourism. India has a growing number of well-educated young people working in financial services and call centres.

3 Advantage – specialisation can lead to a higher output and higher living standards. Firms are able to concentrate on producing those products in which they have a specialisation and further develop their advantage.

   Disadvantage – there is a risk that a country's specialisation could be undermined by others who may gain strong control over the market.

Structured skills practice

1 • The specialisation depends on the quality and quantity of resources available in each country.
   • China especially, but other Asian economies also, have an abundance of relatively cheap labour and the manufacturing skills, and capacity, to make iPhones more cheaply than the USA.
   • The USA has very well-qualified technical expertise, built up over many years, to develop and design iPhone products.

Exam-style multiple choice questions

1 A
2 A

Chapter 37

Progress check questions

1. Globalisation is the term used to describe the ways in which the world is increasingly becoming interconnected through trade, transport and communications.

2. The host developing economy will benefit in terms of job creation, although the extent will depend on the degree of automation of the assembly plant and how many staff move from Germany. Some local firms may benefit through the provision of supporting services for the plant and possibly through supplying components. The balance of payments is likely to benefit since fewer vehicles will now have to be imported. The motor manufacturer may have to pay taxes to the host country government; this revenue can be used for the wider benefit of the population.

3. A tariff is a tax on imported goods. A quota is a physical restriction on imported goods.

4. The government of a developing economy may wish to protect infant industries from external competition as its development strategy is to increase the proportion of GDP generated by industry. A new sunrise firm could be given subsidies to help the competitiveness of its products in domestic, as well as export markets. Import tariffs could give further support. There may also be a short-term case for protecting a declining industry in order to buy time for alternative supplies to be provided.

    The government of a developing economy may also protect its agricultural industry for strategic regions such as safeguarding food supplies.

Structured skills practice

1.
   - The EU is a customs union which primarily seeks to protect the interests of its member states, including their agricultural sectors.
   - Subsidies are used to safeguard the livelihoods of farmers in less efficient producing regions.
   - Subsidies are controversial since they result in higher retail food prices for all EU consumers.
   - The tariffs on imported food are usually levied only on food products that the EU is able to produce for itself, such as dairy products and many types of vegetables.
   - It is a controversial policy since it discriminates against some countries producing similar products to those that are being subsidised. Many of these are developing economies.
   - In conclusion, the evidence would indicate that, on balance, taking a global view, the policies are not fully justified.

Exam-style multiple choice questions

1. B
2. C
3. B

Chapter 38

Progress check questions

1. A floating exchange rate can change frequently through market forces; a fixed exchange rate does not change, other than when the government decides to devalue or revalue its currency.

2. Reasons:
   - to pay for increased imports from another country
   - to pay for a firm moving from its home base to another country.

3. Reasons:
   - when fewer exports are sold to other countries
   - when there is a decrease in the number of international tourists.

4. The depreciation of a currency should lead to a reduction in export prices and a relative increase in the price of imported goods and services. The net effect is important and should lead to less of a deficit on the balance of payments. The increase in the price of imported goods could see consumers switch to locally produced goods. This will increase domestic employment.

5. A fixed exchange rate has the advantage that firms and consumers know what value to plan for when trading. It is more difficult to predict the exchange rate when it depends on so many other factors.

Structured skills practice

1.
   - If the renminbi is over-valued, it means that exports of Chinese goods are cheaper than they should be in their trading partners. Imports of goods into China are in contrast more

expensive than they should be and are often not competitive compared to Chinese-made goods.

- For the US economy, it means a massive import bill for Chinese goods. It can also mean an increase in unemployment in those businesses that are in direct competition with Chinese producers.
- For the Chinese economy, it means that the value of imported goods is less than if the renminbi is revalued. Exports of goods remain competitive.

Exam-style multiple choice questions

1 A
2 C
3 B

Chapter 39

Progress check questions

1 Balance of trade: exports of goods and services − imports of goods and services

   Current account balance: balance of trade + primary income + secondary income

2 These are recorded as 'export of services'.

3 Causes of a deficit in the current account: an overvalued exchange rate which makes import prices relatively cheap; an increase in domestic incomes leading to an increase in demand for imports.

   Consequences of a deficit on the current account: the increased demand for imports is likely to have a negative impact on domestic employment as firms will experience falling demand. The government may have to borrow to finance the deficit.

4 Causes of a surplus on the current account: a strong demand for exports following a depreciation of the currency may lead to a surplus on the current account.

   Consequences of a surplus on the current account: an increase in employment, particularly in export industries. Inflationary pressures due to increased total demand.

5 A depreciation of a currency should have a positive effect on a country's current balance. The depreciation will lead to a decrease in export prices and a relative increase in import prices. The effect on the balance of trade should be positive depending on the price elasticity of demand for exports and imports. The depreciation of the currency may lead to an increase in receipts from international tourism.

Structured skills practice

1
- A deficit on the current account of the balance of payments is when the trade in goods and services exports is less than the trade in goods and services imports.
- The obvious policy is to cut back on imports and increase exports of goods and services.
- This can be done by a depreciation of the currency or by imposing protectionist measures to reduce imports.
- There could also be a local campaign to get residents to purchase domestically produced goods rather than imports.

Exam-style multiple choice questions

1 B
2 B
3 D

Exam-style structured questions for Section 6

Data response question

a The balance of trade consists of the difference between the exports and imports of goods and services.

   This is a basic definition.

b Pakistan's balance of trade has been consistently in deficit, while Malaysia's has been in surplus. Pakistan's balance of trade has deteriorated, while Malaysia's has been reasonably stable. The fluctuations in Pakistan's balance of trade have been greater than those for Malaysia.

   Include any two of the above, but make sure your answer is a comparison.

c Floating exchange rate. The source material indicates that the Bank of Pakistan 'did not intervene' when the rupee fell by over 3% in one day.

   The answer to a question like this is usually found in the source material as you would not be expected to know the detail.

d Two differences are:

i Primary income includes net earnings from residents working abroad.

ii Secondary income includes gifts and aid.

The above were previously called income and current transfers.

e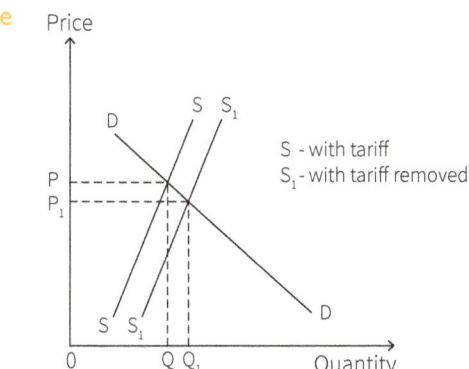

The removal of the tariff results in a fall in the price of imported vehicles from P to P_1. This leads to an increase in the quantity traded from Q to Q_1.

This provides clear reference to the diagram, which is a good way of tackling this question.

f One reason could be that, even after the removal of the tariff, the price of imported vehicles is still not competitive with those manufactured in Malaysia.

Another reason could be non-price factors such as Malaysian consumers preferring to buy locally made vehicles rather than imports or preferring the style of Malaysian vehicles.

A good approach to this question is to answer in terms of the determinants of demand. Another reason could be that incomes in Malaysia have fallen and fewer vehicles are being purchased.

g The fall or depreciation in Pakistan's currency will make imported goods more expensive for consumers in Pakistan. The effect will depend on the price elasticity of demand for these imports – goods that are essential are likely to continue to be consumed at the same level as before the depreciation.

For Pakistan's trading partners, the effect will depend upon the volume and importance of goods they buy from Pakistan. If they do trade, goods from Pakistan will become a little bit cheaper depending on the scale of the depreciation.

The point is understood but the discussion could be improved. The price elasticity of demand for imports and exports should be amplified. A really good point would be to stress the apparent lack of competitiveness of Pakistan's manufactured goods.

h Pakistan has a deteriorating deficit, while Malaysia has a steady surplus. It would seem that the Pakistan government ought to be most concerned because it appears to lack the resources and policies to improve this situation. It is also heavily dependent on the remittances from Pakistani workers overseas.

Malaysia could face the problem of its currency appreciating. This would make its imports cheaper and its exports more expensive. This is maybe not particularly serious, though, compared to Pakistan's position.

Note that the question is about the 'current account position' and not just the balance of trade. Given the evidence, the overall conclusion is that Pakistan should be most concerned. This point should be stressed.

Four-part question

a Free trade occurs when there are no restrictions on the products bought from abroad or sold by firms to other countries.

This is a sound definition.

b Advantage – a more efficient allocation of resources as countries can specialise in producing those goods that they can produce more cheaply than other countries.

Disadvantage – an economy's balance of trade could be adversely affected by the dumping of cheap imported goods.

Two relevant explanations are given.

c Multinational corporations can affect various parts of the current account of the balance of payments such as:

- Primary income – profits gained in the host developing economy are sent back to the home country.

- Balance of trade in goods and services. MNCs may add to the import bill of a developing economy, although this could be offset by export sales. There could also be an impact on trade in services through travel payments and expenditure on financial services.

This is a difficult question in some respects as it requires a link to be explained between the activities of MNCs and the current account.

d   This is a controversial topic. Infant industries can be protected with tariffs (taxes on imported substitutes), quotas (physical limits on similar imports) or subsidies provided by the government. These measures seek to protect an infant industry from foreign competition to allow it to grow, and become more competitive in domestic and overseas markets.

The main disadvantage is that once a protective measure is in place, it becomes difficult to remove it. The industry tends to rely on the protection. Consumers could be disadvantaged by protection – the prices they have to pay in the domestic market could be higher than what they might pay for imports if there were no protection.

Some reference could be made to economies of scale in the first paragraph. There is some discussion but the answer lacks a clear final assessment.

Glossary

Absolute poverty: where people's income is too low to enable them to meet their basic needs.

Actual economic growth: an increase in the output of an economy.

Ageing population: an increase in the average age of the population.

Aggregation: the addition of individual components to arrive at a total amount.

Appreciation: a rise in the value of a floating exchange rate.

Automatic stabilisers: forms of government expenditure and taxation that reduce fluctuations in economic activity, without any change in government policy.

Average fixed cost: total fixed cost divided by output.

Average revenue: the total revenue divided by the quantity sold – which is the same as price.

Average total cost: total cost divided by output.

Average variable cost: total variable cost divided by output.

Balance of payments: the record of a country's economic transactions with other countries.

Barrier to entry: anything that makes it difficult for a firm to start producing a product.

Barrier to exit: anything that makes it difficult for a firm to stop making the product.

Birth rate: the number of births in a year per 1000 population.

Budget: the relationship between government revenue and government spending.

Budget deficit: government spending is higher than government revenue.

Budget surplus: government revenue is higher than government spending.

Capital/capital goods: human-made goods used in production.

Capital-intensive: the use of a high proportion of capital relative to labour.

Casual unemployment: unemployment arising from workers regularly being between periods of employment.

Central bank: a government-owned bank which provides banking services to the government and commercial banks and operates monetary policy.

Changes in demand: shifts in the demand curve.

Changes in supply: changes in supply conditions causing shifts in the supply curve.

Circular flow of income: the movement of expenditure, income and output around the economy.

Claimant count: a measure of unemployment which counts as unemployed those in receipt of unemployment benefits.

Collective bargaining: representatives of workers negotiating with employers' associations.

Commercial banks: banks which aim to make a profit by providing a range of banking services to households and firms.

Competitive market: a market with a number of firms that compete with each other.

Complement: a product that is used together with another product.

Conglomerate merger: a merger between firms producing different products.

Consumer goods: goods and services purchased by households for their own satisfaction.

Consumer prices index (CPI): a measure of the weighted average of the prices of a representative basket of goods and services.

Consumption: expenditure by households on consumer goods and income.

Contraction in demand: a fall in the quantity demanded caused by a rise in the price of the product itself.

Contraction in supply: a fall in the quantity supplied caused by a fall in the price of the product itself.

Contractionary fiscal policy: cuts in government expenditure and/or rises in taxation designed to reduce total demand.

Contractionary monetary policy: cuts in the money supply and/or an increase in the rate of interest designed to reduce total demand.

Corporation tax: a tax on profits of a company.

Cost-push inflation: rises in the price level caused by higher costs of production.

Current account balance: a record of the income received and expenditure made by a country in its dealings with other countries.

Cyclical unemployment: unemployment caused by a lack of total demand.

Death rate: the number of deaths in a year per 1000 population.

Declining industries: old industries which are going out of business.

Decrease in demand: a fall in demand at any given price, causing the demand curve to shift to the left.

Decrease in supply: a fall in supply at any given price, causing the supply curve to shift to the left.

Deflation: a sustained fall in the prices of goods and services.

Demand: the willingness and ability to buy a product.

Demand-pull inflation: rises in the price level caused by excess demand.

Demerit goods: products which the government considers are not fully appreciated by consumers in terms of how harmful they are and which will therefore be over-consumed if left to market forces. Such goods generate negative externalities.

Dependency ratio: the proportion of the population that has to be supported by the labour force.

Depreciation: a fall in the value of a floating exchange rate.

Depreciation (capital consumption): the value of capital goods that have worn out or become obsolete.

Deregulation: the removal of rules and regulations.

Devaluation: a fall in the value of a fixed exchange rate.

Directives: state instructions given to state-owned enterprises.

Direct provision: where a government provides essential goods and services.

Direct taxes: taxes on the income and wealth of individuals and firms.

Diseconomies of scale: higher long run average costs arising from a firm or industry growing in size.

Disequilibrium: a situation where demand and supply are not equal.

Disinflation: a fall in the rate of inflation.

Disposable income: income after income tax has been deducted and state benefits received.

Division of labour: workers specialising in particular tasks.

Dumping: selling products in a foreign market at a price below the cost of production.

Dynamic efficiency: efficiency occurring over time as a result of investment and innovation.

Earnings: the total pay received by a worker.

Economic agents: those who undertake economic activities and make economic decisions.

Economic development: an improvement in economic welfare.

Economic good: a product which requires resources to produce it and therefore has an opportunity cost.

Economic growth: an increase in the output of an economy and, in the long run, an increase in the economy's productive potential.

Economic problem: unlimited wants exceeding finite resources.

Economic system: the institutions, organisations and mechanisms that influence economic behaviour and determine how resources are allocated.

Economically active: those in the labour force, both the employed and the unemployed.

Economically inactive: those not in the labour force.

Economies of scale: lower long run average costs resulting from a firm or industry growing in size.

Elastic demand: when the quantity demanded changes by a greater percentage than the change in price.

Elastic supply: when the quantity supplied changes by a greater percentage than the change in price.

Elasticity of demand for labour: a measure of the responsiveness of demand for labour to a change in the wage rate.

Elasticity of supply of labour: a measure of the responsiveness of the supply of labour to a change in the wage rate.

Embargo: a ban on imports or exports.

Emigration: the act of leaving a country to live in another country.

Employment: being involved in a productive activity for which a payment is received.

Enterprise: risk bearing and key decision making in business.

Entrepreneur: a person who bears the risks and makes the key decisions in a business.

Equilibrium price: the price where demand and supply are equal.

Excess demand: the amount by which demand is greater than supply.

Excess supply: the amount by which supply is greater than demand.

Exchange control: a limit on the amount of foreign currency that can be obtained.

Expansionary fiscal policy: rises in government expenditure and/or cuts in taxation designed to increase total demand.

Expansionary monetary policy: increases in the money supply and/or a reduction in the rate of interest designed to increase total demand.

Extension in demand: a rise in the quantity demanded caused by a fall in the price of the product itself.

Extension in supply: a rise in the quantity supplied caused by a rise in the price of the product itself.

External benefits: benefits enjoyed by those who are not directly involved in the consumption and production activities of others.

External costs: costs imposed on those who are not directly involved in the consumption and production activities of others.

External diseconomies of scale: higher long run average costs arising from an industry growing too large.

External economies of scale: lower long run average costs resulting from an industry growing in size.

External growth: an increase in the size of a firm resulting from it merging or taking over another firm.

Factors of production: the economic resources of land, labour, capital and enterprise.

Fiscal policy: decisions on government spending and taxation designed to influence total demand.

Fixed costs: costs which do not change with output in the short run.

Fixed exchange rate: an exchange rate whose value is set at a particular level in terms of another currency or currencies.

Flat taxes: taxes with a single rate.

Flexible labour force: a labour force which adjusts quickly and smoothly to changes in market conditions.

Floating exchange rate: an exchange rate which can change frequently as it is determined by market forces.

Foreign direct investment (FDI): setting up production units or buying existing production units in another country.

Foreign exchange rate: the price of one currency in terms of another currency or currencies.

Free good: a product which does not require any resources to make it and so does not have an opportunity cost.

Free international trade: the exchange of goods and services between countries without any restrictions.

Free rider: someone who consumes a good or service without paying for it.

Frictional unemployment: temporary unemployment arising from workers being in between jobs.

Full employment: the lowest level of unemployment possible.

Genuine Progress Indicator (GPI): a measure of living standards which takes into account a variety of indicators including income, leisure time, distribution of income and environmental standards.

Geographically immobile: incapable of moving from one location to another location.

Globalisation: the process by which the world is becoming increasingly interconnected through trade and other links.

Gross domestic product (GDP): the total output of a country.

Gross investment: total spending on capital goods.

Horizontal merger: the merger of firms producing the same product and at the same stage of production.

Hot money flows: the movement of money around the world to take advantage of differences in interest rates and exchange rates.

Human Development Index (HDI): a measure of living standards which takes into account income, education and life expectancy.

Hyperinflation: a very rapid and large rise in the price level.

Improvements in technology: advances in the quality of capital goods and methods of production.

Increase in demand: a rise in demand at any given price, causing the demand curve to shift to the right.

Increase in supply: a rise in supply at any given price, causing the supply curve to shift to the right.

Index-linking: changing payments in line with changes in the inflation rate.

Indirect taxes: taxes on goods and services, that is, taxes on expenditure.

Individual demand: a consumer's demand for a product.

Individual supply: supply from one firm.

Industrial action: when workers disrupt production to put pressure on employers to agree to their demands.

Industry: a group of firms producing the same product.

Inelastic demand: when the quantity demanded changes by a smaller percentage than the change in price.

Inelastic supply: when the quantity supplied changes by a smaller percentage than the change in price.

Infant industries: new industries with relatively low output and high cost.

Infant mortality rate: the number of deaths in a year per 1000 live births.

Inferior goods: a product whose demand decreases when income increases and increases when income falls.

Inflation: a rise in the price level of goods and services over time.

Inflation rate: the percentage rise in the price level of goods and services over time.

Informal economy: that part of the economy that is not regulated, protected or taxed by the government.

Internal diseconomies of scale: higher long run average costs arising from a firm growing too large.

Internal economies of scale: lower long run average costs resulting from a firm growing in size.

Internal growth: an increase in the size of a firm resulting from it enlarging existing plants or opening new ones.

International Monetary Fund (IMF): an international organisation which promotes international trade and global financial stability and helps countries with balance of payments problems.

Investment: spending on capital goods.

Labour: human effort used in producing goods and services.

Labour force: people in work and those actively seeking work.

Labour Force Survey (ILO) Measure: a measure of unemployment which counts as unemployed people who identify as such in a survey.

Labour-intensive: the use of a high proportion of labour relative to capital.

Labour market participation rate: the proportion of the working-age population who are in the labour force.

Labour productivity: output per worker hour.

Land: gifts of nature available for production.

Liquidity: being able to turn an asset into cash quickly without a loss.

Local government: a government organisation with the authority to administer a range of policies within an area of the country.

Long run: the time period when all factors of production can be changed and all costs are variable.

Lottery: the drawing of tickets to decide who will get the products.

Macroeconomics: the study of the whole economy.

Market: an arrangement which brings buyers into contact with sellers.

Market demand: total demand for a product.

Market disequilibrium: a situation where demand and supply are not equal at the current price.

Market economic system: an economic system where consumers determine what is produced, resources are allocated by the price mechanism and land and capital are privately owned.

Market equilibrium: a situation where demand and supply are equal at the current price.

Market failure: market forces resulting in an inefficient allocation of resources.

Market structure: the conditions which exist in a market including the number of firms.

Market supply: total supply of a product.

Menu costs: costs involved in having to change prices as a result of inflation.

Merger: where two or more firms join together to form one new firm.

Merit goods: products which the government considers are not fully appreciated by consumers in terms of how beneficial they are and which will therefore be under-consumed if left to market forces. Such goods generate positive externalities.

Microeconomics: the study of the behaviour and decisions of households and firms and the performance of individual markets.

Mixed economic system: an economy in which both the private and public sectors play an important role.

Mobility of capital: the ability to change where capital is used or in which occupation.

Mobility of enterprise: the ability to change where enterprise is used or in which occupation.

Mobility of labour: the ability of labour to change where it works or in which occupation.

Monetarists: a group of economists who think that inflation is caused by the money supply growing more rapidly than output.

Monetary inflation: rises in the price level caused by an excessive growth of the money supply.

Monetary policy: decisions on the money supply, the rate of interest and the exchange rate taken to influence total demand.

Money: any item which is generally acceptable as a means of payment.

Monopoly: a market with a single supplier.

Mortgage: a loan to help buy a house.

Multinational companies (MNCs): companies which produce in more than one country.

Multiplier effect: the final impact on total demand being greater than the initial change.

National champions: industries that are, or have the potential to be, world leaders.

National debt: the total amount the government has borrowed over time.

National minimum wage (NMW): a minimum rate of wage for an hour's work, fixed by the government for the whole economy.

Nationalisation: moving the ownership and control of an industry from the private sector to the government.

Natural monopoly: an industry where a single firm can produce at a lower average cost than two or more firms because of the existence of significant economies of scale.

Negative net investment: a reduction in the number of capital goods caused by some obsolete and worn out capital goods not being replaced.

Net immigration: more people coming to live in a country than people leaving the country to live elsewhere.

Net investment: gross investment minus depreciation.

Net migration: the difference between immigration and emigration.

Nominal GDP: GDP at current market prices and so not adjusted for inflation.

Normal goods: a product whose demand increases when income increases and decreases when income falls.

Normal profit: the minimum level of profit required to keep a firm in the industry in the long run.

Occupationally mobile: capable of changing use.

Opportunity cost: the best alternative forgone.

Optimum population: the size of population which maximises the country's output per head.

Output: goods and services produced by the factors of production.

Perfectly elastic demand: when a change in price causes a complete change in the quantity demanded.

Perfectly elastic supply: when a change in price causes a complete change in quantity supplied.

Perfectly inelastic demand: when a change in price has no effect on the quantity demanded.

Perfectly inelastic supply: when a change in price has no effect on the quantity supplied.

Planned economic system: an economic system where the government makes the crucial decisions, land and capital are state-owned and resources are allocated by directives.

Population pyramid: a diagram showing the age and gender structure of a country's population.

Potential economic growth: an increase in an economy's productive capacity.

Price: the amount of money that has to be given to obtain a product.

Price elasticity of demand (PED): a measure of the responsiveness of the quantity demanded to a change in price.

Price elasticity of supply (PES): a measure of the responsiveness of the quantity supplied to a change in price.

Price fixing: when two or more firms agree to sell a product at the same price.

Price mechanism: the system by which the market forces of demand and supply determine prices.

Price stability: the price level in the economy not changing significantly over time.

Primary income: income earned by people working in different countries and investment income which comes into and goes out of the country.

Primary sector: covers agriculture, fishing, forestry, mining and other industries which extract natural resources.

Private benefits: benefits received by those directly consuming or producing a product.

Private costs: costs borne by those directly consuming or producing a product.

Private good: a product which is both rival and excludable.

Private sector: businesses owned by individuals or shareholders.

Privatisation: the sale of public sector assets to the private sector.

Production: total output.

Production possibility curve (PPC): a curve that shows the maximum output of two types of product and the combination of those products that can be produced with existing resources and technology.

Productively efficient: when products are produced at the lowest possible cost and making full use of resources.

Productivity: the output per factor of production in an hour.

Profit maximisation: making as much profit as possible.

Profit satisficing: sacrificing some profit to achieve other goals.

Progressive tax: one which takes a larger percentage of the income or wealth of the rich.

Proportional tax: one which takes the same percentage of the income or wealth of all taxpayers.

Public corporation: a business organisation owned by the government which is designed to act in the public interest.

Public good: a product which is non-rival and non-excludable and hence needs to be financed by taxation.

Public sector: the part of the economy controlled by the government.

Purchasing power parity (PPP): an exchange rate based on the ratio of the price of a basket of products in different countries.

Quaternary sector: covers service industries that are knowledge based.

Quota: a limit placed on imports or exports.

Rate of interest: a charge for borrowing money and a payment for lending money.

Rationalisation: eliminating unnecessary equipment and plant to make a firm more efficient.

Rationing: a limit on the amount that can be consumed.

Real GDP: GDP at constant prices and so adjusted for inflation.

Real GDP per head: real GDP divided by size of population.

Real income: income adjusted for inflation.

Recession: a reduction in real GDP over a period of six months or more.

Regional unemployment: unemployment caused by a decline in job opportunities in a particular area of the country.

Regressive tax: one which takes a larger percentage of the income or wealth of the poor.

Regulation: various means by which governments seek to control production and consumption.

Relative poverty: where people are poor in comparison to others in their country; their income is too low to enable them to enjoy the average standard of living in their country.

Resources: factors used to produce goods and services.

Revaluation: a rise in the value of a fixed exchange rate.

Savings ratio: the proportion of household disposable income that is saved.

Scale of production: the size of production units and the methods of production used.

Scarcity: a situation where there is not enough to satisfy everyone's wants.

Search unemployment: unemployment arising from workers who have lost their jobs looking for a job they are willing to accept.

Seasonal unemployment: unemployment caused by a fall in demand at particular times of the year.

Secondary income: transfers between residents and non-residents of money, goods or services, not in return for anything else.

Secondary sector: covers manufacturing and construction industries.

Shoe-leather costs: costs involved in moving money around to gain high interest rates.

Social benefits: the total benefits to a society of an economic activity.

Social costs: the total costs to a society of an economic activity.

Socially optimum output: the level of output where social cost equals social benefit and society's welfare is maximised.

Specialisation: the concentration on particular products or tasks.

State-owned enterprises (SOEs): organisations owned by the government which sell products.

Strategic industries: industries that are considered important for the survival or development of the country.

Strike: a group of workers stopping work to put pressure on an employer to agree to their demands.

Structural unemployment: unemployment caused by long-term changes in the pattern of demand and methods of production.

Subsidy: a payment by a government to encourage the production or consumption of a product.

Subsistence agriculture: the output of agricultural goods for farmers' personal use.

Substitute: a product that can be used in place of another.

Sunk costs: costs that cannot be recovered if the firm leaves the industry.

Supernormal profit: profit above that needed to keep a firm in the market in the long run.

Supply: the willingness and ability to sell a product.

Supply-side policy: measures designed to increase total supply.

Sustainable economic growth: economic growth that does not endanger the country's ability to grow in the future.

Tariff: a tax on imports.

Tax: a payment to the government.

Technological unemployment: unemployment caused by workers being replaced by capital equipment.

Tertiary sector: covers industries which provide services.

Third parties: those not directly involved in producing or consuming a product.

Total cost: the total cost of production.

Total demand: the total demand for a country's product at a given price level – it consists of consumer expenditure, investment, government spending and net exports (exports minus imports).

Total revenue: the total amount of money received from selling a product.

Total supply: the total amount of goods and services that domestic firms are willing to supply at a given price level

Trade bloc: a regional group of countries that remove trade restrictions between themselves.

Trade in goods: the value of exported goods and the value of imported goods.

Trade in goods deficit: expenditure on imported goods exceeding revenue from exported goods.

Trade in goods surplus: revenue from exported goods exceeding expenditure on imports.

Trade in services: the value of exported services and the value of imported services.

Trade in service surplus: revenue from exported services exceeding expenditure on imported services.

Trade union: an association which represents the interests of a group of workers.

Transfer payments: transfers of income from one group to another not in return for providing a good or service.

Unemployment: being without a job while willing and able to work.

Unemployment rate: the percentage of the labour force who are willing and able to work but are without jobs.

Unit cost: the average cost of production. It is found by dividing total cost by output.

Unit elasticity of demand: when a change in price causes an equal change in the quantity demanded, leaving total revenue unchanged.

Unit PES: when a change in price causes an equal percentage change in the quantity supplied.

Value added: the difference between the sales revenue received and the cost of raw materials used.

Variable costs: costs that change as output changes.

Vertical merger: the merger of one firm with another firm that either provides an outlet for its products or supplies it with raw materials, components or the products it sells.

Vertical merger backwards: a merger with a firm at an earlier stage of the supply chain.

Vertical merger forwards: a merger with a firm at a later stage of the supply chain.

Vicious circle of poverty: a situation where people become trapped in poverty.

Voluntary export restraints (VERs): agreements with other governments to restrict their exports to the country.

Wage differential: the difference in wages.

Wage–price spiral: wage rises leading to higher prices which, in turn, lead to further wage claims and price rises.

Wage rate: a payment which an employer contracts to pay a worker – the basic wage a worker receives per unit of time (e.g. an hour) or unit of output.

Wants: desires for goods and services.

Wealth: a stock of assets including money held in bank accounts, shares in companies, government bonds, cars and property.

World Bank, The: an international organisation which provides long-term loans on favourable terms, to promote development.

Index

absolute poverty, 155
appreciation, 180, 181
average fixed cost, 99
average revenue, 100
average total cost, 99
average variable cost, 99

balanced budget, 119
banking, 73
    central banks, 73
    commercial banks, 73
barrier to entry, 104
birth rate, 159
borrowing, 77
broad measure, 126
budget, 119
    balanced budget, 119
    deficit budget, 119
    fiscal policy and, 119
    surplus budget, 119

capital, 7
central banks, 73
change in supply, causes of, 38
changes in demand, causes of, 32
claimant count, 140
collective bargaining, 85
commercial banks, 73
competitive markets, 103–4
    features of, 103
complements, 32
consumer price index, 144
contractionary fiscal policy, 123
contractionary monetary policy, 127
costs of production, 99
    average fixed cost, 99
    total cost, 99
    variable costs, 99
current account:
    balance of payments stability, 189
    structure of, 186–7
current account balance, 187
current account deficit:
    causes of, 188
    consequences of, 188
current account surplus:
    causes of, 188
    consequences of, 188

death rate, 159
decrease in demand, 33
deficit budget, 119
deflation, 144
    causes of, 147
    consequences of, 147
    policies, 147
demand, 27
    changes in, 32
    conditions of, 32
    contraction in, 31
    curve, 30
    decrease in, 33
    definition of, 29
    demand schedule, 30
demand-pull inflation, 145
demerit goods, 62
depreciation, 180, 181
direct provision, 67
direct taxes, 120
diseconomies of scale, 92–3
    internal, 93
disequilibrium, 43
disinflation, 144
disposable income, 75
division of labour, 83

earnings, 79
    differences in, reasons for, 81–2
economic agents, 23
economic development, 164
    factors affecting, 166
    reasons for differences in, 164–5
economic goods, 3
economic growth, 113, 114, 133
    benefits and costs of, 136–7
    policies to promote, 137
    and PPC, 136
    recession, 135
economic problem, 2–3
economic systems, 25
    market. See market economic system
    mixed, 65
    planned, 25
economies of scale, 92–3
    internal, 93
elastic demand, 49
    curve, 49

elastic supply, 54
- curve, 54

emigration, 159

employment, 139
- changes in pattern and level of, 139–40
- full employment, 115, 139

enterprise, 7

entrepreneurs, 7

equilibrium price, 42

equity, 121

expansionary fiscal policy, 123

expansionary monetary policy, 127

extension in demand, 31

extension in supply, 37

external benefits, 61

external costs, 61

external growth of firms, 91

factor immobility, 63

factors of production, 6–7

firms, 89
- causes of the growth of, 91–2
- classification of, 89
- diseconomies of scale, 92–3
- economies of scale, 92–3
- objectives of, 101
- small firms, 90

firms and production, 95
- demand for factors of production, 95–6
- labour-intensive/capital-intensive production, 97
- production and productivity, 96

fiscal policy, 122
- and budget, 119
- contractionary, 123
- effects on government macroeconomic aims, 123
- expansionary, 123
- government spending, reasons for, 119
- measures, 122

fixed costs, 99

fixed exchange rate, 181
- advantages and disadvantages of, 183

floating exchange rate, 180
- advantages and disadvantages of, 183

foreign exchange rate, 180
- causes of exchange rate fluctuations, 182
- consequences of change in, 182
- determination of, 182

free goods, 3

free trade
- benefits of, 176
- methods of protection, 176–7
- reasons for and consequences of protection, 178

full employment, 115, 139

geographical mobility, 8

globalisation, 175

government, role of, 110

government macroeconomic aims, 113–14
- effects of supply-side measures on, 131

government spending, reasons for, 119

households, 75
- borrowing, 77
- saving, 76–7
- spending, 75

increase in demand, 33

indirect taxes, 66, 120
- impact of, 121

individual and market supply, 36–7
- effect of change in price on supply, 37
- supply schedule, 36–7

individual demand, 29

individual supply, 36

industry, 89

inelastic demand, 49
- curve, 49

inelastic supply, 54
- curve, 54

inflation, 144

information failure, 62

internal diseconomies of scale, 93

internal economies of scale, 93

internal growth of firms, 91

international specialization. See specialisation of countries

labour, 7
- division of, 83
- quality of, 9
- quantity of, 9
- trade unions. See trade unions

labour force, 8, 9

Labour Force Survey Measure, 140

labour-intensive/capital-intensive production, 97

land, 6

living standards, 152
- and income distribution, 153
- real GDP per head as indicator of, 152

low unemployment, 115

macroeconomic aims of government, 113–14
    balance of payments stability, 116
    conflicts between, 116
macroeconomics, 22
    decision makers in, 23
    and microeconomics, 22
market demand, 29
market disequilibrium, 27, 43
market economic system, 27, 57–8
    advantages and disadvantages of, 58
market equilibrium, 27, 42
market failure, 60
    causes of, 63
    costs and benefits, 61
    demerit goods, 62
    information failure, 62
    merit goods, 62
    nature of, 60
    private goods, 62–3
market structure, 103
    competitive markets, 103–4
    monopoly markets, 104–6
market supply, 36
markets' role in allocating resources, 25
    economic systems, 25
    price mechanism, role of, 27
    three fundamental economic questions, 25
maximum price, 66
merger, 91
    types of, 92
merit goods, 62
microeconomics, 22
    decision makers in, 23
    macroeconomics and, 22
minimum price, 66
mixed economic system, 25, 65
    government intervention to address market failure, 67
    maximum price, 66
    minimum price, 66
    role of government, 110
    subsidies and indirect taxes, 66–7
mobility, 7
mobility of factors of production, 7–8
monetary policy, 126
    contractionary, 127
    expansionary, 127
money, 72
    characteristics of, 72
    functions of, 72

money supply, 126
monopolies, 104–6
    advantages and disadvantages of, 106
    comparing two markets, 105
    natural, 104, 110
monopoly power, abuse of, 63
multinational companies (MNCs)
    benefits and costs of, 176
    role of, 175

narrow measure, 126
nationalisation, 67
natural monopoly, 104, 110
net migration, 159
non-wage factors, 79

objectives of firms, 101
occupational mobility, 8
opportunity cost, 12
    influence on decision making, 12
optimum population, 160
organic growth of firms, 91
over-production, 61

planned economic systems, 25
population growth
    effects of changes in size and structure of population, 160
    factors affecting, 159
    reasons for different rates of, 160
population pyramid, 160
poverty
    absolute poverty, 155
    causes of, 155
    policies to alleviate poverty and redistribute income, 156
    relative poverty, 155
price
    demand and, 29
    supply and, 36
price changes
    causes of, 45
    consequences of, 45–6
price determination, 42
    market disequilibrium, 43
    market equilibrium, 42
price elasticity of demand (PED)
    calculation of, 48
    definition of, 48
    determinants of, 50

price elasticity of supply (PES)
- calculation of, 53
- definition of, 53
- determinants of, 54–5
- elastic and inelastic supply, 54
- implications, for decision making, 55
- interpretation of, 54

price mechanism, 25
price stability, 115
private benefits, 61
private costs, 61
private sector, 57, 58
privatisation, 67
production, 95
- factors of. See factors of production
- and productivity, 95

production possibility curves (PPC), 15, 114
- movements along, 16
- shifts of, 17

productivity, 9, 95
profit:
- normal, 104
- supernormal, 104

progressive tax, 120, 121
proportional tax, 120
public goods, 62–3
public sector, 57, 58
purchasing power parity (PPP), 152

quality, 8
quantity, 8
quantity and quality of factors of production, 8–9

real GDP, 133
real GDP per head, 133, 152
recession, 135
- causes of, 135
- consequences of, 135
- and PPC, 135

redistribution of income, 116
regressive tax, 120, 121
regulation, 67
relative poverty, 155
resources, 2
revaluation, 181
revenue, 100–1
- average revenue, 100
- total revenue, 100

saving, factors influencing on, 76–7
savings ratio, 76

scarcity, 2
small firms, 90
- advantages and disadvantages, 90
- reasons for, 90

social benefits, 61
social costs, 61
specialisation, 83
specialisation of countries, 172
- advantages and disadvantages of, 172–3

spending, influences on household, 75
subsidies, 66
- and indirect taxes, 66–7

substitutes, 32
supply, 27
- change in, 38
- conditions of, 38–9
- contraction in, 37
- definition of, 36

supply-side policies, 130
- effects on government macroeconomic aims, 131
- examples of, 130
- measures, 130

surplus budget, 119

taxation:
- reasons for, 120–1
- types of, 121

third parties, 61
total cost, 99
total demand, 113
total revenue, 100
total supply, 113
trade union membership, advantages and disadvantages of, 87
trade unions, role in economy, 85

under-consumption, 61
unemployment, 139
- measures of, 140
- policies to reduce, 141

unemployment rate, 115, 140

variable costs, 99

wage determination, 80–1
wage factors, 79
wage rate, 79
wants, defined
workers, 79
- difference in earnings, reasons for, 81–2

Acknowledgements

I would like to thank my co-author of AS/A Level Economics, Susan Grant, for producing an excellent new edition of her coursebook for IGCSE and O Level Economics. This has been of great help to me in producing this companion Revision Guide.

My thanks also go to Susan Ross of Ross Economics and Editorial Services Ltd for her fastidious work in ensuring what I have produced reads well and is in line with Cambridge Assessment International Education requirements. Thanks also to Amanda George and Neil O'Regan of CUP for managing the production process. Finally, I would like to thank Diane Bramley for her assistance with word processing.

The numbers of students studying IGCSE and O Level Economics continues to grow. My hope is that knowledge of economics at this level will inspire further study at A Level and maybe university.

I hope that this revision guide will be of value to teachers and to students and help students achieve the grade that they deserve.

Colin G Bamford

Emeritus Professor

Huddersfield Business School